A CENTURY
OF
PROTESTANT
THEOLOGY

A CENTURY OF PROTESTANT THEOLOGY

by
Alasdair I. C. Heron

THE WESTMINSTER PRESS
Philadelphia

Published by The Westminster Press ®
Philadelphia, Pennsylvania

PRINTED IN THE UNITED STATES OF AMERICA
9 8 7 6 5 4 3 2 1

Library of Congress Cataloging in Publication Data

Heron, Alasdair.
    A century of Protestant theology.

    Bibliography: p.
    Includes indexes.
    1. Theology, Doctrinal—History—19th century.
2. Theology, Doctrinal—History—20th century.
3. Theology, Protestant—History. I. Title.
BT28.H425   230'.044'0904   80-17409
ISBN 0-664-24346-0

Contents

Acknowledgements

Permission is gratefully acknowledged for the use of quotations from the following:

Karl Barth, *Evangelical Theology*, Weidenfeld & Nicolson, London, 1963; *God, Grace and Gospel. Scottish Journal of Theology Occasional Paper* No. 8, Edinburgh, 1959.
Emil Brunner and Karl Barth, *Natural Theology*, Geoffrey Bles, London, 1946.
Rudolf Bultmann, *Faith and Understanding*, Harper & Row, New York, and S.C.M. Press, London, 1969.
Eberhard Busch, *Karl Barth*, Fortress Press, Philadelphia, and S.C.M. Press, London, 1976.
Ewart H. Cousins (ed.), *Hope and the Future of Man*, Fortress Press, Philadelphia, and Garnstone Press, London, 1973.
Gustavo Gutiérrez, *A Theology of Liberation*, Orbis Books, New York, and S.C.M. Press, London, 1974.
H. Richard Niebuhr, *The Kingdom of God in America*, Harper & Row, New York, 1937.
Reinhold Niebuhr, *Faith and History*, Charles Scribner's Sons, New York, and Nisbet & Co., London, 1949.
Albrecht Ritschl, *Justification and Reconciliation*, vol. 3, T. & T. Clark, Edinburgh, 1900.
Thomas F. Torrance, *Address* at the Sixth Presentation of the Templeton Foundation Prize for Progress in Religion, Lismore Press, Dublin, 1978; also in T. F. Torrance, *The Ground and Grammar of Theology*, Christian Journals and University of Virginia Press, 1980.

Introduction

It is more than three years now since the Revd Alec Gilmore of
the Lutterworth Press invited me to plan this book as a companion
to Dr R. E. Clements' *A Century of Old Testament Study*. The
task has taken me rather longer than I at first anticipated, and I
am grateful to the Press for the generosity of the patience shown
to me as I endeavoured amid the pressures of other work to complete it.

The aim of the following chapters is the modest one of offering
an introductory survey of the main themes and movements in
Protestant theology in recent times. One word of explanation is
probably called for by the title, for a good fifth of the material
covered dates from more than a hundred years ago. Whereas Dr
Clements could begin his admirably clear and concise account
with the work of Wellhausen, who in the 1870s heralded a new
age in Old Testament research, the dawn of a fresh era in theology
came rather earlier—not with Wellhausen's contemporary,
Albrecht Ritschl, but with Schleiermacher and Hegel at the beginning of the nineteenth century; and they in turn demand to be
set against the background of the Enlightenment. The title, *A Century of Protestant Theology*, has therefore had to be interpreted
in a somewhat elastic sense; but as *most* of the developments described fall between the 1870s and the 1970s, I hope I may be
forgiven.

The field to be covered is of course a vast one, and the cover-
age necessarily selective. It would be quite impossible in such

brief compass to attempt a comprehensive history, for the words, 'Of the making of many books there is no end,' are an apt comment on modern theological writing. This is, rather, a broad outline intended simply to trace the main currents, to identify the distinctive proposals of leading thinkers, and to offer some comment upon them. It will serve its purpose if it proves useful in giving a general orientation—and if, as I hope it will, it encourages some readers to travel on to more detailed study.

The arrangement of the chapters is broadly chronological rather than thematic, for a sense of the dynamics of the development is essential if we are to appreciate the reasons for the emergence of particular lines of thinking. Theology does not fall from the sky, ready-written; it is always conditioned by its setting and by what has gone before—whether it continues along the same lines or reacts against them. A certain amount of shuttling back and forth has however been required in order to give attention to developments in different countries: so the latter part of chapter 2 and the whole of chapter 6 concentrate on British and American work contemporary with the European theology previously described. Swiss and German theologians of both the nineteenth and the twentieth centuries are given an especially prominent place: not only have many of the main impulses to fresh thinking come from them, but theological work is conducted in these countries with a unique intensity and engagement. It may be, as some have maintained in recent years, that the old Teutonic dominance is passing; and it is certainly true that the reception accorded to European theology in Britain and America has never been universally enthusiastic; but there can be little doubt where the centre of gravity has lain. Finally, while the main theme of the book is Protestant theology, the last chapter looks out more widely to the new horizons opened up by the encounter with Roman Catholic and Eastern Orthodox theology, with other religions, and with natural science.

Special thanks must be given to the editorial staff of the Lutterworth Press and the Westminster Press and to their readers for helpful and penetrating comments upon the manuscript, and to four friends and colleagues who offered valued assistance in its writing: Professor David Harned, Professor James Torrance, Dr Iain Torrance and Dr Frank Whaling. My wife Helen by her love, her humour, and her generous toleration of the eccentricity of an occasional writer's timetable, is a steady support and encouragement: such a formal recognition as this can in no way adequately thank her. Nor can I forget Jeanette and Patricia, the seven- and five-year-old theologians of the family, whose colourful artistic works surround my desk, and whose constant invasions, usually at hours when they should long since have been peacefully sleeping, relieve the tedium of the typewriter, even if they have probably also delayed completion of this book by a space of weeks. In token of a further and inexpressible debt to those who have gone before, I would place here the names of their great-grandparents.

In Memoriam
The Reverend William Heron (1881–1961)
Jessie Harvie Heron (1888–1979)

New College, Edinburgh, 1980   Alasdair Heron

1

The Challenge of the Enlightenment

At the peak of the Middle Ages, around the year 1200, Christianity was more or less solidly established as the religion of Europe. Europe itself made up the greater part of what Europeans regarded as the known world. It was bounded and threatened to south and east by the forces of Islam, which were eventually to submerge the ancient eastern Christian Empire with its capital in Constantinople. In western Europe, however, was the world of Christendom, undergirded and sustained, in spite of all internal conflicts, by the Christian faith. All the emerging nations (at least nominally) acknowledged the spiritual authority of the Roman pope; the church was seen as the divinely instituted ark of salvation, riding the storms of the world and history, and mediating to men both the infallible truth of God and the sacramental means of grace as guide and nourishment to their souls upon the pilgrimage to the life beyond; and theology was regarded—and not only by theologians—as 'the queen of the sciences', the supreme intellectual discipline. Church and society alike were hierarchically ordered. On the one hand were pope, cardinals, bishops and abbots, priests and laity; on the other emperor, kings, princes, nobility and common folk. These hierarchies supplied the (God-given) structure of society, the framework within which each individual found his appointed place and travelled on his path towards heaven (or hell). The entire interwoven pattern constituted an essentially static unity, whose focus was found in the spiritual authority of Rome.

This magnificent vision of church and society united as an organic whole was, however, doomed to disintegrate. With the expansion of trade and the growth of powerful merchant classes, economic forces were unleashed which eroded the older social structure and undermined the established order and authorities. The world beyond Europe began to be opened up with voyages to India, China and America, and this transformed men's horizons in a way fully as dramatic as space travel in our own time. The world was found to be vaster, more varied, and full of previously undreamt-of possibilities. At the same time, new attitudes were formed both to the past and to the natural world. In the Renaissance, which began in Italy in the fifteenth century, ancient art and literature began to be rediscovered with a freshness which inspired a new confidence in man's capacity to enquire into and understand the past as it had really been, and a desire to emulate its achievements for himself. The scientific approach to the world of nature developed as a way of looking to see what was actually there and interpreting it in the light of its own evidence instead of simply accepting received, traditional wisdom. The net result of all this was a new, critical attitude to traditional authority, and a fresh impulse towards creative exploration and the opening of new horizons, along with a huge shift of interest towards the investigation and exploitation of this present world.

While the Protestant Reformation of the sixteenth century cannot be wholly explained simply in terms of this general cultural and social upheaval, it was most certainly part of it. It was not only other ancient literature that was opened up for new understanding by the Renaissance: the Bible too began to be read with new eyes, eyes no longer focused simply by the authoritative teaching of the church. These eyes began to discern in the Bible distinctive themes and emphases which did not harmonise with the official theology. Thus the unique authority of the Bible as the inspired Word of God came to be stressed with a quite new sharpness over against the established teaching. In the Bible the voice of God was to be heard speaking with its own authentic power and force: there and there alone was divine truth authentically and immediately available. At the same time there was a good deal of variation in the ways in which the Bible was understood and interpreted by different groups of reformers, and this led to a further fragmentation of the previously unified world of Christendom. So, for example, in the England of the seventeenth century, Anglicans, Puritans, Presbyterians and others all made the same appeal to the Bible; but their different convictions about what the Bible was chiefly saying often seemed more prominent than their shared allegiance to it.

As the centuries passed, the seeds already sown produced much fruit, not all of it necessarily palatable to the now multifarious churches or to theology. Politically, the road ran via numerous conflicts—the Hundred Years' War, the English Civil War, the French Revolution and the American War of Independence, for example—to the emergence of modern democracy, and through more recent upheavals to the communist alternative. Economically, the rise of capitalism, the industrial revolution, the appearance of the social classes we know today, and the phenomenon of urbanisation have transformed the pattern of human life almost beyond recognition, bringing about the consumer society with its practical and all-pervasive materialism which so dominates life in the affluent west. At the same time, the astonishing flowering of science and technology has made it possible to organise and exploit the world and its natural resources on a scale which no earlier civilisation could have imagined; it has also bred a widely held belief, verging on the mythical or superstitious, that 'science is the solution to all our problems'. We have been carried very far indeed away from the medieval vision of society, of Christendom, of the place of the church and of theology as the crown of genuine knowledge. In effect, for all practical purposes, modern western man assumes that the human race is thrown upon its own resources to cope with life and discover what meaning, if any, it may have. Even if he is also religious—as he often enough still is—his religion is most commonly seen as a private, individual affair, divorced to a greater or lesser degree from the everyday concerns of the public world. The broad movement of society and culture has tended to squeeze religion out of the centre of human concern. While that movement has nowhere been wholly completed and has gone less far in some countries than in others, there is no western nation where its effects cannot be seen.

These developments face the churches and theology with a whole series of difficult and delicate questions. What place should religion or theology claim in this kind of society? Should theology accept the valuation which its contemporary world appears to

3

place upon Christianity, or should it reject it? What might theo logy for its part have to say about the direction that world seems to be taking? What responsibility does it have to try to influence the human outlook? How does theology stand *vis-à-vis* other disciplines, such as the natural sciences, which have come to be so important and successful with the passing centuries? These and similar questions have been forced on to the theological agenda by the way in which the modern western world has grown. They help to mark out the field within which the theologian has to work and to discover what his own role and contribution should be. In short, theology is no longer simply taken for granted or even accepted by society at large. This is a situation of which modern theologians have been well aware—often too much so for the comfort of many in the churches—and with which they have tried in various ways to deal.

Within that wider development, the credibility of Christian faith itself first came to be seriously challenged in the seventeenth and eighteenth centuries—in what is commonly called the *Age of Reason* or the *Enlightenment*. The chief mark of that period was a new confidence in the power of reason, as opposed to acceptance of authority, to discover truth: we find things out, not simply by believing what someone else tells us, but by considering the evidence, reflecting upon it, and accepting what can 'prove itself at the bar of reason'. The challenge posed by this new outlook can be illustrated from three great areas of conflict between Enlightenment rationalism and the orthodox belief of the same period— the authority of the Bible; the possibility of miracles; the idea of 'natural religion'. To these must be added two further issues which became more central towards the end of the eighteenth century: the problem of knowledge and of the limits of reason, and the question of history. These emerged as the movement represented by the Enlightenment itself became more self-critical and less brashly confident in its own rationalism; but that does not make them any the less significant or challenging for theology. If anything, they have subsequently been more important and have played a more central role in theological debate than the earlier orthodox/rationalist debating points. But we must first say something about the earlier arguments.

4

We have already noticed the new weight that the Reformation came to place upon the Bible. This led on in later generations to a widespread belief among orthodox Christians that the Bible should be looked upon as a compendium of truths directly revealed by God, inerrant and totally consistent in all its parts, and thus the supremely authoritative source of information not only on points of doctrine but on any other matters on which it might touch. With the rise of rationalism in the Enlightenment period, this conviction came to be questioned on two scores. First, an increasing gap opened up between the new scientific understanding of the universe as developed by men like Copernicus, Galileo and Newton, and the picture which orthodoxy generally believed it could find in the Bible, especially in the accounts of creation in the first two chapters of Genesis. Second, the developing study of the biblical documents themselves began to undermine the rather monolithic orthodox understanding of it. Investigation of the manuscripts and of the history of the transmission of the text of the Bible (what was later to be called 'lower criticism') revealed a mass of variant readings, often with quite different senses. Where in all this was the clear and straightforward infallible message? The orthodox answer was on the surface clear and precise enough, 'in the original text'—but this was little help if the original text could not with certainty be recovered.

More serious still were the questions raised by the emergence of what would later be termed 'higher criticism'. This studied the texts by the techniques of literary and historical analysis, attempted to separate out historical material from legend or poetry, and even began to raise sensitive problems of authorship—as, for instance, whether all the first five books of the Old Testament were in fact written by Moses. Once it was accepted that this kind of question could be raised, the way was open to the conclusion that the Bible should simply be treated as a collection of ancient religious literature with no special claims to be heard or accepted except where it happened to express some general religious 'principle' that could be recognised as universally valid—the kernel within the husk.

The fundamental issue which underlay this conflict between rationalism and orthodoxy was not merely the factual question

5

whether or not 'what the Bible says is true'. At bottom, the difficulty was religious and psychological. Could you at the same time treat the biblical texts as objects of critical scientific study *and* as the medium of a message from God? That question itself was not peculiar to the Age of Reason. It had been faced and dealt with in the early centuries of the church and later along the lines that the inspiration of the Bible did not mean that God simply dictated the words, or that the authors ceased to be human and fallible. That had also been the view of the great Reformers, such as John Calvin. But Protestant orthodoxy in the generations after the Reformation had inclined to treat the Bible in a rather hardened and absolute fashion, and to search in it for a wider range of information than the Reformers were looking for. On the other hand, the broad unity and homogeneity of the Bible itself had not been really seriously challenged in earlier centuries, whereas it could now appear to be falling apart under the impact of the new critical approaches of the eighteenth century. It is this that explains the sharp opposition which developed between the two contrasting attitudes, and the antithesis that came to be sharply drawn between 'reason' and 'authority'. The echoes of that conflict reverberate around us still, though as we shall see in later chapters, the issues need not be posed in quite the fashion of the Age of Reason.

Miracles

As the authority of the Bible began to be questioned, its defenders commonly appealed to the miracles recorded in it as guarantees of the truth of its message. These events, they argued, demonstrated that the hand of God himself was at work in the history with which the Bible deals, and so served to authenticate the Bible's own divine origins. This, however, rapidly proved a double-edged weapon. The same critical and questioning attitude which was forming the new approach to the Bible was at the same time stimulating scientific study and experiment and discovering the regularities in the natural order—what were and commonly still are called 'the laws of nature'. This scientific attitude did not by any means always lead to a denial of the reality of God; but it did not encourage the anticipation that God would actually intervene in the ordinary course of events; nor, when faced with a strange or unexpected occurrence, would it immediately turn to God as the only possible explanation. Rather it would presume that there must be some natural cause which was as yet unknown. This was the stance adopted in *deism*, a rationalist movement in theology which became prominent in England in the seventeenth and eighteenth centuries. Deists believed in the existence of God, and held that he was the necessary 'First Cause' and 'Supreme Architect' of the universe. But they also held that the universe itself was rather like a vast machine, which, once started off, ran according to its own inbuilt laws and patterns. God was therefore seen as the ultimate explanation of everything, but not as the particular, immediate cause of specific, individual occurrences. A not dissimilar attitude was later expressed with classic simplicity by the great French astronomer Laplace. When Napoleon asked him where God came into his theory of the cosmos, he replied shortly, 'I have no need of that hypothesis.'

From this point of view, which could make no place for miracles understood as cases of divine, supernatural interference with the laws of nature, reports of alleged miracles could only be regarded as evidence of credulity and ignorance on the part of those who originated and passed on the stories. The Bible's miracles, so far from supporting its claim to supernatural authority, served rather to undermine its credibility. So the same kind of stark opposition grew up between orthodoxy and rationalism on the matter of miracles as on the authority of the Bible; and the issues raised then have surfaced again in a number of forms since.

Before we move on, it is worth noticing that just as the debate about the Bible rested to a large extent on a rather dubious notion of what kind of authority was in question, so too the argument about miracles was one in which both sides generally shared an equally questionable concept. Rationalist and orthodox alike defined a miracle as a supernatural interference with the natural order of things: what they disagreed about was whether such interferences actually happened. Both had in the background the idea that the universe is a machine which is normally wholly determined by causal laws, and that a miracle is a temporary suspension of these laws. While that conception of the matter was a natural one in the world of thought of the Enlightenment period, in which the emerging sciences were dominated by the model of a machine-like world, it is open to serious scientific and theological challenge. The new frontiers opened up by the development of the sciences through the nineteenth and twentieth centuries have taken them far beyond the model of the machine and revealed a far greater degree of randomness and unpredictability in the fundamental structure of the universe. From a theological point of view on the other hand, it is more than debatable whether the notion of 'the suspension of natural law' is an adequate paraphrase of 'miracle'. The very terms in which the question was posed need to be critically reconsidered.

Natural Religion

The new outlook we have been outlining as coming to stand over against Christian orthodoxy was by no means necessarily irreligious or anti-religious. It could hold, as deism did, to belief in God; it could believe that religion is a 'natural' and proper element in human life, and that spiritual and moral truths are preserved in the Bible and in Christian teaching. This led some to speak of a 'natural religion' implanted in the human heart and necessary to human well-being. But this natural religion need not be grounded specifically upon the authority of the Bible or the Christian tradition, though it might allow these a place. Ultimately, it would attempt to find its basis elsewhere—in rational proofs of the reality of God, in the (assumed) self-evident truth of ethical and religious principles, in the spontaneity with which religion in diverse forms arises in human communities. This kind of desire for a natural—and 'reasonable'—religion developed strongly in deism, and led to the same kind of conflict with orthodoxy as with the Bible and miracles. On the one side the appeal was to reason; on the other, to faith and special divine revelation. The titles of some of the books which were published in the golden age of deism well illustrate the terms of the debate: Locke's *The Reasonableness of Christianity* (1695); Toland's *Christianity not Mysterious* (1696); Collins' *The Grounds and Reasons of the Christian Religion* (1724); and, on the other side, Butler's *The Analogy of Religion, Natural and Revealed* (1736) and Dodwell's *Christianity not Founded upon Argument* (1742). This same period also brought, especially in England, much criticism of traditional Christian creeds and doctrines, notably that of the divinity of Jesus Christ, and the emergence of Unitarianism—a form of Christian belief which rejected Christ's divinity and the doctrine of the Trinity, holding simply (as its name indicates) to the oneness of God the Father as the only God. With this the criticism of traditional orthodox formulations, which had long been regarded as absolutely central and essential to Christian belief, came on the stage in a new way and ushered in a debate which has continued up to the present.

A particularly famous instance of the search for a natural religion is to be seen in the early years of the French Revolution. In 1794 Robespierre made his short-lived attempt to replace Christianity, not with atheism, nor yet with the adoration of Reason, but with 'the worship of the Supreme Being', worked out along lines earlier suggested by Jean-Jaques Rousseau (1712–78). In *The Social Contract* (1762) Rousseau had advocated such a religion, to be maintained by the state, and to include five articles of faith: the existence of a divinity who is omnipotent, intelligent and benevolent, and who foresees and provides; the future life; the happiness of the good; the punishment of the wicked; and the sanctity of the 'social contract' (on which society itself is based) and of the law. This programme for a natural religion has its own importance as making explicit something which is often enough assumed, but has been heavily criticised in much modern theology—the idea that religion functions chiefly to safeguard the good ordering of society. Apart from that, it also shows how wide a gulf had opened up between this sort of natural religion and classical Christianity. The earlier deists were not so sharply aware of this gulf, and often believed themselves to be defending Christian faith by offering it a solid foundation. With Rousseau and Robespierre it is clear that what is being offered is not a support for Christian belief, but a rival.

The search for this sort of natural religion in fact threatened Christianity in two related ways. First, by drawing a distinction between what it regarded as the natural (and therefore genuine) core of religion and the complex of authorities, traditions, institutions and doctrines which went to make up the forms of Christianity, it implied that much, indeed very much of the latter was redundant and could safely be jettisoned. In the process everything distinctively Christian was eliminated: the baby was thrown out with the bath water. Second, and by the same token, the way was opened to setting Christianity on exactly the same footing as any other religion. All might preserve some religious truth and meaning, but none could be allowed to make any absolute claims, though each would be acceptable to the extent—but only to the extent—that it conformed or could be made to conform to the standard of natural religion, conceived of as a set of beliefs or principles which could stand very well on their own feet.

The appeal of such a position is of course very considerable, and seems no less strong today than two centuries ago. Those, and there are many, who believe that there is certainly value and truth in Christian belief, but are unhappy about what they feel to be an arrogant and intolerant insistence on the uniqueness of Jesus Christ, still commonly seek to follow the trail blazed by Rousseau. But it may be observed that the general movement of culture offers little support to anyone who would pin his hopes for the future of man as a spiritual being on this kind of natural religion. Robespierre's experiment was, scarcely surprisingly, a dismal failure; and while the delicious dream of a universal, natural and reasonable religion may have an understandable attraction for those who are influenced by but not wholly committed to Christian (or some other) belief, it does not appear capable of offering any very stable resting-place, or any adequate defence against the more radical challenges to religion as such which have been raised from without and within Christian theology in modern times.

At the same time, the conflict between reason and natural religion on the one hand, and faith and authoritative revelation on the other, opened up an area in which theology had to listen to both sides, to learn from both, and to attempt to find its own way without necessarily falling into either of the sharply polarised alternatives. The desire for natural religion reflected an awareness that religious faith has to do with the inner life of human beings, that it connects up with profound needs, drives and searchings at the core of our existence. Against an orthodoxy which at that time was inclined to reduce faith to the mere acceptance of 'the truths' in the Bible or in the teaching of the church—an acceptance which could leave one's inmost self unaffected, and could even involve the toleration in blind obedience of contradictions and incoherences in the offical system of belief—the voice pressing the claims of reason and the inner self needed to be heard. It is significant that this same era saw the rise to prominence and widespread influence of several movements within the churches which strove to integrate warm personal commitment with the reaf-

10

firmation of the broad pattern of orthodox belief. Pietism and the Moravian movement on the Continent and the Evangelical Revival and Methodism in Britain and America can all be seen as attempting to hold together these two sides. And to a large extent the subsequent history of theology has been determined by the struggle to find the balance between them and to chart a course which will take proper cognisance both of the demands of the inner human self and of the need to hear and recognise the voice that speaks to us from beyond ourselves.

The Enlightenment debates about the Bible, miracles and natural religion all throw into relief one of the characteristic new attitudes of the age, acutely expressed in Pope's lines from his *Essay on Man* (1733–4),

> Know then thy-self, presume not God to scan,
> The proper study of Mankind is Man.

On the rationalist side in each case the enquiry begins from what may be called an anthropological starting-point. Man begins with himself in his search for understanding. The Bible is treated primarily as a human product; the world is explored by human investigation, and only what can be established rationally and scientifically is to be believed; religion itself must be validated by reference to human experience, human values and human reason. Here lies the key to the outlook of the Age of Reason. One of its outstanding early proponents had been the French mathematician and philosopher René Descartes (1596–1650). He maintained that all genuine and certain knowledge begins with your own awareness of your own reality: *cogito, ergo sum*, 'I think, therefore I am.' Having thus established his own reality, he proceeded by working out from there to 'prove' the existence of the external world, of other people, and of God. The details of his arguments need not concern us here: it is the point of departure that is important. Conflict could not but arise between this new attitude and the traditional Christian conviction that man, in and by himself, is *not* the measure of all truth. Essentially, that is the issue in the debates which opened up in the Enlightenment period, and it has remained central in theology ever since.

Still in the eighteenth century, however, the rather confident and aggressive forces of rationalism were to be shaken into a more humble estimate of the power of human reason itself. At least three distinct developments, all flowing out of the Enlightenment, contributed to this. First, there was a powerful and widespread revolt against the rather cold and abstract notion of reason which had earlier held the field, and a fresh interest in the whole range of human experience, including feeling and emotion. This can be seen in the religious movements mentioned above which reacted against an orthodoxy which in its own way had a distinctly rationalist colouring, even though it was opposed to humanistic rationalism. But it can also be recognised more widely in the Romantic movement which began with Rousseau, and was the predominant influence in literature and culture generally from the latter part of the eighteenth century and well into the nineteenth. Romanticism is notoriously difficult to define, and includes a host of diverse movements in art, literature, philosophy and science. Broadly, however, it tended to emphasise the natural as against the artificial, the spontaneous as against the imposed, experience and emotion as against cold rationality, inwardness and imagination as against the outward and formal. Where rationalism was inclined to search for 'the eternal truths of reason', and to disregard or dismiss from serious consideration anything more mundane, the Romantic was one who sought to appreciate and sense the rich diversity of life and wonder over its multifarious forms and expressions. Romanticism has had an immensely powerful impact on the modern outlook, and we shall see in the next chapter how it fed into theology at the beginning of the nineteenth century.

The second major shift came when the concept of reason itself was subjected to a fresh critical examination, especially by David Hume and Immanuel Kant. The third was connected with a new awareness of history, of the fact that human societies and institutions have developed through long centuries and have taken on many different shapes at different times and in different places— an awareness which was especially sharply focused by the work of Gotthold Lessing. The work of Hume, Kant and Lessing was to be of especial significance for theology; for while they undermined the earlier kind of rationalism by restricting the claims and powers of reason and pointing to the sheer variety and diversity of history, they raised equally sharp questions for theologians. These same questions have remained close to the heart of theological debate ever since: How do we know what we know, and how can we be sure that we really know it? and, What is the importance of the history recorded in the Bible for Christian faith?

The Limits of Reason

The deists and Christian rationalists of the Enlightenment believed that rational argument could demonstrate the existence of God, just as Descartes had maintained before them. In this, they followed a venerable tradition. For two thousand years and more the branch of philosophy known as metaphysics had dealt with arguments and proofs about the existence and nature of God, his relation to the world and human beings, and such related matters as human freedom and life beyond death. These were widely (though never universally) held to be demonstrable by appeal either to direct awareness or intuition, or, more often, by indirect argument starting off from ordinary human experience of ourselves and the world around us. Theology had long been familar with this kind of argument, and had on occasion made very extensive use of it. The outstanding example is to be found in the work of the greatest of the medieval theologians, Thomas Aquinas, who died in 1274. He offered a series of philosophical proofs of God's existence—the 'Five Ways'—which could supply a 'natural theology', a theology which could be established, at least in principle, by the exercise of natural human powers of reasoning. This natural theology was then supplemented and completed by 'revealed theology', which drew on scripture and the teaching of the church. Thus he held together the two things which in the Enlightenment tended to fall apart, and to be defined in opposition to each other— faith *against* knowledge, revelation *against* reason. This is not to say that his own particular method of synthesising them was necessarily valid, but it does underline the extent to which the modern problems spring from the disintegration of the medieval framework.

Essentially, the proofs of the reality of God appealed to him as the only adequate explanation for the existence of the world. The arguments could be developed in several quite different forms, and we need not list them all. Three, however, were both characteristic of the general approach and especially central in the eighteenth century: the argument from causality, the argument from design, and the ontological argument. Put very simply, the

13

argument from causality runs like this. Everything that happens is caused by something before it. Therefore the universe itself must have a cause. But there cannot be an infinite series of causes stretching back endlessly; for in that case, no matter how far back we were to look, we should never find a beginning of the whole process, and that in turn would make it quite impossible to understand how it could ever have got off the ground, let alone reached its present state. Therefore there must be a First Cause which itself is *uncaused*; and this can only be God. The argument from design is fairly similar. The world and everything in it shows signs of order and pattern, but such signs are inexplicable without the mind of a Planner. Therefore there must be an Architect and Designer of the universe.

The ontological proof is rather more subtle. It took different forms, but all of them turn on the idea that 'God' *means* something like 'supremely perfect being', and that supreme perfection must include the fact of actual existence. Being real is thus seen as one of the defining attributes of God, just as having three sides is one of the defining attributes of a triangle. The argument readily connected up with the thought that the existence of God is *necessary*: God *could* not *not*-exist. This also found expression in the cosmological argument, which in structure resembles those from causality and design: all that exists is real, but only *accidentally* so; for it might not have existed, may cease to exist, and can certainly be conceived of as non-existent. Therefore it cannot exist simply from itself: it must depend upon the necessary being of God.

Arguments of this sort were devastatingly attacked by David Hume (1711–76) and Immanuel Kant (1724–1804). The main thrust of their philosophical work, as it was carried through especially in Hume's *Enquiry Concerning Human Understanding* (1748) and Kant's *Critique of Pure Reason* (1781/7), was to raise with a quite new sharpness the question of *epistemology*, of the character and basis of genuine knowledge and understanding. The result was to draw the boundaries of certain knowledge much more narrowly than before.

Hume argued that all our knowledge of facts (as opposed to what he called 'relations of ideas', as he termed the necessary, ideal truths of, for example, mathematics) is drawn from experience and must be firmly based upon it. We run into immense difficulties as soon as we attempt to project our minds any distance at all above or beyond the area of our concrete experience, for then our reasoning and arguing cannot be properly controlled. This focus on experience (in Greek *empeiria*) is expressed in the standard description of Hume's type of philosophy as *empiricist* rather than rationalist; and empiricism of this stamp has been especially influential in British philosophy in more recent times as well. It led Hume to be extremely sceptical of the kind of jump that is made when we attempt to argue from the existence of the world to the reality of God beyond the world. We are, he observed, only too willing to make this sort of leap, and not only in the field of theology (Hume was also very critical of what he saw as the pretensions of the science of his day to uncover the 'hidden springs' of things), but we need to be much more modest and cautious, to realise how limited the scope of our experience and knowledge is, and how liable our minds to go astray when they over-reach themselves and fish in waters too deep for their lines to plumb.

This general modesty about the rights and powers of human reason might not appear a very dangerous threat to natural theology, but the way in which Hume sharpened and applied it was to have a quite shattering impact. He singled out for particular attention the concepts of cause and effect, which we use and take for granted in everyday life, which are central to scientific study, and which were also essential to the theological argument from causality. Where, he asked, do we discover that there is some kind of necessary connection between two events, so that we can confidently affirm that A 'causes' B? Do we actually perceive a link between them? No! All we in fact observe is that A is regularly followed by B. This consistent association leads us to connect the two in our own minds, to expect A always to be followed by B, and this we then express by saying that A is the cause of B and B the effect of A. This is all perfectly in order, and indeed it is through such links and associations that we build up an ordered and coherent conception of the world around us and make sense of our experience of it. But we are wrong, he insisted, if we then imagine that we have discerned some mysterious necessity, some metaphysical connection binding A to B, or if we attempt to project and extend the chain of cause and effect entirely beyond the realm of our direct experience. When God is posited as the First Cause, the very ideas of cause and effect are being torn out of the context in which they properly belong, that of the perceived regularities in the world of which we are aware.

Hume's line of thought was equally destructive of the argument from design. That argument rests on the claim that the universe displays the hand of its Architect in the same way as a human artefact is recognisable as the work of an intelligent designer. How do we know this, however, of human artefacts?—simply because we have had repeated experience of them and of the people who make them. If we were to come across an object the like of which we had never before encountered, we would be in no position to determine whether it was an artefact or not, or to conclude with certainty that it had actually been designed and made by human beings. A single instance of B, and of B on its own, cannot enable us to associate it with A. The universe as a whole, however, is just such a single instance: we have no direct experience either of other worlds or of world-designers. On what basis, then, can we demonstrate that the world has been *made*, like an artefact, and not simply grown, like a vegetable? Is there not even something rather arrogant about the assumption that the human mind and capacity to make things supply the only proper model for conceiving of a supreme reality? Thus, he argued, while we may well *believe* that the world is in fact designed by God, we cannot *prove* it. Reasoning up from our restricted experience cannot supply any definite and conclusive demonstration of the reality and character of God.

Following Hume, Kant subjected human reason to an analysis even more radical and far-reaching. In the *Critique of Pure Reason* he called for a 'Copernican revolution' in our ideas about knowledge. Copernicus had shown that the apparent movements of the planets as observed from the earth cannot be satisfactorily or coherently explained on the assumption that the earth itself lies immobile at the centre of the universe. Rather, it too is moving, and our observations are affected by that movement, which must therefore be taken into account in interpreting them. In the same fashion, Kant maintained, the nature of our knowledge cannot be understood if we assume that it is simply fed into us from outside ourselves, and that we are merely passive recipients of information from the world around us. Our experience and understanding are shaped by our own minds, and necessarily so; for they are *our* experience and *our* understanding. We have no access to 'things in themselves' apart from our experience of them; a 'thing in itself'

16

(*Ding an sich*) is in fact utterly inconceivable to us, for any possible conception that we can form of anything at all will necessarily draw upon some real or imagined experience of it. Knowledge is the product of an interaction between our *percepts* mediated by sense-experience and the *concepts* which arise in our minds as the means of ordering and interpreting the percepts. 'Percepts without concepts are blind; concepts without percepts are empty.'

Further—and this was where Kant moved decidedly beyond Hume and everyone else before him—even the most fundamental categories which we use to supply the framework of our knowledge of the world, those of space and time, must be set in this light. They are essential postulates or presuppositions of all experience and reflection, and without them no coherent understanding would be possible. But we have no means of proving their objective validity in a world behind or beyond our own experience, nor do we 'know' space and time in themselves. This does not invalidate them or render them somehow doubtful—for they are indispensable—but it locates them and their validity firmly within the context of the mind's encounter with experience rather than elsewhere.

On this basis, knowledge of God could only be established if either God himself were immediately accessible to our awareness, or 'God' were a category demonstrably necessary, like those of space and time, to the ordering and shaping of our understanding. But he is not directly accessible in any ordinary sense, nor can the necessity of the concept of God for the interpreting of our experience be demonstrated, at least so far as pure reflection on the nature of our knowledge can take us. All the traditional proofs of his existence, Kant argued, ultimately involve an appeal to the ontological argument. But, he insisted, the concept of a 'necessarily existent Being' rests on a confusion between *existence* and *attributes*. Particular attributes or qualities may indeed be part of the very definition of something, and therefore inseparable from it. But the question whether a particular thing exists in reality is a factual one, which cannot be settled simply by defining it as necessarily existing. Accordingly, no valid demonstration of God's existence can be founded on the concept of a necessary Being.

The situation is, however, rather different when we move from 'pure' to 'practical' reason, from the analysis of the conditions and character of knowledge to the consideration of morals and action.

The core of morality was seen by Kant in the 'categorical imperative', the unconditional demand upon us to do what is right for its own sake. This imperative he saw as disclosing three 'postulates of practical reason', three presuppositions or fundamental conditions without which the categorical imperative itself would lack any ultimate basis. These were, first, our freedom as responsible moral agents, for the 'ought' of the categorical imperative implies the 'can' of our ability to obey it or to refuse to obey it; second, immortality, which brings with it the prospect of reward and punishment, and the advance towards higher and fuller good than can be attained in this life; third, God himself as the supreme Good, the ultimate guarantor of the moral order of the universe. Thus while the reality of God cannot be proved by 'pure reason', it can reasonably be believed in the context of 'practical reason'. So Kant sought by 'limiting knowledge to make room for faith', and to connect faith with moral awareness and action.

Where the work of Hume and Kant has been taken fully seriously, theology has faced a choice between two options. Either it might see what could be done within the area which Kant had left to it; or it might ask whether there might not after all be rather more to be said about the way in which genuine knowledge of God is made possible. As we shall see, both options have been taken up in subsequent thinking.

The Relevance of History

We have already touched on the challenge which the beginnings of modern historical study posed for theology by questioning a certain understanding of the authority of the Bible. In the second half of the eighteenth century, two fresh problems came into the open, particularly through the work of Gotthold Ephraim Lessing (1729–81). Lessing was a man of many parts—writer, literary critic, historian, advocate of religious tolerance—who also made pioneering contributions to the study of the New Testament, and was from time to time embroiled in the continuing controversies between rationalism and orthodoxy. It is in that setting that these two problems belong.

The first was relatively straightforward. Once the Bible began to be approached as historical material, open to critical historical study, it was natural that the New Testament, and in particular the life and personality of Jesus himself, should come to be re-examined. Might not Jesus himself have been rather different from the picture given of him in the gospels and the subsequent teaching of the church? Could not the 'real Jesus' or, as later generations were to term him, the 'historical Jesus', conceivably have been quite a different sort of figure from the Christ who was subsequently preached and described in the terms of the Nicene Creed as God made man? At any rate, should not the New Testament material be studied critically and carefully with these questions in mind? One of the first of a long series of attempts to reconstruct the facts behind the records was undertaken by Hermann Samuel Reimarus (1694–1768) in his *Apology for the Reasonable Worshippers of God*. (The title itself reflects Reimarus' own rationalism, and the scepticism with which he approached all supernatural elements in the gospel accounts.) He himself never published this work, but after his death Lessing brought out parts of it as *Fragmente eines Unbekannten* ('Fragments by an Unknown Author'). This ushered in what was to become known in Germany as the *Leben-Jesu Forschung* ('Life of Jesus research') and in English as 'the quest of the historical Jesus'. We shall have more to say about this in the next chapter: it was to produce a quite bewildering variety of 'reconstructions' of Jesus' personality and history, having for the most part only one thing in common—the conviction that whatever the truth about him might be, it was not the traditional Christian picture of him.

The second problem was of a more subtle kind, and was well formulated by Lessing himself. Although he published Reimarus' work, he was not primarily concerned with the correctness or otherwise of the particular interpretations there offered, but with a more fundamental question altogether. As a historian, Lessing was sharply aware of the difficulty of uncovering the past and interpreting the evidence with accuracy; he was also conscious of the great differences between one period and culture and another, and in particular of what more modern writers have sometimes called the 'cultural gap' between the New Testament and the modern world. This led him to doubt whether authentic religious belief can properly be tied to and bound up with particular historical events.

Two famous remarks of his mark out the dimensions of the question. First, 'There is a broad, ugly ditch of history that I cannot jump across.' The past by its nature is only indirectly available to us; we cannot enter it with the same immediacy as the present. How then can religious certainty be based upon the inevitably shaky foundation of historical investigation? Second, 'The accidental truths of history can never become the proof of the necessary truths of reason.' If religious truth is genuine, surely it must be so eternally and universally? Historical events do not have that character at all: they do in fact occur in one way rather than another, but they could all conceivably have turned out quite differently. It is true, for instance, that God is good; and it is also true that Julius Caesar invaded Britain. These are not, however, the same kind of truth; for the first holds for all time and every place, whereas the second has to do with a specific event which as a matter of fact took place at a particular point in history. So, Lessing maintained, the first kind of truth cannot be demonstrated by the second, nor brought down to the same level. Religious truth is of a different order from the truths of history. An equally famous expression of the same view was given by Kant's pupil, the philosopher Fichte (1762–1814), 'The metaphysical only, and not the historical, can give us blessedness.'

What then is the place of history, and in particular the relevance of the events recorded in the Bible? Lessing offered his solution in *The Education of the Human Race* (1780). History is the arena in which, first through the period of the Old Testament, then by the teaching of Jesus in the New, the way has been prepared for the gradual purifying and refining of man's religious sense which will lead to a third, future era, in which religious values will be seen to shine in their own light as 'necessary truths of reason'. Until that happens, creeds, dogmas and the Bible itself have a necessary but essentially temporary and provisional authority. The 'revelation' to which they witness offers nothing that the development of a rational religious sensibility would not in time be able to discover for itself. Past history is thus significant as the occasion by which we have been enabled to see what otherwise we might have failed to grasp; but the real content of the revelation is in principle detachable from the particular history through which it has been manifested.

In focusing thus sharply on the question of the relation between religious faith and historical knowledge, Lessing put his finger on what was to prove a more or less permanently controversial topic in theology from his day to this. Like Kant, he leaves theologians with two broad choices: either to accept this account of the situation, with its absolute distinction between the relativities and contingencies of history and the truth of religion, or to search for some other framework within which to set up the question. The chief motive which would naturally encourage Christian thinkers to look for such an alternative is that Lessing's horizon necessarily scales down to merely relative and passing significance the events on which Christian faith itself depends—the history recorded and interpreted in the Bible, and in particular that of Jesus himself. The last two centuries have brought a variety of attempts in theology to cope with these questions, and both the alternatives bequeathed by Lessing have been followed.

2

New Beginnings:
From Schleiermacher to the First World War

The nineteenth century saw the flowering of a rich and diverse crop of theological approaches, reflecting both the challenge of earlier developments and the complex changes rapidly sweeping over western society. In the churches, traditional orthodoxy of a more or less pre-Enlightenment character fought to retain its footing, but alongside it grew other movements ranging from what today would be called Conservative Evangelicalism to those which were consciously progressive, liberal and modern. New philosophies, new scientific theories about man and the natural world, new interpretations of history, economics and politics, and a deepening interest in non-Christian religions all came to appear variously as enemies or allies of theology. Out of this maelstrom we can select only a few thinkers and those ideas which stand out in retrospect as marking out the major developments and as setting the scene for more recent times. This can best be done by concentrating primarily, though not exclusively, on Germany, and on three broad lines which may be distinguished there. (For a fuller account, which gives a much more rounded picture than is possible here of such thinkers as Schleiermacher, Hegel and Kierkegaard, and which also gives special attention to British and American theology, Claude Welch, *Protestant Thought in the Nineteenth Century*, vol. 1: 1799–1870 (1972), is especially to be recommended.)

The first line begins with the man who has justly been termed 'the father of modern theology', Friedrich D. E. Schleiermacher (1768–1834), who was Professor of Theology in Berlin from 1809; and leads on to Albrecht Ritschl (1822–89), Professor in Göttingen from 1864, and those who under his influence formed the school of what is now generally known as Liberal Theology.

A second and much more broken line runs from Schleiermacher's contemporary Georg W. F. Hegel (1770–1831, Professor of Philosophy in Berlin from 1818), and includes such diverse figures as the theologian A. E. Biedermann (1819–85), the New Testament scholars F. C. Baur (1792–1860) and D. F. Strauss (1808–74), and the philosophers Ludwig Feuerbach (1804–72), Karl Marx (1818–83) and Søren Kierkegaard (1813–55).

In both of these lines one central issue was that raised by Lessing of the relation between theology and history. This was made even more pressing through the nineteenth century by the growth of a sharper historical awareness, by the general influence in the intellectual culture of the time of the ideas of evolution and progress, and by the advances made in historical study of the Bible and past history in general.

Our third theme will be the way in which the questions these developments raised were illustrated towards the end of the nineteenth and the beginning of the present century in the work of Albert Schweitzer (1875–1965), Johannes Weiss (1863–1914), William Wrede (1859–1906), Martin Kähler (1835–1912) and Ernst Troeltsch (1865–1923). Thereafter we shall very briefly outline some of the main trends in theology beyond Germany in the same period.

Schleiermacher and Ritschl

The most important of Schleiermacher's many writings, so far as we are concerned here, are his *Addresses on Religion, to its Cultured Despisers* (1799) and *The Christian Faith* (1821/2; a second and considerably altered edition appeared in 1830/1). The *Addresses* offered a general analysis and defence of religion, which Schleiermacher wished to commend to the intelligentsia of his own day who were tempted to dismiss it as mere primitive superstition, while *The Christian Faith* is a comprehensive and systematic presentation of the main themes of Christian teaching. It is very much longer and fuller, and also very much more definite about

Christian affirmations, than the *Addresses*; but the ground-plan of his thought is recognisably the same in both. *The Christian Faith* spells out in detail the kind of overall understanding of Christian theology which was opened up by the conception of the nature of religion presented in the *Addresses*.

In both, Schleiermacher can be seen attempting to chart a middle way between traditional orthodoxy and cold rationalism, to find a means of re-stating classical Christian convictions in a fresh and modern way which will not reduce them or dilute them, but rather uncover their real force and depth. It should be said that his range of original and indeed trail-blazing contributions to modern theology was wider even than this. He was a renowned preacher, a pioneer critic of the New Testament, one of the founding fathers of the discipline of hermeneutics (the philosophy or science of interpretation); but it is with his fundamental work on the nature and basis of theology itself that we must deal.

Schleiermacher was deeply impressed by Kant's philosophy, and accepted Kant's demolition of rational, philosophical knowledge of God. But where Kant then found a place for religious faith in the realm of practical reason, in ethics and morals, Schleiermacher held that this too was inadequate. Neither metaphysics nor ethics is the home of religion, nor does either hold the key to its real nature. Where religion is reduced to either, and treated as if it were simply a form of *knowing* or a form of *doing*, it is lost to sight altogether. It has to do rather with the infinite, universal wholeness of all things, of that all-embracing totality which may or may not be labelled 'God', but which includes and enfolds everything within itself. Our knowledge and our moral values inevitably reflect and are marked by our own finitude and all its limitations, and to scale religion down to them is to sow the seeds of fanaticism and intolerance by giving them a more absolute standing than they properly deserve. But there is in us another level of being which lies deeper than knowing or acting, and it is at that further depth that the genuine religious impulse arises and lives. He describes this deeper level in terms of 'feeling', 'consciousness', 'immediate awareness'. Propositions 3 and 4 of the second edition of *The Christian Faith** (referred to

* The propositions from the first and second editions of *The Christian Faith* are quoted from *The Christian Faith in Outline*, Friedrich Schleiermacher, translated by D. M. Baillie, Edinburgh (W. F. Henderson), 1922.

hereafter as CF^2), summarise the essential points he makes about it.

> §3. The piety which forms the basis of all ecclesiastical communions is, considered purely in itself, neither a Knowing nor a Doing, but a modification of Feeling, or of immediate self-consciousness.
>
> §4. The common element in all howsoever diverse expressions of piety, by which these are conjointly distinguished from all other feelings, or, in other words, the self-identical essence of piety, is this: the consciousness of being absolutely dependent, or, which is the same thing, of being in relation with God.

This immediate consciousness of dependence is something which in Kantian language might be called 'transcendental'. It lies below and beyond the distinctions between subject and object which are inbuilt in ordinary experience at the level of knowledge and action; so it opens up a direct awareness of the God on whom our existence hangs as given in and with our deepest awareness of ourselves. There is thus, for Schleiermacher, an inherently religious awareness at the very core of our own existence as human beings: it is both inherent in ourselves, and inherently bound up with the reality of God. Self-awareness, at its deepest level, involves at one and the same time awareness both of our finitude and of the infinity on which we depend.

Schleiermacher's theology is commonly described as centred on 'religious experience'. The description is a valid one provided it is remembered that he does not build on special or peculiar 'religious experiences' of a mystical or emotional kind. What he appeals to is, he believes, primordially *human*, the foundation and basis of *all* other experience. It is also sometimes called a theology of 'feeling', and he himself uses this language. But again, he does not mean by this to reduce religion to emotion, though he is clear that emotion plays a part in it. What he is trying to describe, and to find terms to name, is what would later be called 'existential awareness', an awareness which includes and involves *ourselves* by contrast with any more or less detached knowledge of facts and truths quite external to ourselves. 'Immediate self-consciousness' is thus a less misleading description than 'feeling' taken by itself.

It should also be said that while he speaks of 'absolute dependence', he does not mean to imply that we have no personal freedom or responsibility, that we are mere puppets in the hands of omnipotence. Rather, his argument is that our consciousness of

ourselves conveys to us that we are not self-enclosed or self-suf-
ficient, not our own cause or our own explanation. This brings
as its corollary the awareness of the one on whom we depend. It
was a complete caricature of Schleiermacher when Hegel
remarked that on this account a dog must be more religious than
his master, because even more completely dependent. Obedient
passivity and emotional dependence are not at all what Schleiermacher was talking about, though some of his language, taken out
of context, could give that impression.

In the background to this central theme in his thought lie two
major influences upon him which interacted with each other and
with the impulses derived from Kant. First, both in his childhood
home and in his education in Moravian schools, he was imbued
with a deep and warm Christian piety which never left him; but
at the same time he reacted against what he felt to be a too strict
insistence by his father and his teachers on doctrinal principles.
This certainly helped to open up in his mind a sense of the gap
between religious dogmas and the essentially religious attitude and
awareness. Second, he was very much a Romantic, with all the
Romantic's preference for the vital, inward and spontaneous over
the static, outward and formal. In this, he reflected not only the
spirit of his own age, but a wider temper and habit of mind which
is still very much alive, and not least among many Christians. That
is part at least of the secret of his continuing appeal.

The consciousness of absolute dependence, which he can also
sometimes call simply, 'God-consciousness', might at first sight
seem a slender thread indeed on which to suspend a comprehensive statement of all the themes of Christian theology. One might
expect it to lead only to a rather vague pantheism which could
make no real place either for religious institutions or for specific
doctrines and formulations. And at points in the *Addresses* that does
seem to be the direction in which Schleiermacher is heading. They
were not, however, his last word; and in *The Christian Faith* he
builds broad and high on this apparently unpromising foundation.
It supplied him with nothing less than the key to a fresh overall
grasp of theology which was able to cope with the most serious
challenges proffered in the previous century. It did so only at a
price; but it is the measure of his greatness that few others in
ancient or modern times have attempted, let alone carried through,
a comparable essay in the reorientation of Christian thought. (It

is also remarkable how commonly ideas similar to his have kept re-surfacing up to the present day, often without any apparent awareness on the part of their authors that Schleiermacher had already developed them, or that the subsequent movement of theology was to expose serious inadequacies in them.) Three aspects of his reconstruction demand special attention: his account of the nature of theological doctrines; his general account of religion; and his reinterpretation of the inner meaning of the Christian faith itself.

The character of doctrines. In a nutshell, 'Christian doctrines are accounts of the Christian religious affections set forth in speech' (*CF*[2] §15). Christian teachings are expressions of the religious awareness in its Christian form. They can only be understood, and their truth can only be measured, by reference back to that awareness. To treat them simply as statements of objective fact, to be proved or disproved by appeal to observation of the world around us, to the speculations and arguments of metaphysical philosophy, or even to the authority of the Bible understood as a collection of 'divine truths', is to misconceive their nature and function. To say, for example, that God is the Creator and Preserver of the world, is to give particular expression to the awareness of absolute dependence; and it is in and through that awareness that the meaning and truth alike of the doctrinal affirmation are opened up. This is not to imply that the Bible has *no* authority: it plays an essential role in shaping and informing the Christian God-consciousness. But the centre of gravity lies in that consciousness itself. So Schleiermacher offers to religious language a new foundation and point of reference, one with inbuilt defences against the attacks of the Enlightenment. The essential religious awareness, if only it is allowed to address us, will supply the needed evidence.

The awareness which finds expression in doctrines is not something purely private and individual. It is shaped and nurtured in a religious community, and its expression grows and develops through history. The work of the theologian is set by Schleiermacher in that context. He has to serve the church by articulating its teaching, and at the same time, and as part of the same task, to explore and clarify the understanding it contains. 'Dogmatic theology is the science which systematises the doctrine prevalent in a Christian church at a given time' (*CF²* §19). This is not merely a matter of re-stating what had already been said; it involves a genuine progress and advance towards a fuller and clearer understanding enabled by the onward movement of history. At the same time, the present stands in continuity with the past out of which it has grown, and the Christian theologian and the Christian church are bound in particular to the origins in Jesus and to the teaching of the Bible, especially the New Testament.

This twofold emphasis upon religious consciousness and on the task of theology in the present brings with it a major shift in the understanding of the character of theological and doctrinal statements—a shift from the *objective* to the *subjective* pole, from *the truth to be affirmed* to *the awareness and intention of the person or community affirming it*. This becomes quite clear in some of the significant details of Schleiermacher's account. So, for example, 'All attributes which we ascribe to God are to be taken as denoting, not something special in God, but only something special in the manner in which the feeling of absolute dependence is to be related to him' (*CF²* §50).

Again, he distinguished between those doctrines which give *direct* expression to the religious awareness, and those which do so only *indirectly*. The doctrine of the Trinity 'is not an immediate utterance concerning the Christian self-consciousness, but only a combination of several such utterances' (*CF²* §170); that is, it serves to combine and hold together the different affirmations of the Christian consciousness concerning God the Father, Jesus, and the Holy Spirit, but it is essentially a theological construction which has its place *in theology* but should not be taken as expressing the truth *about God*. It 'has not equal value with the other proper doctrines of the faith, but is simply a summary statement' (*CF¹* §187). Therefore, while he could indeed describe the doctrine of the Trinity as 'the true coping-stone of the system of Christian doctrine' (*CF¹* §186), he relegated it to an appendix in both editions of *The Christian Faith*.

Religion and religions. The fundamental religious awareness 'leads necessarily in its development to fellowship or communion' (*CF²* §6), and so forms the different religious communities and traditions of mankind. Each particular religion is marked off from others in two ways—outwardly, by its origins and history, and inwardly, by the particular way in which it gives expression to the essential religious consciousness (CF^2 §10). That expression may itself vary in two major respects. First, it may be scattered and diffused among a variety of objects of devotion, as in polytheism; or it may have a single focus, as in monotheism. The monotheistic forms of religion are the higher, for they more clearly and purely bring the God-consciousness to expression, 'and all others are related to them as subordinate forms, from which men are destined to pass on to those higher ones' (CF^2 §8).

Second, it may 'subordinate the natural in human conditions to the moral', or, alternatively, 'subordinate the moral to the natural' (CF^2 §9). Of the monotheistic faiths, Islam, with its passive fatalism (as Schleiermacher saw it), does the second, whereas Judaism to some degree and Christianity more perfectly emphasise man's ethical freedom and responsibility. They are thus more 'moral' or, as he can also say, more 'teleological' than Islam, for they discern and hold out an ethical purpose and direction for human life. All these definitions and distinctions come together in Schleiermacher's famous definition of Christianity itself,

> Christianity is a monotheistic faith of the teleological type of religion, and is essentially distinguished from other such faiths by the fact that everything in it is related to the redemption accomplished by Jesus of Nazareth (CF^2 §11).

In this way, Schleiermacher was able to include Christianity alongside other faiths under his general conception of religion, and at the same time to affirm its distinctiveness and indeed superiority over all other contenders. To do this he did not need to make any apparently arbitrary appeal to particular revelation or received authority. The analysis of religion as such shows that in the Christian faith it has received its highest, clearest and fullest expression. This leads on now to its distinctive mark: by its history and by its inner meaning alike, it is bound up with 'the redemption accomplished by Jesus of Nazareth'. But what exactly did Schleiermacher understand by that?

The meaning of Christian faith. Schleiermacher's interpretation of Jesus and of the meaning of redemption is linked in two ways with his controlling conception of God-consciousness. First, that consciousness, like every element of our experience, involves the awareness of both pleasure and pain (CF^2 §62). It is the antithesis between these that Schleiermacher takes as the introduction to the doctrine of redemption, which occupies the second (and larger) of the two main divisions of *The Christian Faith*. He unfolds it there as the antithesis between sin and grace. The God-consciousness which is aware of its own limitations, and beyond that, of its own imperfection, becomes a consciousness of sin. That is the painful aspect. The other side is the consciousness of perfection and blessedness which we recognise as mediated to us through Jesus and communicated to us by him. So, 'the distinctive feature of Christian piety lies in the fact that whatever alienation from God there is in the phases of our experience, we are conscious of it as an action originating in ourselves, which we call Sin; but whatever fellowship with God there is, we are conscious of it as resting upon a communication from the Redeemer, which we call Grace' (CF^2 §63). Both sin and redemption are therefore describable in terms of God-consciousness in its negative and positive aspects.

Second, God-consciousness also supplies the key to the person of the Redeemer and the redemption he has accomplished. Jesus was divine in the sense that he was 'distinguished from all (other men) by the constant potency of his God-consciousness, which was a veritable existence of God in him' (CF^2 §94). Similarly, 'The Redeemer assumes believers into the power of his God-consciousness, and this is his redemptive activity' (CF^2 §100). The awareness of God which is fragmentarily and partially there in all men was fully and perfectly formed in Jesus, and spreads from him to those who believe in him. This is the essential meaning of the old dogma which described him as God incarnate and as our Saviour and Redeemer. It is also the meaning of the doctrine that he alone was perfect and wholly free from sin.

The Christian consciousness of God is thus, for Schleiermacher, inextricably bound up with Jesus himself, and derived from him. It is not simply a general or universal awareness of God, though it gathers up and refines the more general consciousness to be found in other religions and at the very core of human existence as such. But it is only in and through the Christian modification of the God-consciousness that the significance of Jesus can be grasped, and it is in terms of God-consciousness that his person and work, who he was and what he achieved, must be interpreted.

By working from this new standpoint, Schleiermacher aimed to bypass the antitheses which had emerged so sharply in earlier generations between reason and revelation, natural religion and received authority, the natural and the supernatural, and to offer a fresh synthesis in which both the authentic and distinctive character of religion and the special nature of the Christian faith would be preserved.

It is impossible in a few words to do justice to Schleiermacher's stature and impact. He ushered in a new era in the study of religion and of theology; he brought a new conception of what the disciplined and ordered study of both could be; he underlined in epoch-making fashion the importance of the subjective aspect of religious awareness, pointing to what lies deeper than intellectual formulations, yet is not reducible to inchoate and diffuse 'feelings'; he attempted to grasp and express in an original and modern way the abiding significance of Jesus, and to uncover the living and personal meaning of what were in danger of being dismissed as merely the fossilised accretions of doctrine. In all these ways, he set his stamp on theology and decisively altered its course. This is more remarkable since in his own lifetime he had but few enthusiastic followers, nor did a school grow up around him to carry on his work. Yet he so influenced or anticipated what was to come that he remains still the great point of departure for modern Protestant theology. In spite of the weaknesses in his attempted synthesis, the same can be said of him in the context of the theology of the last century and a half as of Sir Christopher Wren on his tomb in St Paul's Cathedral, *Si monumentum requiris, circumspice*—'If you would see his memorial, look around you.'

This said, however, it must be added that the weaknesses in his system are very considerable. His analysis of doctrines as expressions of the religious consciousness leaves a fair measure of uncertainty whether what is said is in any sense true *about God*, or only about *our understanding* of God. The sting of this question was to some extent drawn for Schleiermacher himself by the fact that he so closely identified immediate self-consciousness with God-consciousness as to believe that he had found a real and solid bridge between the two sides of the matter. But that identification itself is open to question. Schleiermacher had no doubts about it: it was the fundamental axiom of his whole system. But it is hard indeed to see how that axiom itself could be made more convincing either to a purely humanist philosophy or to a theology which maintained that God is something more and other than the obverse of our finitude. Again, is it adequate, or even in principle correct, to interpret the divinity of Jesus and his work of redemption in terms of God-consciousness? Is there here a tendency to reduce Christianity simply to a movement within history, describable in the favourite Romantic categories of inner awareness and historical development?

Finally, while he is indeed very careful to underline the distinctiveness and uniqueness of Jesus and of Christianity, do hidden thorns lurk in his description of Christianity itself as 'a religion' which can be classified along with other 'religions'? It is no denigration of his immense achievement to point to these real difficulties which it raises. We shall see as we continue how they have repeatedly emerged in later discussion. The fundamental issue is whether this essentially Romantic vision of history, of religion, and of the nature of theological truth and the reality of God, is an adequate vehicle for the reformulation of Christian faith.

Forty years passed after the publication of the second edition of *The Christian Faith* before a comparable essay in constructive restatement of Christian doctrine appeared. This was Albrecht Ritschl's *The Christian Doctrine of Justification and Reconciliation*, which came out in three volumes between 1870 and 1874 and launched the movement which was at first called 'the Ritschlian theology', but is now generally labelled 'Liberal Theology'. (The label, 'liberal', has been used in a variety of ways in theology. Older books surveying the theology of the nineteenth century, such as John Oman's *The Problem of Faith and Freedom* (1906), commonly applied it to extreme radicals, and spoke of Ritschl as neither 'liberal' nor 'orthodox' but 'mediating'. Other writers have used 'liberal' as a blanket term for the whole broad line of development which runs from Schleiermacher. More recently, however, Liberal Theology has become a recognised description of the Ritschlian school, and it is in that sense that it is used here.)

Its leading figures included the theologians Wilhelm Herrmann of Marburg (1846–1922), Theodor Haering of Tübingen (1848–1928), Julius Kaftan of Berlin (1848–1926) and the church historian Adolf von Harnack, also of Berlin (1851–1930). It had very considerable influence in Germany up to the First World War, and also, in somewhat diluted form, in both Britain and America (see chapter 6). Mention should also be made of the French theologian Auguste Sabatier (1839–1901), through whom the movement also made some impact on the French Roman Catholic Modernists, notably A. F. Loisy (1857–1940). Indeed, like the thought of Schleiermacher, the main themes and concerns of Liberal Theology are still very much with us, though often anonymously and unrecognised. While Ritschl was certainly not, as some of his more enthusiastic followers confidently believed, a second Schleiermacher, he was nonetheless a major figure whose work also raises serious issues which cannot be ignored.

Ritschl's own attitude to Schleiermacher and his work was somewhat ambivalent. He could and did talk at times as if he were simply continuing Schleiermacher's programme, and described Schleiermacher as his predecessor in the matter of *method*. Indeed there are strong resemblances between them, especially when one looks back on them from the present day and across all that has happened in theology since Ritschl. He too insisted on drawing a clear line between theology and philosophy; he accepted Kant's demolition of any philosophical natural theology, and insisted that theology must be permitted to proceed with its own work without dictation from speculative metaphysics or the imposition upon it of alien concepts and patterns of thought and investigation. He too worked out a general conception of religion, and saw Christianity as its highest and purest form. He too approached the task of talking about God very much from *our* side, the side of the believer or the theologian, exploring the meaning of theological statements for those who made them, and seeking in that way to disclose their authentic basis and character. In all these respects he reminds us today of Schleiermacher. But there were also very significant differences, and it was upon these that Ritschl himself laid greater weight. They are chiefly associated with his distinctive emphases on *historical revelation* and on the *ethical* rather than *mystical* nature of religion.

Ritschl's *bête noire* was mysticism in any way, shape or form. What he meant by mysticism was belief in a direct, immediate experience of God (or of Jesus) which dissolved the distinction between God and man or between Christ and ourselves, a rapture of union which could carry us beyond time and history and the challenge and responsibility of the present. This kind of religious outlook he regarded as neither biblical nor Protestant. It was characteristic of him that his last work, and his greatest apart from *Justification and Reconciliation*, was a three-volume *History of Pietism* (1880–6), in which he applied his very considerable erudition to demonstrating that Pietism represented the improper infusion into German Protestantism of alien, Roman Catholic conceptions of the Christian life. His own aim was to return to the message of the Bible via the teaching of the Reformers, and on that basis he wished to outline a very different conception of the nature of Christian faith and life. In place of God-consciousness, for which he had little time, he wanted to put on the one hand the revelation made in Jesus and recoverable through the historical study of the New Testament, and on the other the moral and spiritual response to Jesus which issues in Christian living and acting. Both of these are of course present in Schleiermacher too; but they do not supply the framework of his system as they do for Ritschl.

To this end, Ritschl offered a fresh account of the nature of religion, an account which began by considering what religion is *for*. Its purpose, he argued, is not to supply immediate or direct knowledge of God; it is rather to enable the overcoming, with God's help, of the contradictions which run through human existence. For man is a divided being. At bottom this division is based on the fact that he is at one and the same time part of the natural order—along with the elements, plants and animals—yet also a spiritual and personal being who feels a destiny and calling to rule over the natural world. But other aspects of the matter can also be discerned: there is also a contradiction between the way human beings actually live and behave and God's purposes for them, and there is consequently a gulf and alienation between God and man. The keynote of Christian faith, however, is *reconciliation*, and this in turn rests upon *justification*, the making of man right with God.

Justification had been the great theme of the Reformers, especially of Martin Luther, and Ritschl aimed to restore it to the centre of theology by drawing out its consequences and implications in reconciliation, and opening up the force and meaning of Christianity from that centre. Reconciliation is worked out, made concrete and extended in the establishing and development of a new, ethical human community, which the New Testament calls the kingdom of God. This was what Jesus had come to bring about.

So Ritschl offered his own definition of Christianity, which resembles yet also differs strikingly from Schleiermacher's,

Christianity is the monotheistic, completely spiritual and ethical religion, which, on the basis of the life of its Founder as redeeming and establishing the kingdom of God, consists in the freedom of the children of God, includes the impulse to conduct from the motive of love, the intention of which is the moral organisation of mankind, and in the filial relation to God as well as in the kingdom of God lays the foundation of blessedness (*Justification and Reconciliation*, vol. III., E.T. 1900, p. 13).

In a figure which he was fond of using, Christianity is not a circle with a single centre, but an ellipse with two foci. One focus is Jesus, who reveals the love of God for us, and so reconciles us to God; the other is the spiritual and ethical community which he founded. This community is the church, but its goal is the transformation of the whole of human society into the kingdom of God. A fair summary of the whole might be 'the brotherhood of man and the Fatherhood of God, revealed in Jesus' teaching and example, and set before us as the goal which we are called to realise'.

It is very clear here that Ritschl had moved back behind Schleiermacher towards Kant's linking of religion with 'practical reason'. In other respects too, he is strongly reminiscent of Kant. For one thing, Kant himself had developed the thought that the kingdom of God is to be identified or interpreted as the ethical organisation of human society. For another, Kant had made a sharp distinction between 'judgements of fact' and 'judgements of value', between 'This is the case,' and 'This is what this means for me'; and that distinction had been further developed by the philosopher Lotze (1817–81). Like them, Ritschl believed that religious and theological statements are essentially judgements of value-for-us. So to say, 'Jesus is God', does not imply or claim that we have made direct observation of a hidden 'divine nature' in him, or explored his relationship with the Father from the inside. It means rather that he 'has the value of God for us' because in him the love of God towards us is made known. Here, Ritschl was following up a famous dictum of Luther's younger contemporary and associate, Philip Melanchthon in his *Loci Communes* of 1521, 'To know Christ is to know his benefits, not ... to contemplate his natures.' It is only through the work of Christ, through the impact on us of what he has done, that we can recognise him as divine and describe his person in divine terms.

On this ground, Ritschl was critical of much previous theology, and especially of the way the doctrine of the person of Christ had developed in the early centuries. The dogmas of his consubstantiality with the Father and of his possessing two natures in one person, can only mislead us if they are taken as objective, factual descriptions of the constitution of his being. What they really refer to and bring to expression is his meaning for us; and their significance is to be grasped afresh, not by their simple repetition, but by returning behind them to the history of Jesus' life and teaching, and to the message of his cross and resurrection. *That* is the dynamic, historical revelation of the Father's love, which draws us into the community of faith and sets us to work in the service of the kingdom.

An enormously popular and influential exposition of Liberal Theology was presented by Harnack in a series of informal lectures which were published in 1900 as *Das Wesen des Christentums*, 'The Essence of Christianity' (E.T. *What is Christianity?* 1901). The essence was to be found in Jesus' teaching, which Harnack summarised under three heads: the coming of the kingdom of God; the Fatherhood of God and the infinite worth of the human soul; the 'higher righteousness' and the command of love. This had been Jesus' gospel; it concerned the Father only, not the Son— for Jesus had not proclaimed himself. At the same time, he did embody his own message, so that it could be said that in him, 'the divine appeared in as pure a form as is possible on earth'. As a result, even within the New Testament documents, a shift towards an intensified emphasis upon Jesus himself could be traced; and thereafter the early church had been increasingly preoccupied with speculation about his 'divine nature'. This had then led to the classical dogmas of the Trinity and the incarnation, which Harnack described in his great *History of Dogma* as 'the fruit of the Greek spirit on the ground of the gospel', the product of the 'hellenisation of Christianity'. Harnack himself defended that development as necessary for the survival of Christian faith in the ancient Graeco-Roman world, but believed it must now be transcended, for it brought with it the immense danger of transforming the original and authentic gospel of love preached and exemplified by Jesus into abstract intellectual formulae, of confusing the husk with the kernel. Fortunately the unbiased historical study of the New Testament, set free from the crippling restrictions of dogmatic assumptions, could once more uncover the heart of the matter and present modern men afresh with the abiding message and enduring essence of Christian faith.

Like the thought of Schleiermacher, Liberal Theology has its own coherence, attractiveness and plausibility; but it too is open to damaging critical questions from several angles. These questions are all the more important in that the picture it paints of the real meaning of the New Testament, of Jesus' message, and of the essential nature of Christianity, accurately reflects an understanding of the matter which is still very widespread among Christians in the present day, though usually in less sophisticated form. Indeed, it is no exaggeration to say that Harnack's exposition expresses the popular conception of Christianity of the contemporary Christian 'man in the street'—a broadly ethical Unitarianism, in which Jesus is seen as a noble teacher and inspiring example of love and heroic self-sacrifice. It is a grave mistake to dismiss Liberal Theology simply as a manifestation of late nineteenth-century German culture, to which no special attention need be paid: it has a far deeper and wider appeal even now. That is certainly a witness to the fact that there is much that is very fine in it, and it would be foolish to pretend otherwise. But it is no less necessary to face up to its weaknesses as a comprehensive interpretation of the meaning of Christian belief.

Many of these weaknesses will emerge more clearly in later chapters, where we shall see how powerfully the pendulum has swung away from the position of Liberal Theology in recent generations, at least among the leaders and pioneers of theological thinking. For the moment, however, we may briefly indicate some of the problems which the Ritschlian approach encounters. Is the category of 'value-judgement' adequate to characterise the nature of theological statements—especially when it carries with it such a sharp disjunction between *value* and *fact*? Again, does the essence of Christianity really lie in its high spiritual, ethical and personal values, in 'the message' and 'the kingdom' rather than in Jesus Christ himself? Can the revelation of God in Jesus of which Christians have spoken from the New Testament onwards properly be interpreted simply by saying that Jesus manifests the divine love in the most perfect form attainable on earth? Can justification, the putting of sinful man right with God, be fully accounted for in these same terms? Is the kingdom of God spoken of in the New Testament simply 'the moral organisation of the human race', or does that conception owe more than the Liberals themselves realised to their own enlightened and optimistic view of the development of Protestant culture in their own day? Is it adequate at all to try in this fashion to interpret religion as a means to an end, and to define that end in progressive humanistic terms as having to do with the elevation and betterment of human society? There is more than ground for the suspicion that throughout, the second focus of Ritschl's ellipse is the dominant one, and the first is made subservient to it. Finally, is the Liberal confidence in its historical study justified? Is the figure of Jesus it claims to have uncovered really there in the New Testament, and is his message the one that Harnack claims? Is the kingdom he preached the kingdom proclaimed by Ritschl, or something quite different? These last questions were already being raised in the heyday of Liberal Theology itself, as we shall find later in this chapter, and with devastating effect. First, however, we must go back to Schleiermacher's contemporary in Berlin.

Hegel and after

In many ways, Hegel appears to be the complete opposite of Schleiermacher—whose relations with him in the years that they were colleagues in Berlin might charitably be described as strained. He too was concerned to move beyond Kant, and to offer a new basis for theology; he too was profoundly influenced by the spirit of Romanticism. But Hegel was a philosopher, and a philosopher who held that the responsibility of philosophy was to work out a universal and all-embracing system of understanding which would include literally everything—God and religion not excepted. This all-enfolding system was to be thoroughly metaphysical and consistently rational. So where Schleiermacher had drawn a sharp line between theology and philosophy, rejected metaphysics as an avenue of approaching truth, and stressed consciousness as lying deeper than rationality, Hegel subsumed theology under philosophy, and gave reason the highest place.

His motto, as stated in the preface to his *Philosophy of Law* (1821), was, 'The real is the rational, and the rational is the real.' Reality does not lie in *things* but in *reason* (*Vernunft*), which lies deeper than mere detached understanding (*Verstand*). Reason directly links the mind with the rationality which is the supreme reality. For this reason, his system has sometimes been called 'Pan-logism', from the Greek *pan* ('everything') and *logos* ('rationality'). More commonly, however, it is known as Absolute Idealism. Idealism here has nothing to do with 'ideals' in the ordinary English sense of ethical or spiritual values: it is connected rather with 'ideas', and serves to label any kind of philosophy which puts the emphasis on mind, understanding and reason rather than on experience and the senses. Hegel's Idealism is 'absolute' in that it sees all reality as gathered up in the all-encompassing, impersonal Mind which is God.

This concept of the Absolute Mind, or Absolute Spirit (the German word *Geist* includes both English senses), is one of Hegel's controlling motifs. Another is the *dialectic*, a pattern of movement which proceeds from a starting-point (the *thesis*) to another which stands over against it in opposition or contradiction (the *antithesis*), and then moves on to a third stage in which the two are reconciled and reintegrated on a higher level (the *synthesis*). In this movement, Hegel saw the very rhythm of reality itself, both as a whole and in every part, and also the dynamics of knowledge and understanding by which the initial gulf between subject and object is bridged in genuine synthesis, the act of cognition.

In the background here lies one of the favourite themes of the Romantics: that of the *coincidentia oppositorum*, 'coincidence of opposites'. They had exploited this idea as doing more justice to the nature of life and movement and the discovery of truth than the older rationalist insistence on the 'law of non-contradiction'. Put crudely, that law states that if A contradicts B, at least one of them must be false. This was felt by the Romantics to be too static, too absolute, too cut-and-dried, and to leave no place for the dynamics of discovery, the interplay of diversities, the movement from partial to fuller understanding, the connection between the inward and the outward, the whole and the part, the individual and the universal. Apparent oppositions, they felt, should not only be tolerated but gloried in: ultimately they would prove to be resolvable in a wider harmony.

Hegel's dialectic brought this sense to a further degree of refinement. A third important feature of his theory is the contrast he drew between *image* (*Vorstellung*) and *concept* (*Begriff*, sometimes also rendered, much less happily, as 'notion'). An image is a pictorial understanding of a kind which is true so far as it goes, but which falls short of full rational clarity, and must eventually be superseded by a concept. The expressions and ideas of religion—that of the Fatherhood of God, for instance—belong in the category of image, and it is the task of the philosopher to break through to a clearer conceptualisation, refining the images into concepts.

With these basic materials, Hegel developed his total system which included and explained everything from the nature of knowledge through the evolution of human society and culture to the whole history of the universe. The world itself is presented as a kind of self-projection of *Geist*, in which it brings itself into being as Nature, and so as over against itself (thesis and antithesis). Then, through the emergence of conscious mind in the world, the *Absolute Geist* returns to itself in a new kind of self-awareness (the synthesis). Finite mind within the world also advances dialectically, from undifferentiated consciousness through objective awareness of things other than itself to the act of understanding in which the subject/object dichotomy is overcome. Similarly, all the forms of human culture—art, law, religion and so on—are objectifications of the human spirit by which it projects itself externally in order then to move on through them to a higher self-realisation. In this process, art can then be seen to belong to an essentially subjective stage of immediate, concrete picturing; religion appears at that of objectifying symbols; and philosophy breaks through to the conceptualisation in which full and genuine understanding is attained.

In this way, Hegel's system itself gives final form to the understanding of the world and of God which is imperfectly represented in all religion, more adequately sketched in Christianity, and at last attains its fullness in Absolute Idealism. There the finite mind of man, which is but a fragment and form of the Infinite, discovers its true identity with the Absolute—and that is at the same time the return of the Absolute to itself, its own self-realisation. The doctrine of the Trinity thus becomes the universal dialectical process, while the dogmas of creation and incarnation speak of Mind's projection of itself as Nature, and witness to the ultimate identity of Infinite and finite Mind.

Unlike Scheiermacher, Hegel had a large number of followers who sought to carry on from the point he had reached. They tended, however, to go off in different directions. The tradition of Absolute Idealism in his own sense was continued chiefly outside Germany by philosophers such as Edward Caird (1835–1908) and F. H. Bradley (1846–1924), eventually leading through Josiah Royce (1855–1916), A. S. Pringle-Pattison (1856–1931) and J. M. E. McTaggart (1866–1925) to a form of Idealism that was more 'personal' than 'absolute', in line with a more general trend towards a personalist emphasis in much other modern philosophy. Within Germany, the Hegelian school divided into a 'right' and a 'left' wing—the right aiming on the whole to retain Hegel's broad framework, the left building on elements in it, but in a way which led to very different eventual results. On the whole, it was the left wing that was the more creative and influential, and it was to it that some of the men we must now mention belonged. The developments which they initiated will serve to highlight some of the major theological issues raised by Hegel's *tour de force* of systematic synthesis.

One point which cries out for consideration is this: do the Christian doctrines which Hegel has transposed into his own metaphysical key still mean the same? Or, to put the question in terms closer to his own, are the principles enunciated in the system of Absolute Idealism really the truth to which these theological teachings point? The force of this question is brought out by the line of interpretation offered by the distinguished Swiss Hegelian theologian A. E. Biedermann (1819–85). Only one feature of his thought can be mentioned here, but it is both central to this sort of Hegelian theology and typical of an approach which has appealed to many others as well. He made a clear distinction between what he called 'the principle of redemption' and the person of Jesus. The principle is the 'idea', the eternal truth, of 'God-manhood', of the unity of finite and Infinite Mind. This eternal idea was brought to light and exemplified concretely in Jesus, and through him it is also made known to us. It is not that Jesus himself *was* God and man in the special and quite unique sense that Christian dogma had so long maintained. Rather, the dogma is a means of expressing the more general principle which he brings to awareness in our religious consciousness. So, under the aegis of Hegelianism, Biedermann comes close to the view earlier stated by Fichte: it is not the historical as such, but the metaphysical, that makes us blessed—not the historical person of Jesus as God and man, but the metaphysical idea of God-manhood, which is simply exemplified, illustrated, and communicated by Jesus.

This leads in turn to what is perhaps the fundamental difficulty in Hegel's entire pattern of thought. While it does set out to include and explicate the sense of the whole movement of history, history itself seems to be in the end rather unimportant. It does not appear as the arena of significant events, of accidental developments which can nevertheless have the most far-reaching consequences, of puzzling loose ends, or of real contradictions and inexplicabilities. It is simply an element in what, in its totality, is seen as the drama of the self-determined unfolding and return to itself of Absolute Mind. Granted that the whole of history may have a meaning, a purpose and a direction—and granted, too, the power and fruitfulness of many of Hegel's ideas—are that purpose and direction so easily uncovered as he suggests? Or does he too quickly take flight from history altogether into a realm of the Absolute?

The same kind of problem arises if the system is looked at from the angle of the natural sciences. They proceed on the assumption, which Hegel also shared, that there is a sense and pattern in the structure and dynamics of reality, and that these can be explored and entered into through experimentation and theorising. But the scientist cannot lay down in advance what the pattern will turn out to be. Significantly, though Hegel himself was much interested in science, especially in astronomy, his own efforts in that direction were none too successful: physical reality tended to be uncomfortably unwilling to accommodate itself to his theoretical predictions. Nor did his philosophy contribute significantly to the development of the scientific enterprise in succeeding generations. It was too much inclined to wrap everything up and regard it as settled.

It was on this general point that another of Hegel's followers, Ferdinand Christian Baur (1792–1860), was particularly critical of him. Baur was the leader of the 'Tübingen school' which opened up new lines of study of the New Testament, and was the most widely influential and controversial movement in biblical criticism in the first half of the nineteenth century. It was regarded by many as dangerously radical and extreme—in much the same style as the 'Bultmann school' in the last forty years—but it did introduce a new epoch in critical New Testament research, most notably by drawing attention to the distinct strands and theologies within the different New Testament documents. The contrasts between the synoptic gospels (Matthew, Mark and Luke) and the fourth gospel, between the various letters ascribed to Paul, and between Paul's theology and that of other leaders in the primitive church, all now came in for serious consideration. In this new study, Baur made considerable use of Hegel's dialectical conception, finding the New Testament to reflect, not a homogeneous movement, but a conflict between an earlier, Petrine theology and a later, Pauline type, which the later New Testament documents were attempting to reconcile in a new synthesis. He also traced the same kind of dialectical movement in the development of the church and theology in subsequent ages. While the procedure was to some extent artificial and led to conclusions that did not always stand up to later study, it did at least mean that the different forms of early Christian teaching could now be admitted for discussion, and the possibility of real conflict between opposing views recognised as a natural and proper element in the development. But while Baur used these ideas of Hegel in this way, he criticised the master's overall system as a new form of *Gnosticism*—the escape from history and its untidiness into an untroubled world of heavenly truth lying far beyond it. He directed the same charge against Schleiermacher as well, and in this paved the way for Ritschl and Liberal Theology (Ritschl himself began his career as a New Testament scholar in the Tübingen tradition).

So far as his own understanding of Jesus himself was concerned, however, Baur resembled Biedermann: Jesus was the exemplary embodiment of an 'idea'. He differed from Hegel in his particular emphasis on historical study of the New Testament, but remained Idealist in his theology. This combination of an insistence on the relativity of history and an attempt to express the significance of Jesus in terms which appeal to something more universal than the concrete particular person of Jesus himself was indeed widely characteristic of much nineteenth-century thought. Liberal Theology went the same way, though it substituted the categories of Ritschl's system for those of Hegel's. (Nor, it may be added, was it only in the nineteenth century that this stratagem was adopted: it has figured in a good deal of more recent writing as well. But the nineteenth century was also to see more radical questioning of this assumption about the proper approach to the matter.)

While Biedermann and Baur were in accord with Hegel's aim

to combine Christianity and speculative philosophy, others drew from him the material for frontal attacks on Christian belief, notably Strauss, Feuerbach and Marx. Strauss began his career as an Idealist theologian and New Testament scholar in the Tübingen mould, but by the end of his life had abandoned Christian faith altogether. Feuerbach's position was more consistent: he was a philosopher who did not believe in God but was on his own admission passionately concerned with religion and theology, whose real object he held to be man himself. Both Strauss and Feuerbach in effect fastened on the hinge of Hegel's system—the identification of finite and Infinite Mind—and, having grasped it, turned it upside down. There is, they held, no supernatural God of the kind Hegel still believed in; there is only man, and it is the human spirit which finds oblique expression in religion and theology. Here, they drew on Hegel's account of religious doctrines and institutions as symbolic objectifications of that spirit. But having snapped the thread which had led Hegel on from there to his speculative Absolute, they turned back to find the real meaning and reference of these objectifications in the subject which had produced them as forms of its own self-expression. Theology was thus transformed back into anthropology.

Strauss' most influential work was his *Life of Jesus* (1835), which was enthusiastically translated into English by George Eliot. Here, he introduced into New Testament criticism the idea of 'myth', and applied it to the supernatural elements in the gospels. In the past, the orthodox approach had been to take these literally, while the rationalists had dismissed them as arbitrary fiction. Strauss maintained that both approaches were equally shallow. These features of the gospels are neither simple history nor redundant embroidery. They are the means used by the writers and the early church to express their own awareness of the significance of Jesus who, as the Founder of Christianity, had been the first to discover the deep truth that God and man are one. But what is said about Jesus really expresses the truth about the human race as a whole. Man himself is the union of the finite and the Infinite, of Spirit and Nature, the miracle-worker in whom Spirit rules over Nature; and mankind as a whole is sinless and destined for perfection in its onward and upward march, symbolised by the New Testament in terms of death, resurrection and ascension.

This new, technical use of 'myth' to mean, not a falsehood, but a truth indirectly expressed, has since become very common in theology—though not always with the same idea about what truth actually is as in Strauss. Similarly, the recognition that what is said about Jesus in the New Testament is the expression of faith in him, and that this side of the matter, though not the only one, cannot be left out of account, has also become a basic axiom of much modern New Testament study. In these ways, the *Life of Jesus* ranks with the work of Baur as epoch-making in New Testament research. But for Strauss himself it represented a stage in what was to become an anguished and sometimes bitter drifting away from even this somewhat diluted and Idealist 'Christianity'.

Feuerbach's position was developed particularly in *The Essence of Christianity* (1841), *The Philosophy of the Future* (1843) and *The Essence of Religion* (1853). It centres in the conviction that the very idea of God is itself a projection in which man seeks to transcend the limitations of his own finitude. Religion reflects man's desire to be the God he imagines. More recent interpretations of religion as illusory self-projection (Sigmund Freud) or as expressions of the structure and self-understanding of human society (Emile Durkheim) owe a great deal to Feuerbach, in whom the broad lines are already laid down. But he did not simply dismiss religion on this score; rather he kept returning to reflect upon it. He believed that once the real heart and living impulse at its core were discerned, it had validity and significance as expressing the nature of man himself. This was the main difference between Feuerbach and the more radical Karl Marx, whose early thought was much affected both by Feuerbach and by the more militantly atheistic Hegelian Bruno Bauer.

Marx maintained that the human consciousness which could project this refracted religious self-image must be a 'false consciousness', profoundly alienated from itself; that it had been brought into this state by the development of divisions within human society between the different social and economic classes; that religion served in that situation as an 'ideology', a system of beliefs functioning to support the established order, and an 'opium' which would keep the proletariat passive in the face of their oppression and exploitation by diverting their attention and hopes to another world and its promised rewards; that it was not enough for the philosopher to understand and diagnose this situation, but that he must go on to change it; and that this involved

45

moving back from Feuerbach's 'critique of heaven' to a fresh 'critique of earth', of economics, politics and society in general, with the aim of changing the structures of the established order and overcoming the forces of division and alienation which both produced religion and drew support from it. Marx also believed that the day of Christianity was already past: it really belonged to an earlier, feudal pattern of society, and had been undermined beyond hope of recovery by the emergence of the bourgeois culture, which had already passed beyond it, and appeared to maintain it only for the most cynical of purposes. While in the nineteenth century, Marx appeared simply as an 'anti-theologian', many of the themes in his work have come to play a role in more recent theological discussion.

These developments on the left wing of Hegelianism, and the work of Feuerbach in particular, throw into high relief a profound ambiguity not only in Hegel's thought, but also in that of Schleiermacher and Ritschl. Although they all speak with great seriousness of God, their procedure concentrates very much on man—whether on his religious awareness, his moral striving, or his rational understanding. Does their theology then really speak about a real God, or merely about man himself? If the former, have they made the point sufficiently clear, shown the foundation on which they are building, and set up adequate defences against Feuerbach's criticisms? While they, unlike Feuerbach, certainly did not intend to turn theology into anthropology, did they nevertheless risk doing precisely that? By focusing attention, albeit in negative and often hostile fashion, on that issue, the radical Hegelians placed on the agenda what was to become an urgent matter in later generations.

The way in which that topic was to explode on to the stage in the twentieth century is anticipated in the frontal attack launched on Hegel's system by the Danish philosopher Søren Kierkegaard. He received but scant attention outside his native land for half a century after his death, but then came to be a major force who made a profound impression on both theology and philosophy. In a literary career lasting only some twelve years, he poured out a steady stream of sermons, pamphlets and books, some under his own name, some with symbolic pseudonyms. Among the most significant for theology were *Philosophical Fragments* (1844), *Stages on Life's Way* (1845) and *Concluding Unscientific Postscript* (1846).

Throughout his work he circled endlessly around the question of what it is to be a Christian, to have faith, to encounter God. He was a brilliant but also a tortured thinker, in many ways a solitary and tragic figure, his personality marked by a tendency to depression, and by the decision he made in 1843 to break off his engagement to Regine Olsen. His profound psychological insight owed a great deal to a neurotic streak, and it was no accident that one of his contributions to subsequent technical terminology was the term *Angst* ('dread'), and that he published books with such titles as *The Concept of Dread, Fear and Trembling* and *The Sickness unto Death*. But he was far from being merely neurotic; rather, he was a visionary of genius comparable with that of William Blake or Fyodor Dostoievsky, one of those rare souls whose work, forged in the fires of their own pain, shatters established perceptions and calls their readers into a new and different world. And against the background of the dominant trends in theology, Kierkegaard offered something very new and different indeed.

His thought was shaped by two distinct but complementary convictions. The first has to do with his understanding of the character of truth and the way in which it is opened up and attained, and is expressed in one of his battle-cries, 'Truth is subjectivity!' By this, he did not mean that truth is simply subjective, merely my own opinion, what I happen to like to regard as true. He meant that the deepest and profoundest truth, the truth that ultimately matters and is in the end really worth grasping, cannot be of the sort that can be contemplated and appropriated in an attitude of serene detachment. It must be seized with passion and entered inwardly. Nor can it be had simply as a possession: it must be 'leapt into' repeatedly and afresh. There are of course all kinds of truths that are not of this sort; but they lie on a lower level altogether. The truth with which faith deals is of the highest and most ultimate kind, and faith itself is a 'leap' and a 'passion', a leap into the truth that can only be grasped on the road of authentic commitment.

The second conviction is, again in his own expression, of 'the infinite qualitative difference' between God and man, the infinite and the finite, eternity and time. From this sense of the immense gulf between God and himself, and between God's holiness and his own sinful existence, arises the pathos of Kierkegaard's understanding of faith itself. Man stands over against the awful otherness of God, by which his own existence is challenged, questioned and judged; but in faith he finds the power nonetheless to live in that encounter with God by which each present moment becomes a meeting with eternity. But in this meeting the absolute difference between the two sides remains: it is not dissolved away in a 'coincidence of opposites', an 'identity in difference', an 'eternal God-man unity'.

The heart of Christianity, for Kierkegaard, lies in the recognition in Jesus of the intersection of time and eternity, the coming together of God and man. But this intersection is not a Hegelian movement from thesis through antithesis to eventual sythesis. It is, rather, what he terms 'the Absolute Paradox', for the absolute difference between God and man remains, even when God becomes man in the incarnation. How he could do so at all is something beyond our finite comprehension, and the full significance of the intersection of eternity with time in Jesus is only grasped along with the awareness that it is beyond our power to understand or explain.

This recognition occurs in a decisive 'moment' in which we find ourselves faced and encountered by the reality of God in Jesus. This 'moment' is itself a point in our own time and history, but insofar as it is also the encounter with eternity, it is the 'eternal moment', and shares something of the quality of the intersection of time and eternity in Jesus himself. And it is itself always also paradoxical, for it discloses what cannot be scaled down to be contained, proved, measured, demonstrated or explained within the framework of finite human reasoning. Jesus is God 'incognito': it is of the very nature of the presence of God as man that it *must* be ambiguous, that it may not be recognised by everyone, that the 'sign' by its very nature may be 'spoken against'. It follows that once a person reaches the level of authentic faith—which he sees as the third and highest stage along the path of life, following others which he terms the 'aesthetic' and the 'ethical'—it is led and governed purely by obedience to God and not by anything merely human, however lofty. The archetype of faith is Abraham, who went out at God's command though he did not know where he was going, and who was prepared at that command even to sacrifice his own son.

This approach led Kierkegaard to tackle the question of the connection between Jesus' history and our own in a quite new fashion.

He did this by contrasting Jesus with Socrates as he is described in Plato's dialogues. Socrates is a teacher, but his function as he himself describes it is to uncover in the minds of those he teaches what they really know already, but have simply failed to recognise or make explicit. He calls himself a 'midwife', and like a midwife, has only a temporary and external role to play in the process of birth. His task is to provoke and stimulate, and it is completed once the lesson is over and the point has been grasped. The approach to Jesus in much of the theology and teaching with which Kierkegaard was familiar tended very much to see him too in that kind of light—as the founder of a religion, as the discoverer and imparter of divine truths, as the exemplar of particular values, which were only accidentally bound up with him, but in principle could be detached from him. We have already noticed how that approach was broadly characteristic of the Hegelians and of Liberal Theology, and Schleiermacher too can fairly be added to the list. They all insist on the centrality of Jesus, but incline then to explain that centrality in terms of something more general or universal, which is thought of as exemplified in him, and then as spreading out from him and moving on through history.

By contrast, Kierkegaard asserted that the whole point is that Jesus is *not* another Socrates. He does not claim to offer us some 'truth' separable from himself, but challenges men to recognise him as the one who *is* the truth, and the truth into which we too are brought out of our own *un*truthfulness when we recognise who he is. That in turn involves much more than simply studying him as a figure of past history, or breathing in his historical influence. It means encountering him as the one who is eternally present before us and who therefore meets us *now*. This is the recognition of faith, and there is no way in which it can be demonstrated to be valid by appeal to merely historical argument about Jesus. The 'believer at second hand', the one who believes through having heard the witness of those who believed 'at first hand', i.e. the original disciples, must make the same leap of faith as they did to break through Jesus' incognito: they have no advantage over him of the kind that a purely historical approach to Jesus might suggest.

Kierkegaard thus rejects decisively and with withering scorn all attempts to present Christian faith in terms of Idealism or moral values, of historical influence and historical study, or of belonging to an established Christian church. Idealism obliterates the infinite qualitative difference between God and man, loses sight of the ineffable paradox of the incarnation, and ends in what Kierkegaard mercilessly pillories as the ludicrous identification of the thoughts of a philosopher with the mind of God. Both the object of faith—Jesus as God in history—and the character of faith itself disappear from view in the Idealist reconstruction. The Infinite becomes merely the extension *ad infinitum* of the finite instead of a reality 'wholly other'. The same is done when religion is reduced to ethics, or treated simply as a movement within history, to be explained and defended, or even proved, by historical research and demonstration. The encounter between time and eternity cannot be fitted into either pattern of interpretation. Finally, 'Christendom' itself has betrayed Jesus by domesticating him as if he were the possession of the church, and by making faith the acceptance of formulae and practices hallowed by the authority of the past. This dissolves the central paradox which is of the very essence of faith, and turns faith itself into an inheritance rather than a permanent passion of risk, commitment and obedience.

The gauntlet thus thrown down against ideas and assumptions so widely current in the Christianity and theology of his own day was Kierkegaard's great contribution. In many ways it must be admitted that his thought was unbalanced and inadequately developed. He worked out his positions very much through polemical critique of others, and tended to be clearer about what was to be rejected than about what was to be put constructively in its place. The categories and concepts he hammered out in his attack on Idealism—many of them of course drawn from Idealism itself, but refashioned by him—are by no means wholly adequate to serve the restatement of Christian theology, and could indeed lead to the emergence of philosophies quite alien to Christianity itself. In resisting rationalism he risks emphasising paradox to the point where it can seem sheerly irrational; his insistence on the otherness of God and the sinfulness of man, and his fondness for some of the more arbitrary-seeming accounts of God in the stories of Abraham and Job, leave much too little place for a positive grasp of grace and mercy, goodness and love, though he does attempt to give them place; his stress upon the centrality of the incarnation of God in Jesus commonly seems to reduce to the bare repetition of the claim that Jesus was also, paradoxically, God, but not fully to work through the implications and purpose of this identification of God with man; his bitter attacks upon 'Christendom' in his latter years reveal rather too much of the solitary individualist who has little sense of the nature of community. Nor has his influence always been entirely healthy: he resembles Nietzsche and Schopenhauer in that it has sometimes been the more morbid and pathological features of his thought that have exercised the strongest fascination on his readers.

When, generations after his death, theology rediscovered him, it also found it necessary to move beyond him. Nonetheless he stands out as a prophetic beacon, a fresh and radical thinker whose radicalism did not lie in attempting a consciously 'modern reinterpretation' of Christian faith, but in struggling afresh with the heart of the matter, and charting out a very different course from those being recommended on all sides around him.

We have just seen how Kierkegaard rejected any idea that faith could be proved by the appeal to historical argument. Earlier we traced the new emphasis which, by contrast, Liberal Theology laid upon the historical approach to the New Testament. The wide gulf between these approaches reveals the extent to which the relation between theological and historical study became problematical through the nineteenth century. Some of the main issues arising here can be illustrated further from the course taken by the historical study of Jesus through the century, and from the rise towards its close of quite new approaches to the study of the history of religions in general.

In 1906 Albert Schweitzer published a lengthy book, *Von Reimarus zu Wrede. Eine Geschichte der Leben-Jesu Forschung* ('From Reimarus to Wrede. A History of the Life of Jesus Research'), translated into English as *The Quest of the Historical Jesus*. In it, he surveyed and criticised a large number of attempts to reconstruct 'the real Jesus', from Reimarus' *Fragments*, published by Lessing in the 1770s, to William Wrede's *Das Messiasgeheimnis in den Evangelien* ('The Messianic Secret in the Gospels') of 1901. The various *Lives* had been written from a variety of standpoints, but he observed that the best of them had been inspired with hate—hate, not of Jesus, but of the 'Christ of dogma'. The general aim was to tear away the wrappings in which orthodox Christianity How far they had been successful was, however, another matter How far they had been successful was, however, another matter entirely: the main effect of Schweitzer's brilliant study was in fact to put an end to that quest, at least in its most widely popular form.

In the period he covered, Schweitzer distinguished three broad stages, in which three distinct issues were successively at the centre of discussion. The first ran up to Strauss' *Life of Jesus*, and struggled with the question whether the supernatural and miraculous elements in the gospels should be accepted. Strauss had settled that question by treating them as myths, in which the significance of Jesus was indirectly expressed. Similarly, theologians such as Schleiermacher had moved away from the idea of a miracle as a supernatural intervention in the normal processes of nature, and were in essential harmony with Strauss' conclusions.

As a result, the key to the meaning of Jesus had come to be looked for, not in supernatural accreditation by miracles, but in his personality, his consciousness of God, his teaching and his impact upon his followers. This had then opened up what Schweitzer described as the 'psychologising' approach to Jesus, which set out to explore his understanding of himself, tracing his awareness of God, his key ideas, even the development of his teaching through the career which ran from Galilee to Golgotha. Schleiermacher's own account of Jesus relied heavily on such psychological study; so, for that matter, did that of Liberal Theology; and so too did those which saw Jesus only as a particularly heroic and noble representative of the human race, as did the immensely popular *Life of Jesus* by the Frenchman Ernst Renan (1823–92). Just this approach had, however, been rendered impossible by the development of the second and third stages in critical New Testament study, for they had removed any real basis for it.

The question in the second stage, which was ushered in by the work of Baur, was raised by the manifest differences in style and content between the synoptic gospels and the gospel of John. Baur, and the generality of leading New Testament scholars after him, had come to hold that the fourth gospel was not a reliable historical source. It was much later than the others; it was the product of hellenistic circles in the church of the early second century; it was therefore altogether remote from the life and times of Jesus himself. Once it was felt not to be reliable as evidence for Jesus' own history and teaching, however, most of what the psychological biographies had chiefly depended upon was removed along with it. Without the fourth gospel there were very few sayings which could be taken as directly expressing what Jesus' own self-understanding might have been; for most of these statements are in it, not in the synoptics. Without it, too, there was no longer a clear chronological framework within which to set and arrange the events and stages of Jesus' ministry; for most of the indications of dates and journeys are in it. The biographical approach to Jesus' life, and the psychological study of his own mind, were thus left with far too little to work with. That was bad enough; but worse yet was to come in the third stage.

That third stage had been introduced by the work of Johannes Weiss in his *Die Predigt Jesu vom Reiche Gottes* ('The Preaching of Jesus concerning the Kingdom of God'), published in 1892. Weiss was Ritschl's son-in-law, and had set out to investigate the theme of the kingdom of God in the synoptic gospels with a suspicion that it amounted to something rather different from what Ritschl had made of it. The suspicion proved amply justified. Weiss found that the kingdom Jesus preached belonged in the apocalyptic, eschatological framework of contemporary Jewish thought. Jesus was not inviting men to join a spiritual and ethical community directed towards the moral organisation of mankind. He was proclaiming the imminent end of the present world, and the coming victorious rule of God which would break in from beyond. This showed, Schweitzer forcefully argued, that the entire quest of the Idealists, Liberals and humanists had been utterly misconceived. The New Testament message was consistently eschatological, having to do with the end of the present order of things and the coming of something quite new; and Jesus himself represented the final flowering of the apocalyptic spirit of late Judaism.

As Reimarus had long since argued, *that*, rather than the intention of 'founding Christianity', was the key to his preaching and teaching. The real Jesus could not have been more removed from Renan's 'amiable carpenter' who spoke beautifully about the lilies of the field in order to convey a new and simple principle of love; the 'historical Jesus' of so many searches and 'discoveries' was not historical at all. As Schweitzer's contemporary, the Roman Catholic Modernist, George Tyrrell, remarked, the biographers of

Jesus 'looked into the deep well of history, and saw there only the reflection of their own faces'.

A final nail in the coffin had been hammered in by Wrede. By studying the gospel references to the apocalyptic Jewish figure of the 'Son of Man'—whom Jesus sometimes appears to identify with himself, but sometimes not—Wrede had come to the conclusions that Jesus had not in fact applied the title to himself; that after his resurrection the church had come to anticipate his return; that it had then identified Jesus himself as the coming Son of Man; and that the impression given in the gospels of a 'messianic secret' that Jesus in his lifetime conveyed only to his closest disciples, and charged them not to reveal to others until the proper time came, was a mere literary device to support that identification. The general conclusion reached here was that any attempt to get behind the early church's proclamation of Jesus to what Jesus himself had actually believed about himself could only be built on psychological conjecture and historical guesswork.

The importance of Schweitzer's study is twofold. Along with Weiss, he forced theology to approach with a new seriousness the eschatological element in the New Testament and in Jesus' message. They look beyond history as such to the activity of God, and set the movement of history itself in that light. While Schweitzer tended to dwell too exclusively on this aspect, he was certainly justified in stressing it. Second, he effectively demolished the picture of Jesus and his teaching which had been developed in the 'progressive' theology of the previous generations.

The further question of where now theology ought to be going was one he was less equipped to tackle. His own answer to it was in some ways remarkably similar to those he attacked, for it added up to this: historical study cannot bring Jesus down to our own time; rather, it reveals his strangeness to us, and he loses all colour and significance if we attempt to tear him out of his own historical and religious setting in late Judaism. So too his *message* of the coming kingdom cannot be lifted out and carried over to the present: that message was refuted when Jesus himself attempted to provoke the intervention of God and bring about the end of history by challenging the powers and authorities of his own day. He attempted to stop the wheel of history, but the wheel turned on and crushed him on the cross. But there is something else: what Schweitzer calls the 'spirit' of Jesus. That lives on, and we are called and challenged to share it, to hear the words once spoken by the lake-side, 'Come, follow me.' And Schweitzer's own subsequent work in Africa, whose guiding principle he described as 'reverence for life', stands as a monument to his understanding of what that spirit and that following meant. It is however noticeable that while on the point of history he was directly opposed to Liberal Theology, his appeal to a 'spirit' somehow detachable from the Jesus of history, and his practical application of it, run very much along similar lines to the Liberal approach.

Some years earlier, the same issues had been opened up from a more consciously theological angle by the Halle professor Martin Kähler. In his *Der Sogennante historische Jesus und der geschichtliche, biblische Christus* (E.T. *The so-called historical Jesus and the historic, biblical Christ*, 1966) published in 1892, he took issue with the underlying aims and presuppositions of the 'life of Jesus research'. The question he broached was whether or how far the historical approach to the New Testament is appropriate as a means of uncovering the truth about Jesus and supplying a solid basis (or correction) for Christian belief. That question was already implicit in his title, with its distinction between the adjectives *historisch* (corresponding to the noun *Historie*) and *geschichtlich* (from *Geschichte*). Both *Historie* and *Geschichte* may be translated as 'history', and both *historisch* and *geschichtlich* as 'historical'; and there is no easy way directly to represent in English the contrast he drew between them. *Geschichte* as Kähler used it refers to past history as such; *Historie* to history as studied by the means and methods of historical study. But the distinction carried other overtones as well, which have become even more central in more recent applications of the distinction. *Historie* can be seen as describing the past *as past*, and as fragmentarily reconstructed by the detached, scholarly and scientific method of the historian; *Geschichte* as describing a past which in some fashion also impinges upon and involves the present, a past which must be approached via subjective commitment rather than by a purely objective analysis of a more neutral kind.

Kähler rejected any purely *historisch* approach to the figure of Jesus for three main reasons. First of all, the available evidence is not of the right kind. The gospels do not furnish us with the materials for a modern-style biography, nor do they give us a window into Jesus' mind by which we could peer into his inmost soul.

They were written to proclaim him as the Christ, the anointed of God, the revealer of the Father, and to elicit the appropriate response of faith and trust in him. Second, any reconstruction of Jesus' personality must involve, like all such reconstructions, the general principle of *analogy*. We must assume that he was a man like ourselves, and apply our own experience and use our own sympathetic imagination to visualise and enter into his mind. But, Kähler insisted, precisely this principle cannot be relied upon in the case of Jesus, because of the witness of the Bible and of Christian experience of him that he is unique, perfect and free from sin. There is a difference of kind, not merely of degree, between him and ourselves. Third, all purely historical study by its very nature can offer only provisional results. If faith is to be solidly grounded at all, it must rest on some more secure foundation than that. Otherwise a 'papacy of the professors' would be set up between Jesus Christ and those who believe in him. By its very nature, faith rests and must rest in a 'storm-free territory' which mere historical consideration and reconsideration cannot in any way disturb.

Overall, historical (*historisch*) study of Jesus attempts to reconstruct the kind of real Jesus whom the historian, for whatever good or bad reasons of his own, thinks to be worth finding. Faith, by contrast, approaches Jesus with a radically different attitude, recognising in him the revelation of the invisible God, believing that it is true that 'he who has seen me has seen the Father'. This is not the artificial 'historical Jesus', but the Jesus who was and is seen and trusted as the Christ of God, the Christ of *Geschichte* rather than the mere Jesus of *Historie*.

Kähler's insistence that faith and historical research are not the same thing is obviously valid. But it is nonetheless questionable whether his statement of the difference is entirely adequate. How far is the wedge to be driven between *Historie* and *Geschichte*? Is ordinary historical study wholly irrelevant to the approach of the believer to Jesus? Kähler's thought, and the distinction he drew, were to find many echoes in later debate, along with the work of Schweitzer, and we shall meet these questions again. For the moment it is enough to observe that the *Historie/Geschichte* dichotomy *could* very easily end up looking rather like Lessing's between the accidental truths of history and the necessary truths of reason, or Fichte's between the historical and the metaphysical, and thus lead to a position open to the same charge of Gnosticism that Baur had laid at the door of Hegel and Schleiermacher.

A wider but related set of matters was brought to the fore around this same period by the 'history-of-religions school' (*Religionsgeschichtliche Schule*), which may be reckoned to have begun with Otto Pfleiderer's *Primitive Christianity* (1887; E.T. 1906). This shared and to some extent grew out of the Ritschlian emphasis on history and historical investigation, and was concerned to set the history of the beginnings of Christianity in the wider context of the culture, philosophy and religion of the ancient world. Powerful impulses in this direction had been supplied by the immense development in the study of antiquity throughout the nineteenth century. As more and more material was uncovered, the interest of students of both Old and New Testaments had extended to take in increasingly large tracts of the surrounding fields, and to seek to locate the biblical material in that broader setting.

The most radical thinkers in the *Religionsgeschichtliche Schule*—such as Richard Reitzenstein (1861–1931) and Wilhelm Bousset (1865–1920)—inclined to treat Christianity itself as an eclectic synthesis of religious and philosophical ideas flowing in from a variety of sources in the ancient world. Reitzenstein in particular pushed to its extreme limits a view, which was to be held by others in the following generation, notably Rudolf Bultmann, that the ideas of redemption displayed in the New Testament were in fact derived from pre-Christian gnostic mythology. Other members of the group, notably Johannes Weiss, were more cautious. Their approach, however, inevitably raised further questions both about the assumptions on which it was based, and about the implications for the standing of the Bible and for the uniqueness and distinctiveness of Christianity of this kind of historical comparison with non-biblical sources. These led on to the further issues of the relation between Christianity and other religions in general, and of the impact of the critical study of religions on Christian theology; for that study too had made huge strides through the nineteenth century. The most systematic theological reflection on these problems was offered in this period by Ernst Troeltsch.

Behind Troeltsch stands the philosopher Wilhelm Dilthey (1833–1911) who in turn drew much of his inspiration from Schleiermacher. Dilthey set out to construct a philosophy of history which would disclose the real nature of historical knowledge and establish its significance for modern culture. Basic to it is a distinction, which he took from the English philosopher John Stuart Mill (1806–73), between 'natural science' and 'moral science', which he rendered in German as *Naturwissenschaft* and *Geisteswissenschaft* respectively. In natural science, we study the phenomena of the world around us, the world of *things*, of *objects*. There, we are always in the position of observers, looking in, as it were, from without. We are necessarily at a distance from them, detached. In moral (or human) science, by contrast, we deal with that with which we have immediate contact within ourselves—the human spirit and the forms in which it expresses and manifests itself. This is what enables us in historical study to bridge the gulf between the present and the past, to enter into the experience and awareness which are opened up for us in the thoughts, beliefs, practices and social customs and institutions of other times and other cultures. The various forms of religion in particular reveal the human spirit facing the ultimate questions about the meaning of existence, and by studying them our own understanding can be deepened and extended. In this, however, we are not dealing directly with *God*—Dilthey bracketed off the question of God himself—but with religion as a human phenomenon. In the process we become aware of the *diversity*—and therefore also of the *relativity*—of the different particular forms it has taken. But the enduring constant is the spirit of man in which we also share.

Troeltsch himself worked in three main fields. He sought to develop further Dilthey's philosophy of history, seeing the modern awareness of history as the key to the nature of our culture. He developed a sociological approach to the study of church history in his *The Social Teaching of the Christian Churches* (1911; E.T. 1931), where he distinguished three main social forms of religious institution: the church-type, the sect-type, and individual mysticism. Finally, he devoted a good deal of attention to the problem of the implications of his general historical approach for understanding the character of Christianity itself, particularly in *The Absoluteness of Christianity* (1901; E.T. 1972), the unfinished *Der Historismus und seine Probleme* ('historicism and its problems'), published in 1922, and a lecture written just before his death on 'The Place of Christianity among the World Religions'. In *The*

Absoluteness of Christianity he rejected the idea that any historical phenomenon, including the Christian faith, could be absolutely and universally valid, but still tried to hold that Christianity was nevertheless in some fashion the 'normative' form of religion. By the end of his life, his position was somewhat more relativist, and that can fairly be seen as the result of the consistent working-through of his earlier principles.

Troeltsch's approach to the question follows the lines of a general study of the religious history of mankind. That study follows three basic principles: of *criticism, analogy* and *correlation.* Criticism demands that all evidence must be critically weighed, and all conclusions open to revision in the light of fresh evidence. Analogy means that the events being investigated are essentially similar in kind to those of which we ourselves have direct experience. Correlation specifies that every event in history is connected with others, and the whole of history is a kind of network of these inter-relations. There are no breaks in it in the sense of special divine interventions; and while every event is in its own way particular, individual and unique, none is qualitatively of a wholly different kind from all others.

The net result is that no religion can be 'absolute' or 'final', and Troeltsch eventually rejected the attempts of Schleiermacher and Hegel to establish the uniqueness of Christianity in any absolutely distinctive sense. Historical study cannot make place for any such absoluteness, let alone demonstrate it. At very best, any particular religion can be normative or valid only for those who happen to subscribe to it. Within that horizon, its doctrines may of course be affirmed and presented as true; but the wider and more ample perspective of the study of religion in general cannot permit such restrictions—though it may be engaged in by one who *also,* as a personal matter, adheres to a particular faith. Christian *dogmatic* theology as traditionally practised is an aspect of Christian *practical* theology, the working-out of the mode of expression of Christian beliefs in a Christian context. The disciplined study of religion reaches out more broadly to cover all the forms of religious experience.

In Troeltsch, the focusing of attention on 'religion' which had been so central for Schleiermacher and Liberal Theology is thus intensified to the point where its separation off from Christian theology becomes inevitable. In this way, Troeltsch anticipated the further expansion through the twentieth century of the study of religion by comparative, psychological, anthropological and sociological means. This study has been and doubtless will continue to be enormously fruitful in many ways, but the question which Troeltsch's own work so clearly poses needs to be faced. How far is this inevitably relativising method of study compatible with genuine religious belief and commitment? In particular, how can it be held together with Christian conviction.

In Troeltsch's own case, it is very clear that even when he sought—as he also did—to function as a Christian theologian, and to work out a pattern of Christian doctrine, his approach was deeply coloured by the relativism of his wider approach to the study of religion. He was able to tolerate this because he did have a kind of ultimate theological perspective of his own: in a style that owed a good deal to Hegel, he believed that all history is a movement of the spirit which is on the way to a return to God, and will at the last find its home in God. All religion could therefore be seen as an immanent reflection and intimation of the ultimate reality of God himself. And some such ultimate perspective is required if Troeltsch's method of study is not to dissolve into complete scepticism about genuine truth in religion. But is this broad and almost pantheistic frame of reference in itself any more valid than, for example, the traditional Christian affirmation of the absolute uniqueness of Jesus as the incarnation of God? The initiative in theology in the closing years of Troeltsch's life was already passing to those who held that it was not, and that the whole direction of thought which could be seen as culminating in him needed to be put into reverse. One negative consequence of this has been that positive Christian theology on the one hand and the study of religion on the other have very largely tended to go their separate ways; and this too does little to resolve the problem posed by Troeltsch himself. His solutions may not be acceptable; but others must be found.

Other Nineteenth-century Trends

So far in this chapter we have concentrated on only a small selection of the most creative and influential thinkers in theology from Schleiermacher to the turn of the century. A full survey even of German theology in that period would have had to mention very many more, and to bring out a far wider range of approaches and issues; but we have attended particularly to those whose legacy did most to shape the background to more recent thought. Before we leave that age, however, we must at least mention some others, especially in Britain and America, and note some further themes in their work.

While Schleiermacher was working in Berlin, ideas in some respects similar to his were being advanced in less systematic form in England by Samuel Taylor Coleridge (1772–1834), particularly in his *Aids to Reflection* (1825) and *Confessions of an Enquiring Spirit*, published in 1840. Like Schleiermacher, Coleridge rejected any attempt to prove the truth of religion by appeal to rational, philosophical proofs: this seemed to him completely to miss the character of faith, which he described as having to do, not with *theory*, but with *life*. This does not mean that faith itself is irrational, nor is it mere emotional 'feeling'. It is an imaginative reaching out to grasp the reality of God, to encounter and respond to his will, and to find in him living truth. Coleridge thus moved beyond Schleiermacher in stressing the personal in God's own being, though, like Schleiermacher, he too tended to place the theological centre of gravity in the inner experience of faith.

He was to have a wide, if rather scattered, influence in English theology through the nineteenth century, and served to introduce into it some of the same impulses that Schleiermacher brought in Germany. He also played a part in developing in England, even before the full force of the new historical criticism of the Bible had been felt there, an understanding of the authority of the Bible which did not rest simply on regarding it as the inspired and inerrant compendium from which the truths about God could be read off in literal and rationalist fashion. Instead he insisted that the truth of God is to be found in it when it is approached in the proper way—by one who is searching in awareness of his own need. Self-knowledge and knowledge of God are closely bound up together. Here the new voice of the nineteenth century can be clearly heard, with its insistence upon self-awareness, self-expression and self-discovery—an insistence whose dangers we have already remarked upon where it is taken to extremes, so that the human self entirely fills the horizon. But that was not Coleridge's intention. He stood more in the classical Christian tradition, which insisted that self-knowledge and knowledge of

God are intimately connected, but that they are not at all the same thing.

A somewhat similar note was being struck at the same time in Scotland by the lay theologian Thomas Erskine of Linlathen (1788–1870). His concern, especially in *The Unconditional Freeness of the Gospel* (1828) and *The Brazen Serpent* (1831), was to set a fresh insistence on God's love and forgiveness over against the rather rigid and authoritarian Calvinism which (at least in theory) dominated his native land. Calvinism as it had developed and hardened had tended to place a huge emphasis on man's total depravity and sinfulness, to limit the forgiveness offered in Jesus Christ to the 'elect', and to speak as if faith were a condition of forgiveness, our side of a bargain made with God. Erskine sought to put this into reverse: forgiveness is there *for all* in Jesus Christ, who is the representative head of the whole human race, and faith is the glad recognition that we are forgiven and reconciled to God through him.

A position very like Erskine's was also represented by his friend John McLeod Campbell (1800–72). He was deposed from the ministry of the Church of Scotland in 1831 for teaching that 'assurance of salvation' is attainable, and is indeed part of genuine faith, and for views on the atonement incompatible with the *Westminster Confession*. His teaching found its fullest form in *The Nature of the Atonement* (1856). Here he rejected the widely accepted 'penal theory', according to which Jesus bore on the cross the punishment which God must exact from sinners if he was once more to be gracious to them. This approach tended to stress law and judgement as primary in God's attitude towards sinners, and to see grace, love and mercy as secondary, and as available only if the conditions of the law had been satisfied. Campbell set the matter in the directly opposite light. God's love and desire to forgive are primary. Because of this, Jesus Christ as God incarnate identifies himself with sinners, takes their part, vicariously confesses and bears the burden of their sins and the judgement which they bring about. Campbell thus sought to subordinate law to love, and the 'judicial' element in our relation to God to a deeper and wider 'filial' one.

A counterpart to Campbell in America at the same time was Horace Bushnell (1802–81), with his *The Vicarious Sacrifice* (1866) and *Forgiveness and Law* (1874), in which some of the same emphases appear. In themselves they were by no means new—they were indeed centuries old—but they constituted a direct challenge to the rather abstract and clear-cut penal theory which was much subscribed to on both sides of the Atlantic, and to this extent also reflected something of the atmosphere of the new age. The concerns of Erskine, Campbell and Bushnell also throw into relief the fact that Anglo-Saxon theology tended to devote rather more attention than German to the matter of the atonement—indeed the very word 'atonement' is an English one which has no precise German equivalent.

Coleridge, Erskine and Campbell were all among the formative influences upon Frederick Denison Maurice (1805–72), who ranks with John Henry Newman (1801–90) as one of the outstanding English theologians of the whole nineteenth century. Until his conversion to the Roman Catholic Church in 1845, Newman, along with others such as John Keble (1792–1866), Edward Pusey (1800–82) and Richard Hurrel Froude (1803–36), was a leader of the Tractarian movement, which developed into the Anglo-Catholic wing of the Church of England. By contrast with what it saw as the corrosive and unbelieving spirit of the age, that movement was deeply concerned to recover and reinstate the ancient doctrines of the faith, especially the great dogmas hammered out in the early centuries; and with them to restore the sense of continuity and rich unbroken tradition which found its expression especially in ritual and liturgy.

Newman's greatness did not lie chiefly in fresh theological insight, but in the enormous impact of his spirituality, his hymns, and his studies of the church fathers. He did however attempt in his *Sermons Chiefly on the Theory of Religious Belief* (1843) and *The Grammar of Assent* (1870) an analysis of the nature of religious belief which shows some affinity with Coleridge, and includes Newman's own original idea of the 'illative sense' by which we find it possible to proceed through probabilities to certitude; and in his celebrated *Essay on the Development of Christian Doctrine* (1878) struggled with the problem of change and continuity in the expression of Christian faith down through the centuries in a fashion which has helped many others to grasp something of the questions, if not in most cases to accept his answers.

Maurice, in spite of early contacts with the Tractarians, took a very different road. In their emphasis on ritual and doctrine he sensed the same danger of a too purely objective conception of faith as in the rigid understanding of man, sin and atonement in which he had been brought up, and which, like Erskine and Campbell, he rejected. Maurice had a horror alike of all-too-neat theological schemes and systems and of ecclesiastical parties. The central matter to which the gospel points, he insisted, is Jesus Christ himself; and it is in him, as the head and Lord of all mankind, that all men are invited to discover God, their neighbour, and themselves. The gospel does not direct us to our sin and the threat of judgement, but to reconciliation in the kingdom of Christ. This does not mean that sin is unreal: it runs through the whole fabric of our existence, both individual and social. But in him it is overcome, and the church is an instrument for the reconstitution of human community around him. So Maurice could call himself a 'Christian socialist', though his socialism, like that of his associate Charles Kingsley (1819–75), was of a somewhat idealistic and utopian character. Nevertheless, he anticipated both some of the themes and concerns of the Ritschlian theology and the christological emphasis which was once more to come to the centre in the twentieth century. His thought was in many ways inadequately worked out, but he set signposts for the future.

Towards the end of Maurice's life, in 1860, there appeared a collection of papers by seven Oxford dons, entitled *Essays and Reviews*, and these made a great impact in Britain. They were not, by modern standards, especially radical in tone; but they introduced to a wider public the new approaches to the critical study of the Bible which up till then had developed more on the Continent, and only to some extent in the cloistered world of the English universities. So, for example, the paper by Benjamin Jowett (1817–93) 'On the Interpretation of Scripture' pointed out that it was not always easy to know what might be meant by 'proving a doctrine from Scripture', and insisted that the Bible must be interpreted like any other piece of literature. The book raised a storm of controversy, and two of the authors were in fact tried for heresy (though finally acquitted).

The strength of feeling that could be raised by what was felt in many quarters to be the attack of modern criticism on the authority of the Bible was shown again some years later in the Robertson Smith case in Scotland. Smith was Professor of Old Testament in the Free Church College in Aberdeen. In 1875 he contributed an article on the Bible to *Encyclopedia Britannica,* in which he considered and in part accepted the hypothesis of Wellhausen that the first five books of the Old Testament were composites, made up of different interwoven literary strands. After some years of controversy (in which, admittedly, Smith himself did little to smooth things over, tending if anything to exacerbate the situation by his own behaviour), he was finally deposed from his chair in 1881. Fortunately for him, he was very soon offered instead the chair of Arabic in Cambridge. The effect of the case, however, was the reverse of what some of his critics had hoped for: attempts to bring similar charges against others failed, and the right and indeed duty of biblical scholars to explore these questions came to be tacitly accepted in Scotland as elsewhere.

An indication of the gradual change of climate was another collection of papers published thirty years after *Essays and Reviews.* This was *Lux Mundi,* edited in 1890 by Charles Gore (1853–1932). The contributors all came from the Anglo-Catholic wing of the Church of England, but their shared aim was to assist the re-expression of the central Christian doctrines in a way that would be appropriate to their own time, and that would take account of the historical character both of the Bible and of subsequent theology. One emphasis, for which Gore himself was especially noted, was on *kenotic* christology. This approach, which had already been followed by several German theologians in the nineteenth century, especially Gottfried Thomasius (1802–75), took its cue from Philippians 2:7, which speaks of Christ as having 'emptied himself' (in Greek, *ekenosen*). Kenotic christology took this to mean that in becoming man, the Son of God divested himself of his specifically divine attributes, such as omniscience and omnipotence. In this way, it hoped to do justice to the real humanness of Jesus, while still affirming the established doctrine of his 'two natures'. Kenotic christology of this sort did have its own internal problems: on closer examination it is not easy to understand what exactly it can mean to speak of this 'self-emptying', and attempts to make the matter more precise tend to fade into a tangle of artificialities and contradictions. Nevertheless, this emphasis on the fact that Jesus was a real man, and the rejection of what was certainly a widespread tendency to picture him as a purely superhuman (and rather unreal) figure, were clearly necessary: here lies one side of what classical Christian teaching has always held.

A very different response to the critical approach to the Bible was worked out on the other side of the Atlantic by Charles Hodge (1797–1878) of Princeton, the Presbyterian seminary which came to be a veritable bastion of Calvinist orthodoxy. The tradition was carried on after him by his son, Archibald Alexander Hodge (1823–86), and Benjamin B. Warfield (1851–1921). The characteristic emphasis of the Princeton theology was on the inspired and infallible authority of the Bible. While it could and did allow that the discoveries of natural science and of philological and literary criticism of the text could cast light upon the meaning of the Bible, it held that the proper responsibility of the theologian is to interpret the Bible out of itself. Its teaching supplies the data which he must gather and interpret scientifically by tracing the general principles running through it and underlying the particular propositions it contains. In this way, it applied to the Bible the 'inductive method' of scientific study developed in the rise of modern natural science, which similarly aimed to work up from pieces of data to more universal principles or laws. The overall shape of the theology which resulted was strongly reminiscent of the Calvinist systems of the seventeenth century, which these men sought to follow and to update.

This kind of approach is still followed in some branches of Calvinism, especially in America and Holland. But the Princeton theology has also had a much wider influence among more conservative Christians to the present day. There, it has not so much been its Calvinism that has been welcome as its emphasis upon the inerrancy of Scripture. It should however be added that there were important elements, especially in the theology of the two Hodges, which foreshadowed the revival of a fresher form of Calvinist thinking in the twentieth century. Their emphasis on the responsibility of the theologian towards the Bible, and on the need for a disciplined hermeneutic which will allow the Bible itself to speak, will be found again, albeit much modified, in the thought of Karl Barth; as too will Archibald Hodge's principle that 'Christ and his work is the centre around which all Christian theology is brought into order,' as he put it on page 16 of the 1878 edition of his *Outlines of Theology*, which was first published in 1860, and, together with his father's *Systematic Theology* (1871), is a classic textbook of the Princeton method.

To conclude this very selective sketch, one other type of American theology must be mentioned—that of the 'Mercersburg school' of John W. Nevin (1803–86) and Philip Schaff (1819–93), who were colleagues in the seminary of the German Reformed Church at Mercersburg, Pennsylvania, in the years preceding 1853. In that year, the college moved away from Mercersburg, Nevin retired, and Schaff later embarked on an outstanding career as a Church historian at Union Seminary, New York, where he published in 1876 his great *History of the Creeds of Christendom.*

Like Maurice, with whom they had some affinities, Nevin and Schaff had a horror of party-spirit and sectarianism, and also of the individualism they found deeply entrenched in much American Protestantism, especially in the revivalist movements which came more and more to the fore through the nineteenth century. They wanted to recover a wider, more comprehensive vision of the church, one which could include and make room for the different forms in which the church had appeared through history, and in this way to overcome the deeply entrenched divisions between the separated confessions and denominations.

They found a theoretical perspective on the matter by developing Baur's application of Hegel's dialectic to church history. So, for instance, they saw the Roman Catholic Church as representing a 'Petrine' approach, over against which Protestantism had emerged as a 'Pauline' antithesis; and both should ultimately be reconcilable in a 'Johannine' synthesis. In this way, the 'ideal' reality of the church was seen as involved in a continual process of dialectical movement through history, a process in which conflict and separation had their place as necessary but provisional moments in the growth towards a fuller and more complex unity. Theologically, the basis for this understanding lay in Jesus Christ as the one in whose own person God and man are reconciled, and in the vision of the church—the whole church—as the continuation of his life through the centuries. Liturgically, it centred in the sacrament of the eucharist: there was the heart and focus of the life and worship of the church, the key and core of its participation in the life of Christ. While the Mercersburg theology as such was short-lived, and made relatively little impact in its own day, it presaged the emergence of the ecumenical movement some two to three generations later, and to a remarkable extent anticipated some of that movement's central themes and concerns.

3

A Changing Climate

The nineteenth century brought a new kind of search for the basis and foundation of theology itself; a fresh attempt to bring human awareness and experience into the centre of theological study; the forging of more specialised techniques for the literary and historical study of the Bible, techniques whose application helped to raise what were often felt to be disturbing and challenging questions about its meaning and relevance as well as about the standing and authority of established Christian doctrines; and the sharp new question whether Christian theology itself ought not to be subsumed under some more general study of religion and religions. While very different answers to these various questions were offered, the struggle with them reflected a new and consciously *modern* outlook. There was an intensified sense of a gap between present and past, and of the need to find a way of bridging it which would make possible an adequate statement of belief for the present day. There was also a fair amount of uncertainty, as the examples of Kähler and Kierkegaard well illustrate, whether the most fashionable current restatements were in fact adequate. These doubts were to find a wider resonance in the twentieth century.

Theology in the last sixty years or so has naturally built upon and extended aspects of the work of its nineteenth-century predecessors; but it has also gone through some striking changes of direction, especially from the aims and programme of Liberal Theology. This is hardly surprising when it is remembered how far the world has changed in living memory, and in ways which inevitably made their mark on theology itself. The most dramatic and explosive of these changes was the devastating impact upon the social and political fabric of Europe of the First World War. It did not only transform the political and military map: by the destruction which it wrought, unparalleled in previous human history in its scale, it hurled a black question mark against the confidence in the onward and upward progress of Christian civilisation which had so strongly characterised Liberal Theology, and forced the bitter question whether the advanced theological thought of the nineteenth century as a whole had not been far too unaware of the darker side of human nature, too optimistic about innate human capacity for good, too willing to take contemporary culture at its own high evaluation of itself, and overall too disposed to take God for granted, and to assume that he was somehow simply 'given' in what it regarded as the highest ethical, spiritual and religious values of mankind.

These questions have lost nothing of their force in the decades since 1914 as subsequent conflicts have contributed their own appalling demonstration of man's capacity for inhumanity, and as a new sensitivity has developed to the dilemmas facing the human race and to the degree of inequality and injustice in human affairs in general. Human nature and human achievements have come to appear far more ambiguous than the progressive hopes of the nineteenth century admitted. Where the force of the challenge has been felt in theology, it has led not only to a more sober evaluation of man's spiritual and ethical potential, and to more serious reflection on the meaning of human sin, but also to a widespread doubt whether theology itself could really be solidly built on the basis sketched by a Ritschl or even a Schleiermacher. Could one, as it were, argue up to the reality and character of God from the analysis of religious experience or ethical awareness, as they had tended to do? Must not theology, if it were to be possible at all, be established from the other side, by God himself—by the God who makes himself known to us in Jesus Christ rather than the God whom we choose to recognise in him, a God who comes from beyond ourselves to judge, redeem and save? This reversal of the questions which dominated the field at the turn of the century has been characteristic of the main movement in Protestant theology in the last sixty years. It has certainly not been the only movement, nor has it always taken the same form or led to the same conclusions. But this shift of focus, which as we shall see came about with remarkable suddenness through the 1920s, is the primary clue to the shape of more recent developments.

Other far-reaching changes in the modern world have also made their mark on theology, notably the immense advances in science and technology, and the accelerating contact and interaction between different races and cultures in what it is now normal to call 'the global village', The explosion of science and the application of its discoveries have altered the world even of our grandfathers beyond recognition. Virtually no aspect of our lives, especially in the developed countries, has remained unaffected by them, and religion and theology are certainly not exempt. One set of issues has to do with the way in which science and technology so drastically alter previous patterns of life that they erode and undermine the social, ethical and spiritual values which had been encapsulated and preserved in them. The corrosive acids of modernity have powerfully assisted a general movement of 'secularisation', and faced all kinds of religious tradition—Christian and non-Christian alike—with a challenge which cannot be ignored. This is sometimes described by saying that the church has at last entered a 'post-Constantinian era', an era in which the synthesis of Christianity and western culture and society ushered in by Constantine, the first Christian Emperor of Rome, has finally dissolved, and the church once more represents a social minority in an increasingly pluralistic age. Or, to put the matter more succinctly, the age of Christendom is finally over. While there is a good deal of division of opinion both about these attempts to characterise the present situation and about what further conclusions theology should draw from it, there lies here a nexus of issues to which theologians have had to turn their attention, especially since the Second World War.

In another way too, the advance of science has posed a challenge for theology. The natural sciences have proved so enormously successful in modern times that they are now commonly regarded as *the* supremely useful and valid intellectual discipline, and as setting the standard to which all other kinds of enquiry must conform if they are to be taken seriously as dealing with truth and reality. Theology, like other studies in the broad field of the 'humanities' or the 'liberal arts', has been compelled to face the implications of that challenge, and has sought to do so in a variety of ways.

The meeting and mixing of diverse cultures has also had a profound impact on religious life in general, and on Christian theology in particular. This century has seen the rise to prominence on the world-stage of the ecumenical movement, which grew out of the need felt by Christians engaged in foreign mission to overcome the divisions between churches and denominations which made less and less sense in the missionary context. While the progress towards the reunion of separated churches has been much slower than many had hoped, the last sixty years have seen dialogue and joint action at many levels, from the local to the international, between Christian communities which had for long centuries been very largely isolated from each other. One result of this has been that theology itself has become ecumenical in a fashion undreamt of a century ago, and many of the main fronts in theological debate and controversy now run across rather than along denominational boundaries. Bridges are being built between different confessions, and a new atmosphere of mutual respect is slowly helping to find ways of overcoming what were once felt to be absolutely irreconcilable differences. In addition, the rapid expansion of Christian churches in parts of the Third World (contrasting very markedly with what sometimes appears to be a steady decline in the west) has led those churches increasingly to feel the need not merely to copy the styles of life, worship and theology developed in western Christianity, but to develop others appropriate to their own setting. This has brought in a new dimension to recent thinking, and begun to raise sharp questions about what has been called the 'Latin captivity' of western theology.

This fresh ecumenical contact and its opening of new horizons has by no means been restricted to the meeting of Christians with Christians. The question of the relation between Christianity and other world faiths has taken on a new urgency in a time where, for instance, an Indian Christian must take stock of his position *vis-à-vis* his Hindu fellow-countrymen, or a British or American Christian finds himself living alongside adherents of other religions in his own homeland. That issue has been sharpened even further by the fate of the millions of Jews murdered in Nazi extermination camps—a fate for which centuries of Christian antisemitism must bear at least part of the blame. While in this survey we are chiefly concerned with modern Protestant theology, and with its main development in the west, the impact upon it of this new ecumenical awareness cannot be left out of account.

Another subject directly connected with the way more recent theology has moved is that of philosophy—or, rather, of the various kinds of philosophy which have influenced theologians. Behind much of the theology of the nineteenth century stood the towering figures of Kant and Hegel. They remain important influences still, but other schools and approaches have more recently become prominent, and fed into theology at various points. These other approaches for the most part reflect a leading feature of most twentieth-century philosophy—the revolt against Absolute Idealism of the Hegelian type, with its tendency to downgrade the individual, the personal, and the historical in favour of the ideal and impersonal.

The revolt itself has taken many forms, and issued in a variety of quite different conceptions of what philosophy itself is about. On the face of it there are more contrasts than resemblances between, for example, the brand of empirical and then linguistic philosophy which has predominated in England in recent decades, the existentialist thought which has led the way in western Europe, and the critical reflection on human history and society on a broadly Marxist basis which has naturally held sway in communist countries, but more recently come more to the fore in the west as well. Yet each in its own way reflects the rejection of the abstraction and impersonality of Absolute Idealism, and the endeavour to relate philosophy more concretely to the textured fabric of human life and experience. Marxism and Existentialism have exercised the greatest influence upon theology, while in addition the general question of how far theology should permit itself to be influenced by philosophy has also been given a good deal of attention.

Several of the issues just outlined will be given special attention in our last chapter, which will look at the wider horizons opened up for Protestant theology by the ecumenical movement, the encounter with other faiths, and the development of science. Before we come to that, however, it may give a better picture of the dynamics and movement of theology itself if we approach it more chronologically, and deal in turn with the two main impulses stemming from Germany and Switzerland which largely set the

72

tone in the period from 1920 to 1960—those associated above all with Karl Barth and Rudolf Bultmann—with trends outside Germany in that same period, and then with the movements which have received the widest attention in the last twenty years or so. To a large degree, all of these developments can be traced back to a sudden and quite unexpected revolt against the drive and direction of nineteenth century thinking. The man who, more than any other, provoked and personified that revolt was Karl Barth (1886–1968); and the book which, as one critic put it, 'fell like a bomb on the playground of the theologians', was his *Commentary on the Epistle to the Romans*, first published in 1918, when its then virtually unknown author was pastor of Safenwil in his native Switzerland.

4

From Rebellion to the *Church Dogmatics*: The Theology of Karl Barth

Karl Barth had been pastor in Safenwil since 1911. In 1921, the year that the second (and heavily altered) edition of his *Romans* appeared, he was called to a university chair in Göttingen, and thereafter to Münster (1925) and Bonn (1930). His active opposition to the Nazis, the leading part that he played in the *Kirchenkampf*, the struggle against the Nazi attempt to take over the German Evangelical Church, and his refusal to take the oath of loyalty to Hitler, led to his dismissal from Bonn in 1935. He then became professor in Basle, where he remained for the rest of his long life. His early concerns as a parish minister and his active involvement in the cultural and political turmoil of Germany in the 1920s and 1930s are of direct relevance for his theology, and in particular for the passionate conviction that ran through all his work from 1918 to 1968: that Christian faith rests solely on the revelation of God in Jesus Christ, and that the task of theology is to allow that revelation to shine in its own light and stand on its own authority as the Word of God to us. Theology lives out of the Word; and the name of the Word is Jesus.

This positive conviction carried with it the rejection of any attempt to compromise with other sources, authorities or norms, or to establish theology itself on any other foundation. These fundamental axioms were refined, clarified and applied through a long series of debates and conflicts with the Liberal Theology in which he had been trained, and which he had earlier enthusiastically followed, with the claims of the *Führer* to be the chosen instrument of divine providence, and with colleagues, notably Emil Brunner (1889–1966), Rudolf Bultmann (1884–1976) and Friedrich Gogarten (1887–1967), whose approaches, though having some affinities with his own, he felt in the end to be in varying degrees unsatisfactory.

In his years in Safenwil, Barth and his closest friend throughout sixty years, Eduard Thurneysen (1888–1974) engaged in an intense questioning search for the foundation and ultimate rationale of their calling as pastors and preachers. Barth was driven to this not only by his own exceptionally and relentlessly enquiring mind, but also by the shaking of the foundations of the world he had known under the impact of the First World War. In August 1914, as the war broke out, a group of 93 German intellectuals, among them many of his own former theological teachers, issued a declaration supporting the Kaiser's war policy as necessary to the defence of Christian civilisation. This 'black day', as he later called it, convinced the neutral (and strongly socialist) Barth that not only the political ideals of his teachers, but their underlying theology too, could have no future. *Kulturprotestantismus* ('Cultural Protestantism'), the identification of Protestant Christianity with (German) culture, lost all credibility. So too, in this same period, did the *Ehrfurcht vor Geschichte* ('reverence before history') which had loomed so large in the historical concerns of much nineteenth-century thinking, and which in Harnack bade fair to become the great and chief obligation and dignity of the theologian. Neither cultural Protestantism nor reverence before history could tell him what to preach in Safenwil, Sunday by Sunday, while the inheritors of Christian civilisation tore the world apart in the name of their enlightened values.

Several influences combined in this period to help him in the search for an alternative theological approach. Both the philosophy of Kierkegaard and the novels of Dostoievsky spoke directly to his own questions by pointing to the tyranny of power, the pretensions of institutionalised Christianity, and contrasting both with the vital depths of human experience and need and the infinity of God. Closer to home, he found the work of the Swiss philosopher Franz Overbeck (1837–1905), who had been a friend of Nietzsche. Overbeck had launched his own attack on Christianity and Christendom. He insisted that a genuine religion, if such there be, must rest on a supernatural revelation coming from beyond history; and he denounced the 'historicising' of Christianity, by which the original message of Christ and the apostles, a message which spoke of the wholly supernatural kingdom of God, had been betrayed by the transformation of Christianity itself into a social, cultural, and political movement *within* history—a movement which the advanced theologians and Christian apologists of the nineteenth century had then, with complete consistency, attempted to interpret and justify in purely historical and psychological terms. Overbeck's critique connected directly with the recent rediscovery of the eschatological emphasis of the New Testament in the work of Weiss and Schweitzer; and these were powerfully reinforced in their effect upon Barth by the preaching of J. C. Blumhardt (1827–91), which had centred on the call to live in the light of the future coming of the kingdom, in which the victory won by God in the death and resurrection of Jesus would at last become apparent. By contrast with the Liberal understanding, the kingdom as Blumhardt preached it was not gradually evolving through history, nor identified with the moral progress of human civilisation, but would come 'from beyond'. It did have ethical, social and political implications even for life in the present time, but it could not be reduced to these: rather it set the present in the light of God's future.

All this led Barth back to a closer reading of the Bible, and especially of Paul. Here, as he put it many years later, he made the

> discovery that the theme of the Bible—contrary to the critical and the orthodox exegesis in which we had been brought up—definitely could not possibly be man's religion and religious ethics—could not possibly be his own secret godliness, but—this was the *rocher de bronze* on which we first struck—the Godness of God, precisely God's Godness, God's own peculiar nature over against not only the natural, but also the spiritual cosmos, God's absolutely unique existence, power and initiative, above all in his relationship to man (*God, Grace and Gospel*, E.T. 1959, p. 34).

God *is God*, not man writ large; and he cannot be spoken of simply by speaking of ourselves in a loud voice. He cannot be taken for granted as simply 'there' in our religious sense, our spiritual depth, or our moral awareness, for he transcends, he stands over against all of these. He can be met, really met, only in the encounter in which we finite creatures of time and history are confronted by the One who is infinite and eternal, and who remains infinite and eternal and 'wholly Other' than ourselves in that meeting. In biblical language, God makes himself known always and only as the Lord who lays his claim upon us; in that of Kierkegaard, he is the Subject who can never be reduced to an object, but is always the One who challenges us across the gulf of the 'infinite qualitative difference', and so awakens in us the 'infinite passion' of faith.

The implication of this for theology is that if it is really *theology*, it can only take place as God conveys his own Word to us and enables us to hear it; but the Word itself always remains his and not ours. It cannot be trapped in the net of our human thoughts and expressions. Instead, it flashes across between them, coming 'vertically from above', and leaving behind only the marks of its passing, much as lightning scorches the earth where it strikes. There is absolutely no continuity, similarity or resemblance between God and man, no *analogia entis* ('analogy of being') between God and ourselves, or between God and anything else at all. There is only what from our side is neither predictable nor controllable—the coming of the Word from beyond which opens and displays to us the overwhelming advent of God as he makes himself known in the 'eternal moment'. In that moment, the Word which touched time and history in Jesus Christ touches them again, and so the original Word itself is heard, leaping across the distances of time which are no barrier or hindrance to the running of the communication from eternity.

This was the basis of the position which Barth presented with particular volcanic power in the second edition of his *Romans*; but it contained another central element as well. The Word of God is one of both judgement and mercy. It contradicts and condemns us in our pride, our self-sufficiency, our ethics, our politics, *and our religion* which, far from being our point of closest access to God, is the house we build in order to hide ourselves from him, to convince ourselves that we have him in our control. The hurricane of the Word tears away the flimsy structures of our pretensions, the altars of our false gods, the artificial securities to which we love to cling, all that Paul describes as 'the righteousness of the Law'. The cross of Jesus is God's final and decisive 'No!' to all that: it leaves us literally nothing of our own on which we can rely. But that is only the first stage, the negative side of the matter. God's 'No!' to any form of self-reliance on our part is spoken in order to enable us to put our trust solely in him, and to hear behind and beyond his 'No!' the even deeper and more final promise of his 'Yes!' It is only through the cross, only through the 'No!' of judgement and destruction, that God's will to affirm us as his children can be heard; but the affirmation is the real purpose of the negation. It is that that makes real and radical faith possible, faith which lives from nothing in itself, but solely from the promise and invitation of God. Faith is thus not—as in Schleiermacher—a general and universally accessible awareness of absolute dependence, but the response in the 'moment' to the Word of God himself, a Word which continually creates and renews the possibility of faith.

The appearance of the first, and then the second, editions of *Romans* made a considerable and widespread impression. Barth himself later said that he had been like a man who, tripping in the darkness of the church tower, had accidentally caught hold of the bell-rope to steady himself and alarmed the whole country-side. The analogy was an apt one, for the book helped to set in motion the new movement which came to be known as Dialectical Theology, and whose leading lights, apart from Barth himself, were Brunner, Bultmann and Gogarten. The 'dialectic' here was that of Kierkegaard rather than Hegel. It underlined, as Barth had done, the absolute contrast between God and man, the interplay of the 'No!' and the 'Yes!' of the Word to man; and also, following from these, the fact that no human speaking about God could directly or immediately express or contain the truth about him. Rather, all our statements must be qualified, and indeed negated, even as they are made, and only by such affirmation *and negation* is room made to hear the authentic Word of God himself through them.

The new approach which thus came into being and swept rapidly to prominence in Switzerland and Germany was clearly very different in tone and style from the previously established Liberal Theology. But it was not only different: the two were diametrically opposed. Gone now was the concern with 'religion', so central for Ritschl and Schleiermacher, and their desire to commend 'the Christian faith' to their contemporary culture; gone too was the emphasis on inwardness or on history as the avenues into the meaning of the gospel. All that stood under God's 'No!' Here, the Dialectical Theologians took up afresh one of the prominent motifs in the thought of the Reformers: that the kind of religion that man works out for himself is in the end idolatry, for its real object is not the living God, but man's own secret divinity.

Now Feuerbach's critique came into its own within the new movement of theology itself. From this standpoint, the efforts of Schleiermacher and Ritschl came to be diagnosed as effectively displacing God by man, reducing theology to anthropology, resting on the hidden assumption that God and man were ultimately somehow identical, and thus failing to take sufficiently seriously the reality of God himself, the need for revelation, the authority of the Bible as the vehicle of his Word, the finiteness and sinfulness of man, and the radical character of authentic faith. As a result, the nineteenth-century approaches had misconceived the nature of God's Word itself, turning it into a spiritual ideal, a heroic example, or a set of ethical norms, and interpreted Jesus accordingly, instead of recognising in him the perennially contemporary event of the encounter of time with eternity, the intersection of the finite by the infinite, by which everything human and creaturely is contradicted in its self-enclosedness and opened up to the reality of God.

Dialectical Theology thus set out to reverse the approach, and in particular to emphasise, first, the 'Godness of God'; second, the reality of the Word of God in Jesus Christ; third, the impossibility of building theology itself on any other foundation. Within a very few years it succeeded in drastically altering the climate in its own homelands—much to the pain of surviving Liberals, such as Harnack, who saw in the entire regrettable enterprise the swamping of properly respectable theological and historical study by a wave of sheer barbarism, of uncouth and indeed vulgar 'enthusiasm'.

The three emphases just mentioned were and remained central to Barth's theology. In the earlier years, however, it was the first and the third that he most tended to emphasise—the otherness of God, and the impossiblity of climbing up to true knowledge of him by our own efforts—so that even today his thought is widely interpreted as essentially negative, as circling ever around God's 'No!' to human presumption. In fact, however, the second point—the reality of God's giving himself to be known in Jesus Christ—was always the real focus of his concern, and he came to stress it more and more as the years passed, and as he moved away from what he later said to have been the one-sidedness of his earlier writings. (He continued to insist, nonetheless, that that one-sidedness had been necessary, and that the negative points he had made must not be withdrawn, nor even weakened, but merely held together with the positive. The real force and power of God's 'Yes!' can only be heard along with the 'No!' that is necessarily carried with it.)

The core of Barth's theology is not that God is in principle unknowable, nor yet that man is an arrogant sinner who, left to himself, will ever be about the business of fashioning golden calves to worship, but that God has crossed the infinite gulf in Jesus Christ to claim man as his friend and partner. This Barth saw as the irreplaceable basis of Christian theology; and, he insisted, once it had been recognised, there could be no possible reason for casting around in other directions, and certainly not for turning theology back into the contemplation of our own spiritual navels, or for blunting the challenge and promise of the gospel by seeking to reinterpret or 'improve' it in the terms of some alternative (and therefore competing) theological or philosophical frame of reference.

By its very nature, Dialectical Theology was a vital and tempestuous movement, and its leaders were by no means all of the same stamp. As the years passed, they moved away from each other to a greater or less degree. Barth and Brunner had most in common. They were both Swiss, both Reformed (i.e. Calvinist), both theologians rather than historians or biblical specialists, and both men of immense intellectual power and energy, capable of ranging far and wide over the whole spread of Christian thought in search of the resources and materials to fashion the theology which had to be reconstructed. Bultmann was primarily a New Testament scholar, and his theological position, once he had settled it to his own satisfaction, remained more or less inflexible thereafter. Like Gogarten—another systematic theologian—he was German and Lutheran; and he was also much influenced by the Existentialism of Martin Heidegger (1889–1976).

Through the 1920s, a clear gap opened up between Barth and Brunner on the one hand, and Bultmann and Gogarten on the other, though it was only to be later that the full significance of the divergence between them became apparent. Each pair in fact began to gravitate to opposite poles within the horizon which Dialectical Theology had opened up. The emphasis on God's revelation and on the faith that apprehends it raised the further question of what theology itself can speak about directly—*the revelation*, or merely *faith's apprehension of it*? Does God's making of himself known have any abiding content which can be articulated, or can it merely be pointed to and fleetingly glimpsed, but not retained? In the second edition of his *Romans*, Barth had really given the second answer, and Bultmann and Gogarten continued to give it. Accordingly, they concentrated on what *could* be spoken of—the life and experience and understanding of faith. Barth and Brunner moved on from that position and came to focus their attention on the re-working and re-stating of the main classical Christian doctrines, especially of christology, in which they believed the meaning and content of the revelation was explicated. They thus became the outstanding exponents of what has sometimes been called, with a variety of overtones, 'Neo-orthodoxy'; and in the widening gulf between them and the other two there emerges very clearly what one recent writer has aptly described as 'the divided mind of modern theology'. We shall come back to Bultmann and Gogarten later, and for the moment concentrate on the line struck out upon by Brunner and, in particular, by Barth.

The first great public indication of the shift in Barth's thinking came in 1927, when he published the first volume of a projected *Christian Dogmatics*, which was intended eventually to handle in a systematic way all the main Christian doctrines. The title of the volume was significant: *Christian Doctrine in Outline, Vol. 1. The Doctrine of the Word of God, Prolegomena to Christian Dogmatics*. The aim of this introductory study ('prolegomena') was to make clear the basis for the entire enterprise and the methods which it would use, and the emphasis on 'the doctrine of the Word of God' signalled Barth's intention to ground it on God's own revelation of himself and nothing else.

In the book itself he carried through this programme by asserting that theology could not be dictated to by another discipline either about the nature of its object or about the methods appropriate to its study. Echoing Kant, he insisted that any properly objective enquiry could not impose on its material methods worked out in advance or in relation to some other topic; only within the context of encounter with and experience of the object itself could it discover how to speak of it and enquire into it. Theology must take as its starting-point the actuality of God's self-revelation in Jesus Christ, disclosed to us by the Holy Spirit, and set its sights and adjust its compass by that. It must in fact plunge into the heart of the matter in order to lay bare the fundamental conditions which made it all even possible. These conditions of the possibility of Christian theology were on the one hand the actuality of the revelation in Jesus, and on the other the reception of that revelation in faith empowered by the Holy Spirit. Outside that horizon, one might, if one had nothing better to do, endlessly debate whether such a thing as theology might be possible; but there could be no ground for giving a positive answer. Within that horizon, however, it can be seen that God's making of himself known through Jesus has a threefold pattern: he makes *himself* known *in Jesus Christ* and *to us*, and this triadic structure is nothing other than that of the Trinity: that God is Father, Son and Holy Spirit; that the Son is the Word and Image of the Father; that the Holy Spirit is the power who discloses that Image and conveys that Word. The doctrine of the Trinity, so far from being an *appendix* (even if also a coping-stone) to Christian theology, as it had seemed to Schleiermacher, supplies the ground-plan, the inner dynamics of the whole.

This volume was thus very largely taken up with an exposition of the doctrine of the Trinity, not as a second-order theological construction, but as sketching the basis within God himself of the possibility and actuality of his making of himself known to us in Jesus Christ. Within that horizon, Barth went on to distinguish three 'forms' of the Word. The primary form is God's own self-expression, his eternal Word which was made flesh in Jesus; the secondary form is the witness of the Bible in Old and New Testaments to that primary Word, the witness by which the Word itself is mediated and heard; the tertiary form is the proclamation of Jesus Christ in the church as the Word of God to us. In each of these forms, the Word is the Word insofar and only insofar as God really expresses and communicates himself through it; and the special task of Christian *dogmatics* is to refer the present proclamation of Jesus Christ back to its original ground in God himself in order to clear away distortions and misrepresentations so that the Word itself can be heard afresh in its own integrity. Dogmatics thus has a critical function in relation to the present witness and preaching of the church, recalling it to its basis and assisting it to uncover and hear what it is called to say today. It is not merely the study of *dogmas* as accumulated down through the centuries (as in the Roman Catholic understanding of dogmatics), but their critical subordination to and testing by the primary and original *dogma*, which is nothing other than Jesus Christ himself.

It was clear here that Barth was very substantially qualifying his earlier Dialectical approach. He was in fact becoming increasingly dissatisfied with an exclusive concentration on the infinite qualitative difference, and the encounter in the eternal moment. Time and history, and above all the revelation *in* (and not merely *through*) Jesus Christ, were all too likely to be sold short by this. His emphasis on the independence of theology, on refusing to allow any other intellectual discipline to dictate to it, reflected an awareness that his own earlier thought might itself have been guilty of imposing inappropriate categories and of squeezing theology into a strait-jacket. But his new slant sent waves of horrified shock through many of his contempories who had valued the fresh and radical air of Dialectical Theology, but were scarcely prepared for such a wholesale repristination of—of all things!—the doctrine of the Trinity. Was this not, they wondered, a quite disastrous return to the past, a toppling over of the (admittedly partly justified) reaction against Liberal Theology into sheer traditionalism? These critics did not perhaps all observe the extent to which Barth was opening up a new path, for no one before had handled the doctrine of the Trinity in this fashion. We shall notice in a little how he was to build further upon the foundations laid in 1927, and what a distinctive theology resulted.

At any rate, Barth himself was to come to make exactly the opposite criticism of the book, which he later used to call 'my well-known false start'. He subsequently concluded that, in spite of his own intentions, it was still too deeply coloured by the thought of Kierkegaard and Heidegger, that it gave faith a wrong kind of priority over revelation in the arrangement of its material, and that its account of faith was more Existentialist than Christian. Five years later he took up the project again under the new title of *Church Dogmatics*. This time he sought to expunge every trace of Existentialism, but retained much of the material from the first draft, including the elements mentioned above. They were to remain corner-stones of his thought.

A significant stage on the way to the *Church Dogmatics* came with a study of Anselm's *Proslogion*, which Barth published in 1931 as *Fides Quaerens Intellectum* ('faith seeking understanding': the phrase was Anselm's own description of the task of theology). The book ranks as one of the most penetrating modern accounts of Anselm's thought, though it is not without its weaknesses as an interpretation of Anselm himself. But it also served to clarify and develop Barth's own understanding of what theology is about: it has the function of exploring and articulating the rational, intelligible *sense* of what is believed. God's Word is not simply a bare event of encounter with the Subject who stands over against us as Lord. It is also rational with the rationality of God himself. His Word, in Greek, his *Logos*, is not only personal address, but also his own divine intelligibility. This does not mean that that intelligibility can be wholly captured in the formulations or in the mind of the theologian; it does, however, mean that the divine intelligibility comes across to us, that God gives himself to be known and understood, and that the understanding that is made possible in theology is and is intended to be a *genuine* understanding and an authentic *contact* with the intelligibility of God. The Word was made flesh in Jesus Christ; God has given himself to be understood in our terms and on our level; and even in these terms and on that level it is the reality of God that is given for us to understand.

This carried Barth decisively away from Dialectical Theology, and especially from Bultmann. Bultmann too was happy to describe theology as 'faith seeking understanding'; but what he meant by this was faith's *self*-understanding, an understanding having to do with self-awareness and self-knowledge, subjective rather than objective. To Barth, this could only indicate that Bultmann was in effect taking the same path as their nineteenth-century forefathers. He had rejected Romanticism and Idealism, but simply substituted Existentialism for them, without challenging the essentially anthropocentric focus. Nor was Bultmann much concerned to deny the charge

In the same period, a smaller but nonetheless very important gap was also opening up between Barth and Brunner. From the late 1920s, Brunner had become increasingly interested in the question of *natural theology*. By this he did not mean the philosophical proofs of God's existence or the natural religion which had been the focus of so much discussion in the eighteenth centúry, and which he and Barth, like Schleiermacher and Ritschl before them, had rejected. Nor did he mean what he and Barth had joined in attacking in Schleiermacher and Liberal Theology (Brunner being indeed far sharper and harsher against Schleiermacher than Barth ever was: Barth used to insist that only one who was capable of loving Schleiermacher was entitled to criticise him), namely the supplementing of the revelation of God in Jesus Christ by additional sources of a more general religious or ethical kind. Brunner was as insistent as Barth that God is known only by revelation, and that that revelation is Jesus Christ himself.

But that left open a further question which concerned Brunner deeply: what was the connection between that unique revelation and three other more general areas: the whole universe as God's creation; the existence of human beings as 'made in the image of God', albeit as 'fallen' they have in some fashion lost or disfigured that 'image'; and the ordering of human life and society by such institutions as marriage and the state, which theology had traditionally treated as divinely ordained? These three together marked out the 'natural order', marked and disfigured, certainly, by sin and fallenness, but also upheld by God's preserving providence. Therefore the connection between these and the work of revelation and restoration in Jesus Christ must be explored, the 'point of contact' which they offer for the advent of divine grace must be found. Only in this way, Brunner felt, could a theology based, quite properly, on the revelation in Jesus be preserved from operating in a vacuum, and enabled to open up the apologetic and educational perspectives essential to the missionary and pastoral work of the church. Here too he also saw the opening for what he called *eristics*, a kind of 'polemical apologetics' in which the Christian understanding of human life as marked by sin and in need of grace could engage in controversial dialogue with other views in order to clarify the difference made by the message of the gospel.

Barth was deeply suspicious of this entire concern, which he had earlier tried to combat in Gogarten, who through the 1920s had developed a strong interest in the theology of 'the orders of creation'. This appeared to Barth inevitably doomed to dilute the concentration of theology on its proper task by compromising between the revelation in Jesus and other sources and authorities. The Word of God, he held, makes its own 'point of contact', created its own space in which to work, and must be allowed to do so freely. His sense of acute danger here was further sharpened by developments within Germany, as the Nazis sought with the help of *Reichsbischof* Müller and the 'German Christians' to make the church subserve their quasi-religious ideology of 'blood and soil', an ideology in which Hitler was unashamedly presented by the indefatigable Goebbels as a new messiah, commissioned by divine providence to save the German nation and establish the supremacy of the chosen, Aryan race in the 'thousand year *Reich*'. While Brunner naturally had not the remotest intention of supporting anything of this kind, his concern for his own kind of natural theology seemed to Barth to be wholly without adequate defences against it. He was convinced that, in the words of the *Barmen Declaration* which he with others drafted in May 1934 in opposition to the German Christians, 'Jesus Christ as he is attested to us in Holy Scripture is the one Word of God, which we have to hear, and which we have to trust and obey in life and in death.'

Later in 1934, Brunner published a polemical tract against Barth entitled *Nature and Grace*, to which Barth immediately replied with characteristic vigour in *No! An Answer to Emil Brunner*. A fair sample of his style is this retort to Brunner's appeal to the tag *gratia non tollit sed perficit naturam*, 'grace does not destroy nature, but perfects it'.

> Is the change in the human situation through the revelation of God, of which 1 Corinthians 2 and Galatians 2 speak, really a *reparatio*, a restoration in the sense in which Brunner employs it when he says, 'It is not possible to repair what no longer exists. *But it is possible to repair a thing in such a way that one has to say this has become quite new*'? (Italics mine) I must confess that I am quite flabbergasted by this sentence. Had one not better at this point break off the discussion as hopeless? Or should one hope for an angel from heaven who would call to Brunner through a silver trumpet of enormous dimensions that 2 Corinthians 5:17 is not a mere phrase, which might just as well apply to a motorcar that has come to grief and been successfully 'repaired'? (Brunner and Barth, *Natural Theology*, E.T. 1946, p. 93).

This riposte throws into relief the central difference between the two as Barth saw it. In his view, the revelation of God in Jesus Christ, and the repairing and restoring of fallen human nature brought about through it, were nothing less than a miraculous new beginning, an act of creative divine power, whose discontinuity from what had preceded it was signalled by the double miracle of Jesus' birth from a virgin and his resurrection from the grave. (Brunner, on the other hand, rejected the virgin birth, though not the resurrection.) Because there is that discontinuity, the connection can be established only from God's side, not from ours. Therefore we must not speak as if there were any 'capacity' in fallen human nature to receive or prepare for God by itself. That could only prevent the sheer miracle of grace from standing as it must on its own as God's free and loving initiative and movement towards us.

Here Barth applied, in contrast to what Roman Catholic theology called the *analogia entis*, 'analogy of being' between God and man, what he described, following Calvin, as the *analogia fidei*, the 'analogy of faith'. The whole character of faith is that it does not rest on itself, nor on what can be seen as an extension of itself, but on what is quite other than itself, by which its own emptiness is filled. And this is the model, the pattern, which must be seen to run through theology: it is in this fashion that the relation between God and ourselves is to be seen. Accordingly, Barth regarded any theological concern with created and fallen nature apart from its re-creation in Jesus Christ as quite superfluous. Natural theology, even of Brunner's qualified kind, could only be a snare and a delusion, a thing in which one ought to have no interest except that properly shown for an abyss beside the path—the interest whose concern is to avoid falling into it.

Brunner by contrast appealed to the Reformers, and especially to Calvin, in support of his contentions that there is a 'general revelation' of God in the ordering of the created universe, simply because it is of his making and bears his signature, and that this has its subjective correlate in man, made in God's image. Though that image has been defaced by the fall, its *form* if not its *content* remains in our essential humanity, our personhood, our reason and our ethical responsibility. It is this in fact that makes it possible to speak of man as a sinner, deserving judgement, because he is capable of guilt and bears responsibility for what he has made of himself; and precisely here lies the point upon which God's grace in Jesus Christ comes to bear. So Brunner rejected the possibility of an independent natural theology in which man could attain to knowledge of God through the general revelation in nature; for the defacing of the image of God in him had made that impossible. But, he insisted, Barth was simply running to the opposite extreme from the Enlightenment's rejection of revelation in favour of reason, and eroding the theological significance of the natural realm altogether.

While Brunner's interpretation of Calvin was weak at many points—as Barth took a somewhat mischievous delight in pointing out—his claim to stand more clearly than Barth in the line of Calvin was not without foundation. Here in fact we come to the most characteristic and distinctive feature of Barth's whole approach to theology: his absolute, thoroughgoing *christocentrism*. Barth, unlike Brunner and unlike Calvin too, insisted in his mature work on unfolding every aspect of Christian faith in the light of Jesus Christ and *only* in that light. The full implications of this are best indicated if we observe that far more is involved in it than merely the uniqueness of the *revelation* in Jesus, solely the issue whether there is genuine access to knowledge *of God* in any other place. What is also involved—and this was the point at issue between Barth and Brunner—is whether there can be any valid Christian understanding of creation, or nature, or sin, apart from Jesus Christ. Brunner wished to speak of man as created and fallen, as standing in guilt under the wrath and judgement of God, *apart* from Jesus Christ. (The 'eristic' element in Brunner's apologetics also reflects this.) In this, he was following the main line of traditional Reformed theology, and indeed of western theology in general. Its most common approach through long centuries had been a kind of two-pronged one. It dealt with the creation and fall of man, stressed the gravity of sin and fear of divine retribution, and *then* turned to present Christ as the answer and escape. The doctrines of the creation and of sin thus supplied an overall understanding of human life and posed a problem; and Jesus Christ was then brought into that horizon as the solution to that problem. But the horizon and the problem stood, as it were, on their own feet; they could be and were independently established.

The clearest and harshest expression of this twofold approach (and one which certainly brings into the open its ultimate presuppositions) was perhaps the application of the doctrine of predestination in the Federal or Covenant Theology of the seventeenth century as expressed in such classic statements as the *Westminster Confession*, which for centuries held sway on both sides of the Atlantic as the most widely authoritative summary in English of Reformed orthodoxy. According to the *Confession*, God in his free and eternal counsel has predestined some men to everlasting life, some to everlasting death. The reprobate (the condemned) fall under the judgement imposed on man because Adam broke his 'covenant' with God, a 'covenant of works' in which he and his descendants were promised eternal life upon condition of their obedience, which condition he failed to observe, thus plunging himself and all his seed into ruin. The 'elect' are saved from this just punishment because of a new 'covenant of grace' established in Jesus Christ: he fulfilled the terms of the covenant of works, bore the penalty for Adam's breaking of it, and thus became the means of salvation *for the elect*. All men stand under God's just wrath; but the elect have his love opened to them through Jesus. This theology thus drew an outer and an inner circle, and located Christ in the inner one: the outer circle of sin and judgement stood quite independently of him.

Only in the nineteenth century did widespread protests against this kind of thinking break out within the main stream of Reformed theology itself. Such diverse figures as McLeod Campbell, Schaff, Hodge and Ritschl began to insist (even if they did not always fully carry it through) that the person and work of Christ must determine the *whole* shape of Christian thinking. (This was a point on which Barth seems to have given Ritschl little credit; but Ritschl so represented the things against which Barth was having to fight that he could rarely find anything at all to praise in him. He was far fonder of Schleiermacher.) But it was Barth himself who really carried this programme through, insisting that even the doctrines of creation and sin must be grounded in christology, that there is no predestination of God apart from Jesus Christ, that on the cross Jesus himself is the one rejected and abandoned by God, and that both judgement and mercy, reprobation and election, must be seen as worked through in him, All these lines must, so to speak, be carried into the centre where they meet in Jesus Christ himself, and be seen as opening out from him rather than as constituting a distinct frame of reference into which he can be subsequently fitted. There can in this view be no room whatsoever for any separate or even semi-independent perspectives. While Barth had by no means worked through all the implications of this at the time of his controversy with Brunner, the disagreement which came into the open in 1934 can be seen in retrospect as foreshadowing the shape of his own future theology.

The rift between the two was never really healed, and from the 1930s onwards they pursued their separate paths. Brunner never accepted Barth's absolute christocentrism, was sharply critical of the amount of attention that Barth devoted to the Trinity, and saw in the unfolding of the *Church Dogmatics* a relapse into an excessively objective kind of theology. In his *Truth As Encounter* (2nd edn, 1963; E.T. 1964) he maintained that Barth and Bultmann had come to represent the extremes of objectivism and subjectivism, and offered his own attempt to chart a middle way in which both the given truth of God and the need for it to be apprehended in the personal encounter of faith would be given their proper place. This concern to avoid a false polarisation was certainly justified; but it is a real question whether Brunner in fact did justice to Barth in his interpretation of him, or appreciated what Barth was really doing in reconstructing the foundations of theological thinking. So, for example, when Barth came in a later volume of the *Church Dogmatics* to discuss the image of God in man, he did so in a fashion which led Brunner to assert that Barth had now changed his ground, and adopted Brunner's own stance as developed in *Nature and Grace*. In fact, however, Barth's revised (and more positive) treatment of the theme of the image was still grounded in christology, and the essential contrast with Brunner stood unchanged. If Barth was now able to say at least some of the things that Brunner also wished to say, he was doing so within his own perspective—and demonstrating at the same time that that perspective was not as narrow and restricted as Brunner had imagined it must be.

While Brunner's theology was for a time regarded, especially in Britain and America, as more 'moderate' than Barth's, and therefore preferable, he must now be regarded as the less radical and less creative of the two. But if he suffers to this extent by comparison with Barth, he towers over most other theologians of his generation; and it is more than a little sad that two men so gifted and with so much in common should not have managed to remain closer to each other. As Barth once put it, he and Brunner were like the elephant and the whale: both were God's creatures, but it was impossible for them to meet! Perhaps, however, the last word ought to be the message which Brunner received on his deathbed from his old colleague and adversary, 'If he is still alive, and it is possible, tell him again, "Commended to *our* God", even by me. And tell him, *Yes*, that the time when I thought that I had to say "No" to him is now long past, since we all live only by virtue of the fact that a great and merciful God says his gracious Yes to all of us' (Eberhard Busch, *Karl Barth*, E.T. 1976, pp. 476–7).

The *Church Dogmatics* was never completed, but by the time of Barth's death ran to thirteen part-volumes which appeared at intervals between 1932 (vol. I/1) and 1967 (IV/4, Fragment). The centre and focus of the whole is Jesus Christ himself—Jesus Christ as 'true God and true man', and so as the key *both* to the nature and activity of God *and* to the meaning and purpose of human existence. Working from that centre, Barth explores four great intersecting circles which supply the overall structure of the whole: the doctrines of the *Word of God* (vol. I), of *God* (vol. II), of *Creation* (vol. III), and of *Reconciliation* (vol. IV), each being developed with reference to the trinitarian structure of God's own being as Father, Son and Holy Spirit. (A further projected volume on the doctrine of *Redemption* was never begun, let alone completed.) The four circles are not presented as dealing with quite separate topics, such that to move from one to another would be in any sense a change of subject, but rather as four equally fundamental and interlocking dimensions of the same ground-motif that runs throughout: that Jesus Christ is the actualisation and realisation in time and history of God's eternal decision to be God for and with man; he is himself the everlasting covenant of God with us, and in that covenant the meaning and purpose of the created universe itself is contained; and in him too lies the uncovering and overcoming of man's estrangement from God by the divine 'No!' of the cross which leads on to the 'Yes!' of the resurrection.

This concentration on christology is of the very essence of Barth's method, but the greatness of his theological achievement lies not simply in the method and form of the whole, but in the way in which he succeeded by this means in re-integrating and casting quite fresh light on all the great leading themes of classical orthodox belief. Not without reason has his impact on theology been compared with that of Einstein on physics. Where Einstein broke through the previously accepted notions of space and time and re-ordered the fundamental concepts of established physics around the single constant of the velocity of light, Barth undertook a comparable reorientation of theology around the single centre of Jesus Christ. And just as Einstein's work involved a drastic revision of accepted ideas about space and time, mass and energy, velocity and movement, Barth's necessitated a comparable rethinking of established views both of God and of creation in general and man in particular. We have already mentioned one aspect of this in his departure from the predestinarian scheme of classical Calvinism, and many comparable illustrations could be given. Of these we can select here only one or two typical examples.

In respect of christology itself, Barth powerfully defended and re-stated the orthodox doctrine that Jesus Christ is both God and man, 'two natures in one person', as the Council of Chalcedon (AD 451) had described it. But he developed and extended the rather static idea of 'nature' in a dynamic way, tracing in Jesus' person and history a 'double movement' of God to man and man to God. This movement 'down' from God to man expresses and reveals the character and nature of God himself; for his *being* is not separate from his *action*; and in the answering movement 'up' from man to God, we see that human existence itself is grounded upon and made to answer to the divine initiative. Jesus is therefore not simply the human *instrument* of God's purposes, nor simply a man responding to divine grace: he is God come *as man* in order to work out and establish in himself the true destiny of man in friendship and communion with God. So the very being of God and the true nature of man are opened up for us in him.

In respect of God's being, the fundamental axiom with which Barth works is that God is 'eternally and antecedently in himself' what he shows himself to be in Jesus. There is no other God than this, nor is he God in any other way than he here makes known. In Jesus' own relation of sonship to the Father, a relation which is mediated and empowered by the Holy Spirit, the triune structure of God's own eternal being as Father, Son and Holy Spirit is shown as the eternal ground within God of the human person and history of Jesus. (Similarly, the self-relatedness within God's triunity is opened up as the basis on which he calls into being creatures other than himself, creatures whose *raison d'être* is to mirror and participate in his relation to himself.) So the doctrine of the Trinity is presented as intrinsically bound up with the incarnation of the eternal Son as Jesus Christ, and as supplying the ultimate framework for a theology centred and focused in him.

In this way, Barth distanced himself from what had been a very common tendency in much previous theology to separate off very sharply from each other (a) the *being* of God, (b) the *triunity* of God, and (c) the *incarnation*. This had led in a good deal of theology and piety to a concentration of attention on a vaguely unitarian 'God', loosely identified with the Father, and to increasing difficulties in connecting that up in any coherent way with either the Trinity or the incarnation. Barth insisted that the God with whom we have to deal makes himself known in and through Jesus Christ as the Father, Son and Holy Spirit, and that this is the real key to his being as God. For this reason, too, he broke away from the traditional pattern of definitions of the 'attributes of God' in terms of such qualities as omnipotence, eternity, omnipresence, infinity, perfection and so on. Instead he insisted that God as revealed in Jesus is he who has freely bound himself to be God for man, and that his primary essential characteristics are therefore *love* and *freedom*, 'God is he who loves in freedom!'

On the side of man, however, though his very existence depends solely upon the creative love of God, there is a surd element in the equation. This emerges in all its terrifying inexplicability in the fact that the incarnation involves for Jesus humiliation, rejection, and the cross, with the awful cry, 'My God, my God, why have you forsaken me?' God's love for and claim on man are worked out through a judgement and condemnation which disclose a profound alienation and estrangement between man and God, a contradiction in which man has attempted to break away from the tie with God, so that God's claim on him has become a consuming fire. This is the mystery of sin which has no rational explanation, for it is ultimately and radically inexplicable. That God's creatures should revolt against him, and so cut themselves off from the ground of their own being, is an 'impossible possibility' which has nonetheless been actualised. To it, God can only utter the dreadful 'No' which abandons sin to the nothingness that is its own real nature. But this is not his final nor yet his strongest word, for two reasons. First, it leads on from the cross of Jesus to his resurrection, from condemnation to vindication, from destruction to restoration. Second, it is God himself who not only *speaks* but also *hears* that 'No' in the person of the one man who does not deserve to hear it, the righteous one who stands in the place of the unrighteous. He is the real man as none other; for he alone is man as God intends man to be; he alone has travelled to the uttermost limits of the 'far country' of man's estrangement; and in him alone has the judgement been passed, carried out, and overcome to issue in reconciliation. All of this has been enacted and realised and completed in Jesus himself, and the meaning of sin, so far as we are concerned, is only really opened up at the very place where it is borne and done away with.

In spite of the millions of words they contain, and some noticeable shifts of emphasis over the years, the volumes of the *Church Dogmatics* are marked by an immense overall coherence and harmony. The seemingly endless variations and applications all circle round and reflect the single theme. Barth travels far and wide through the Bible, from Genesis to Revelation, and digests, criticises, and re-states a vast amount of material from the previous history of Christian thought, and from contemporary discussion—much of this in lengthy pages of tiny print, which readers are sometimes relieved to discover can be passed over without loss of the main drift (though it should be said that some of the finest passages are to be found in the small print). But all this is contained in a framework which, in its clarity and essential simplicity, has reminded many commentators of Barth's passionate fondness for Mozart. He used to say that he did not want to listen to a man like Beethoven, whose stormy music told his hearers all about himself and his troubles, but rather to hear the pure beauty of musical form, which so far as he was concerned reached its acme in Mozart's classical perfection. The same desire to articulate theology as something of beauty and of joy in the light of the God who has made himself known to us in Jesus Christ runs through all thirteen volumes, and makes them a unique achievement. The mountain peaks of Christian belief are travelled there in a style that has few rivals in the whole history of the church, and none at all in the twentieth century.

A project as ambitiously conceived and energetically executed as this naturally provoked both admiration and criticism from various quarters. Nor indeed did Barth pretend to be beyond criticism, though he was not slow to point out where he thought his critics had misunderstood or misrepresented his views. He commonly observed to his students that it was doubtful whether there was as much joy in heaven as in some places on earth at the rise of the 'Barthian school'—and would add that he at any rate did not belong to it. He also used to remind them that theology, even at its best and highest, was a human activity which could take no pride in itself, but only in its object; it dare not take itself too seriously, but must rather be 'a modest, free, critical and happy science' (*Evangelical Theology*, E.T. 1963, p. 64). This was of a piece with his fundamental conviction that the whole truth about God *and about ourselves* lies in Jesus Christ and must be found there.

What then have been the main criticisms? They vary a good deal depending on the distance between the critics' positions and outlooks and Barth's own. Some stand quite close to him but are unhappy about this or that emphasis or point of detail, or about tendencies which they see running through his work; others differ from him so radically on the nature and basis of theology itself that they in effect reject his approach wholesale. While we cannot discuss these very fully, we may try to sketch some of the main issues raised by each group.

An objection which has been raised by Jürgen Moltmann (see chapter 7) and by others who have been concerned to set our present time in the light of the eschatological emphasis of the New Testament is that Barth and his allies in the 1920s who aimed to recover that emphasis in fact misinterpreted it by twisting it into the 'eternal moment' of the encounter between time and eternity; and that his mature theology distorted it in a different but equally damaging fashion by swallowing up the whole of time and history in the central history of Jesus Christ, and by dissolving that away in turn in the eternal self-determination of God within the council of the Trinity to be 'God for man'. Thus, so the charge runs, he evacuated time and history, and in particular *our* present and future, of real theological significance. Related to this is Brunner's objection that he led theology back into a 'false objectivism', the complaint we shall later find Reinhold Niebuhr making that he does not take the challenge and struggle of Christian life sufficiently seriously, and the widespread feeling that he seeks to approach theology, and especially christology, 'from above', from the side of God, whereas today we must work 'from below', from 'the man Jesus' and 'the human situation'.

Another charge of a similar kind is that Barth was excessively concerned with *ontology*, with the rationale of the *being* of God; that he misused biblical terms and concepts on the one hand by treating them semi-literally as 'ontic', as descriptive of the way things actually *are* when they are often pictorial or metaphorical, and on the other hand by turning the whole of Scripture into a vast allegory of Jesus Christ; and that this reflected a Platonist streak in his thinking which encouraged an unbalanced concentration on eternal realities rather than the actual world of concrete life and experience.

So far as this bundle of interconnected criticisms is concerned, at least two distinct questions can be asked. First, how far did Barth do what he is accused of? and second, to what extent is there here a basis for valid criticism? On neither score is there any universal agreement, and many would deny that the objections are well grounded, holding that they rest on over-simplifications, and that even to the degree that Barth did move in the directions suggested, he nevertheless did not fall into the extreme positions of which he is held guilty. Others, however, would rather maintain that these charges have sometimes been exaggerated, but that they do highlight genuine dangers of which one ought to be aware in reading Barth: dangers which lie partly in what he actually says, but also partly in what he can very easily be *taken* to be saying when his real meaning is subtly but significantly different.

A more radical criticism was formulated by Dietrich Bonhoeffer (see chapter 7), who questioned what he called Barth's *Offenbarungspositivismus*, 'positivism of revelation'. By this he meant that the appeal to revelation upon which Barth laid such emphasis, especially in the 1920s and 1930s, was in the end all too arbitrary and served to evade genuine questions about the basis for theological affirmations. Bonhoeffer's unease was intensified towards the end of his life (in 1945) by a growing sense that not only 'revelation' but all the other categories of traditional 'religious' language were no longer viable in the modern world. In this way, he sought to carry even further Barth's own attack on 'religion'. Similarly, he retained a strong christocentrism, but tried to find a 'non-religious' interpretation of Jesus as 'the man for others' in whom God is indeed present, but present in weakness, suffering and hiddenness rather than in the authoritative majesty which was so markedly appealed to in Barth's earlier writing.

Some elements in Bonhoeffer's criticism were met very adequately by the later development of Barth's thought as the stress on revelation was counterbalanced by others, and the *humanity* rather than the *otherness* of God came to the fore. The fundamental issue, however, was not disposed of by this, and we shall see in chapter 7 how it erupted afresh in the 1950s and 1960s. The question is whether the kind of dogmatic theology which Barth undertook is any longer possible or valid in 'a world come of age', a secularised post-Christian culture. Is his work, to put it at its bluntest, a throwback to an age long past, a magnificent but doomed attempt to breathe life into fossils? Can the classical doctrines of the Trinity and the incarnation continue to serve as focusing and shaping theology for today, or must they give way to some quite different approach? Does the future lie with 'demythologised', 'secular' or revamped Liberal theology of the kinds we shall discuss in the following chapters? Alternatively, is traditional dogmatic theology to be retained, but in a form of synthetic alliance with traditional natural theology of the kind Barth was so determined to avoid? That too, as we shall see, is what some other schools would recommend, especially in England, where the main stream of Anglican theology has been strongly critical of Barth's 'one-sidedness'. Or are those on the right lines who maintain that Barth's broad approach is correct and must be built upon, but at the same time opened up to permit more 'input' into theology from the natural and human sciences, as we shall find attempted, for example, by Moltmann and Torrance?

These questions take us to the very heart not only of recent theological debate about Barth, but of the inner problematic of the entire development of modern theology as we are tracing it. His has been the strongest and most resonant of the voices which have called for a change of priorities. He did not seek so much to *answer* the questions posed from the Enlightenment onwards as to *reverse* them. Where others were most sharply conscious of the crisis posed for theology by the development of modern culture and the change in our self-awareness, he saw the real crisis as lying in the inability of theology to do justice to its object, and called it to look in the opposite direction from that it had been taking. Not our questions about the problem of God, but God's call and invitation to us determined the direction of his thought and shaped his writing; and it was this basic orientation that led him on to the restatement of christological and trinitarian dogma as the foundation and horizon of theology itself. The challenge which he poses is to accept or reject that foundation, to adopt or refuse to adopt that horizon. Either way, the choice involves fundamental perceptions of the source and task of theology as such.

It is not therefore surprising that Barth's work has been and continues to be controversial. In recent years, after an earlier period of reaction, most of the leading German theologians have been post-Barthian in the sense that while they have departed from him in various ways, they have nevertheless taken a basic orientation from him. In Britain and America, there has been a greater variety of attitudes reflecting a wider diversity of theological stances. Those who enthusiastically acknowledge his influence are certainly in the minority; but there are enough to ensure that the debate will continue.

5

Faith, Myth and History:
The Bultmann Question

In 1941 Rudolf Bultmann wrote an essay, 'New Testament and Mythology', whose impact on theology in the years after the Second World War was as great, in a different fashion, as that of Barth's *Romans* a quarter-century before. It and other important contributions to the debate it unleashed can be found in English in *Kerygma and Myth*, ed. H.-W. Bartsch (vol. I, 1953; vol. II, 1962; both volumes combined, 1972); it stands at the beginning of vol. I (pp. 1–44).

Bultmann's field of study was the New Testament, of which he was professor in Marburg from 1921 to 1951. He was widely regarded, and not without reason, as the finest New Testament scholar of his day; and he also numbered among his students several who were to be among the leaders of the next generation—the 'Bultmann school'. Here, we can mention his work on the New Testament only so far as is necessary to lead into the question with which his 1941 essay was occupied; how is the gospel of Jesus Christ to be interpreted and communicated to the people of the twentieth century? This was Bultmann's great theological concern, and both his analysis of the problem and his projected solution of *Entymythologisierung* ('demythologisation') raised a rather different set of issues from those touched upon in the last chapter, and offered an approach which, in spite of some affinities, stands in sharp contrast to those of Barth and Brunner.

In order to set Bultmann against his background, it is helpful to remind ourselves of the previous development of New Testament study as we sketched it in chapter 2. Bultmann stood particularly close, first of all, to Martin Kähler, and he took over Kähler's sharp distinction between *Historie* and *Geschichte*, and between historical study and the approach of faith. Faith, he consistently insisted, was not reducible to belief in historical events in the past, nor could it be proved or demonstrated by appeal to historical argument. It is something living in the present, and it involves decision and commitment. Further, by its very nature, it depends on God and nothing else. To attempt to validate or justify it by historical proofs is to contradict its real nature, and in particular to miss the point of Luther's battle-cry, which Bultmann made his own—we are justified 'by faith alone' (*sola fide*).

Along with this concentration on faith, which placed him quite close to the early work of Barth, Bultmann also took up and carried forward the two major trends in the critical study of the New Testament which had come to the fore in the previous decades. The work of men such as Wrede, Weiss and Schweitzer had demonstrated that the New Testament itself was shot through with theological interpretation of Jesus and his significance, and that theology and christology could not be simply ironed out in order to recover the materials for a straightforward biography of him. The theology of the New Testament—which meant, the theology of the primitive church—must be taken into account in any attempt to understand the documents. Their witness was to Jesus, proclaimed as the Christ of God in the light of Easter, and in the terms developed and applied to him in the earliest Christian communities.

Bultmann himself carried this emphasis further by pioneering with others—notably Martin Dibelius (1883–1947) and Karl Ludwig Schmidt (1891–1956)—the new technique of *Formgeschichte* ('form criticism'). Earlier research had developed *Quellengeschichte* ('source criticism'), which traced the use of sources by the biblical authors. So, for example, it had been found that both Matthew and Luke appeared to have used Mark as a source, and that in addition they had probably derived other material, common to them but not to Mark, from another source, no longer extant, which came to be known as 'Q'. This kind of comparison and reconstruction enabled the mapping of the connections between the gospels in a way which cast fresh light on their probable dating, and on the way in which their material might have been shaped and modified in its transmission from earlier to later stages.

Form criticism pushed the analysis of the material a stage further by concentrating on the 'form', the literary shape, in which particular units in the text were cast, and by detecting there clues to the way in which these segments had been used and interpreted and applied in the decades before they became embedded in the present gospels, rather like fragments of harder rock in a geological stratum. (More recent study has gone on to develop yet a third style of analysis, that of *Redaktionsgeschichte*, 'redaction criticism', which, on the basis of the results of form criticism, then attempts to discern the special theological concerns and convictions of the author(s) responsible for the final form of the material as we now have it in the written gospels, and aims to reconstruct from that a picture of the climate and views current in his or their setting in the early church.)

One of the fateful consequences of this angle of approach, at least in Bultmann's own case, was the conclusion that the New Testament is so much the work of the primitive church, so concerned with the Christ of the post-Easter *kerygma* ('proclamation' or 'preaching'), that we can learn from it relatively little about the historical life and teaching of Jesus himself. This view, forcibly expressed in his early book, *Jesus* (1926; E.T. *Jesus and the Word*, 1934), would of course be very damaging to some types of Christian belief; but it was not so for Bultmann precisely because, as he saw it, the centre of gravity did not lie in 'history' but in the *kerygma* and in faith. 'I often have the impression,' he said once, 'that my conservative New Testament colleagues feel very uncomfortable, for I see them perpetually engaged in salvage operations. I calmly let the fire burn, for I see that what is consumed is only the fanciful portraits of Life-of-Jesus theology, and that means nothing other than "Christ after the flesh"' (*Faith and Understanding*, vol. I, E.T. 1969, p. 132).

The second earlier trend which he carried onward was the history-of-religions approach to the study of the New Testament. Its relating of the ideas and teachings of the Bible to the wider background of ancient culture had a decisive influence on his own thought, and was directly related to the programme of demythologisation. This can most easily be seen if his approach is contrasted with that taken by the broad movement, generally described as

'Biblical Theology', which pursued the new and more specifically theological interest in the Bible that opened up after the First World War, and whose great monument is the multi-volumed *Theological Wordbook of the New Testament*, edited by Gerhard Kittel (1888–1948).

The broad aim of Biblical Theology, which as a movement flourished from the 1920s to the 1950s, was to recover *the distinctive theology of the Bible as expressed in the Bible's own terms*. It explored the ways of thinking and speaking to be found in the Bible, the original force and sense of biblical concepts, and the understanding of God, man and the world encapsulated in them, and sought in that way to enter into the 'strange new world of the Bible' in order to enable contemporary theology to be more solidly based upon it. The movement was a diverse and enormously fruitful one; but in at least some of its forms it was not entirely free of some rather doubtful assumptions and methods. It could and sometimes did tend to isolate the Bible artificially from its context in the environment of the ancient world, to over-stress the distinctiveness of biblical modes of thought, to impose an unreal uniformity on the diversity of its material, and to forget, amid the excitement of exploration, that its strange new world was and is very different from the modern one, and that there are genuine problems of translation from these times and cultures to our own. It would be quite wrong to give the impression that the entire movement was guilty of these failings, or that they wholly invalidated it; but they did occur, and highlight areas of real difficulty which have become increasingly apparent in the last twenty or thirty years.

Bultmann by contrast was very sharply aware indeed of the gulf between the ancient world and our own, of the links between material in the Bible and other ancient sources, and of the problem of *hermeneutics*, of the discipline of interpretation which was required if the message of the Bible was to be heard in the modern world. What came to impress itself upon him was not so much the *distinctiveness* of biblical concepts as their *remoteness*, their anchorage in a wider and, to us, alien culture. In particular, he became convinced that the general view of God and his relation to the world with which the New Testament writers tended to operate was no longer viable in the twentieth century, and that what appeared to be quite central elements in the New Testament *kerygma* were expressed there in terms which were originally non-biblical—notably in those of a 'Redeemer myth' which, following Reitzenstein, he believed to be older than Christianity itself, to have had its roots in Iranian Zoroastrianism, and to have been taken up by the early church as a means of expressing Jesus' radical significance. Both the world-view and the myth of redemption through the descent to earth of a 'heavenly man' must be reinterpreted if the real meaning, the abiding content of the message, was to be heard by the inhabitants of our contemporary scientific and historically conscious age. This brings us to the core of his own position, and to the two lines which there connect up with his distinction between 'history' and 'faith': his critique of 'myth' and his 'existential reinterpretation'.

Bultmann's use of the term 'myth' stands in direct line of descent from that introduced by Strauss a century before. As he applies it, it has several different but related meanings. The 'Redeemer myth' was a dramatic story about a heavenly being who came to earth and appeared as a man to bring a revelation from beyond, and also to suffer and conquer death. The world-view of the New Testament writers was 'mythical' in the sense that they thought of the universe as containing heaven above, the underworld below, and our earth in between, and believed the course of human life and history to be governed by supernatural forces of good and evil. The understanding of God himself in the Bible has 'mythical' elements in it to the extent that it speaks of God as if he were an entity who could be present and active as an agent within the world and history, part of the furniture of the universe, as it were, instead of being utterly transcendent and wholly beyond the world. 'Myth' may thus label a particular kind of dramatic story about the entrance into the world of a heavenly being, a pre-scientific cosmology, or an interpretation of God as 'a being' who exists and behaves in the same sort of fashion as other beings whom we know and of whom we have ordinary experience.

This last emphasis is the most fundamental of the three, and the key to Bultmann's theology. It also links up directly with the great concern in Dialectical Theology to preserve and emphasise the 'otherness' of God, the 'absolute qualitative difference' between God and everything else. Mythical talk about God misrepresents his real nature, and dilutes, indeed destroys his real strangeness by picturing him as 'a being' among others, and fitting him into a supernatural world running somehow parallel to our own, and interacting with it. In effect, it 'domesticates' God. In a pre-scientific culture, however, such a mode of thinking, albeit incorrect, was nonetheless theologically viable, because it was in harmony with the wider assumptions and convictions of the culture. Modern people can no longer subscribe to it, because we no longer believe in such a supernatural realm: we know that the world is ruled by the iron laws of nature, and that these are not interfered with, nor the seamless fabric of history broken, by interventions from beyond. The mythical conception of God has thus become not only theologically insupportable, but also culturally obsolete. This need not, however, destroy belief in God. Rather, just as the destruction of the old quest of the historical Jesus had opened the way to a fresh appreciation of the radical character of faith in him, the erosion of mythical thinking can and must direct us towards a more adequate theology.

For this to happen, however, the mere destruction of mythical thought is not enough. That by itself cannot tell us what the real meaning of the New Testament is. In order to get further, we must discover the real function of the mythical elements in it. What mythical thinking does is to use the distorting medium of objectifying pictures to express indirectly our apprehension of the meaning of our own existence. The mythical description of God reflects and points us towards the authentic reality of the God whom *we* encounter in faith as the one who addresses *us* from beyond the world and its history. The redemption myth attached to the person of Jesus serves to express his significance *for us* as the one in whom that encounter takes place, in whom we hear the Word of God which sets us free from bondage to sin, guilt and the fear of death—which are themselves 'projected' in the New Testament's talk of the 'principalities and powers' from whom Jesus Christ is the liberator. Myth thus articulates in its essentially indirect way the *self-understanding* of faith which has encountered the Word of God in Jesus.

This does not at all mean, so far as Bultmann was concerned, that God himself is, so to speak, dissolved away into the 'self-understanding of faith'. But it is only in the meeting of faith with God that God can be truly spoken of at all, while in faith, even a faith which is seeeking rather than completely finding, God himself is present. (Here, he liked to quote one of the sayings of Augustine, 'Thou couldst not seek me if thou hadst not already found me.') This makes possible and valid a theological concentration on the side of the faith which believes and seeks, and on the self-understanding which it attains, as the only possible avenue of approach to that reality. The task of the interpretation of the New Testament is therefore to explore the self-understanding of faith which it contains and opens up as possible for ourselves. In this sense, Bultmann could say that theology *is* anthropology, that enquiry into God is enquiry into the meaning of human existence before God.

In developing the positive side of his enquiry into the meaning of our existence, Bultmann drew on the thought of Existentialism, and particularly of Martin Heidegger (1889–1976). Existentialism can be seen as standing at the opposite pole to the impersonality of Hegel's Absolute Idealism. Its ancestry can be traced back to Kierkegaard and Dostoievsky, but it is not so much a single school as a broad approach which different thinkers have followed and developed in a variety of fashions, from the atheism of a Jean Paul Sartre (1905–1980) to the Jewish or Christian belief of a Martin Buber (1878–1965), a Karl Jaspers (1883–1969), a Gabriel Marcel (1889–1973), or a Nikolai Berdyaev (1874–1948).

What these and similar thinkers have in common is a concern with the meaning of human existence, coupled with a conviction that that meaning can only be opened up and uncovered from within our own experience as beings in some fashion responsible for our own existence. It cannot be explored in any detached or impersonal fashion, for that would simply cut us off from our point of direct access to it. The question of life is, or at least includes and is brought to focus by, the question of *my* life; the question of death similarly involves the question of *my own* death. The questions which are or ought to be of primary concern to us are precisely those which matter in this way for our own existence, which are 'existential' rather than merely 'factual' or 'theoretical'; and they can only be posed from a committed and engaged standpoint. This may sound excessively self-centred, and some forms of Existentialism—notably in the case of Sartre—do appear self-centred to the point of a rather black absurdity. But other forms have ruled out that kind of egocentrism by insisting that it is in fact only in and through the meeting and sharing with other persons that our own personhood is grounded, while theological

Existentialism goes further still in speaking of the transcendent reality of Being and seeking in this way to approach or translate the meaning of classical language about God.

Heidegger's primary philosophical interest was the nature of Being (*Sein*), which he saw as the central and fundamental question of all philosophy. In his early writings, particularly *Sein und Zeit* (1927; E.T. *Being and Time*, 1962), the avenue by which he attempted to explore it was what he called *Dasein* ('being-there'), which was his name for the specific form of existence which we know and share as human beings, by contrast with the nature of things. In our own *Dasein* lies a 'clearing' in which the character of *Sein* as such is revealed. So while Heidegger's ultimate concern was with the *ontology of Being*, his way of leading into it was along existentialist lines. This led him to analyse the shape and movement of existence, its basic dynamics, and the connection of our *Dasein* with time, the world about us, and other people. His thought and language often seem very strange, if not utterly incomprehensible (especially to non-Germans, who have to struggle with the fact that the 'clearing', the window into *Sein* which Heidegger's *Dasein* possesses, is heavily patterned and coloured by the structures of German speech and thought). This makes it hard indeed to summarise even a few of the main elements in it at all lucidly; but some attempt must be made in order to cast a little more light on Bultmann.

Dasein's chief characteristic is a variety of kinds of *Sorge*, of 'care' or 'concern', which prevent it from resting quietly within itself, but lead it rather to 'project itself beyond itself' in a way which enables it continually to realise and establish itself afresh, and to construct around it a world of objects given meaning by being taken up into its purposes. This process may be further analysed and described in terms of three central concepts which are related to the temporal dimensions of past, present and future: facticity, fallenness and possibility. Of these, the third, *possibility*, is the most fundamental. It is the openness to new possibilities which gives *Dasein* its special character, its capacity and need to 'project itself ahead'. But the possibilities open to us are not unlimited: certain things are 'given' in any situation, and we ourselves are in a manner 'thrown' into the world. We find ourselves here, but do not know why or whence. This givenness and thrownness, the heritage of the past, is described by *facticity*. The self-realisation of *Dasein* in the present moment is enabled by possibility out of facticity: the present is constituted by the future out of the past. Thus the future is not simply—as we normally think of it—the 'not-yet', that which has no reality. Rather, it is the power of possibility which enables the present to move on beyond the past, and is thus constitutive of the present itself as the point of intersection of past and future. It is in this way, too, that possibility is ontologically prior to facticity, and the distinctive feature of *Dasein* by contrast, for example, with the existence of things, mere objects, which belong on the level of facticity except insofar as they are taken up into the purposes of *Dasein* and given new meaning in the horizon of *Dasein*'s own possibilities.

At the same time, however, the very openness which is inherent to and constitutive of *Dasein* is a constant threat which produces *anxiety*—anxiety which is not merely emotional, but has a deeper ground in the nature of *Dasein* itself. This is not merely the ordinary anxiety that may be felt before particular fears or uncertainties of existence, but rather that which arises from the exposed precariousness of *Dasein* as such. This precariousness is of the very essence of *Dasein*—for it is inseparable from possibility—yet it is that of which *Dasein* is most afraid. It is focused most sharply in the inevitability of death, which, for Heidegger, is not merely the termination of existence at some point in the future, but rather, as the threat and reminder of that termination, is *Dasein's* 'ownmost possibility'. It is the moment which discloses with utter clarity the real nature of *Dasein* as an exposed and fragile 'standing out of non-being'. The response of *Dasein* to this anxiety is to seek to escape itself, and to evade responsibility for itself in the face of the threat of non-being by burying itself in concern with the world of things around it, or by submerging its own individual identity in that of the mass of other people—what Heidegger calls 'the they-Self'—where individual responsibility is denied and avoided and *Dasein*'s own loneliness is hidden from. In this way, Dasein *falls*, incurs *guilt* by denying itself, and topples into *inauthentic existence*: it scatters and loses its own real nature. The only way in which it can once more become *authentic* is through the acceptance alike of its finitude, its anxiety, its guilt and its inauthenticity, an acceptance which will enable it once more to realise itself creatively in the present. Authentic existence is thus not something simply 'given', as if it belonged in the realm of facticity; rather it must be repeatedly reached for and discovered afresh in the realm of possibility.

On this basis, Heidegger also offered his own account of the aim of studying the past history of mankind. Taking up the distinction between *Historie* and *Geschichte*, he set the discipline of historical study (*Historie*) in the context of the wider historicity (*Geschichtlichkeit*) of *Dasein*. Because *Dasein* itself is historical, set to realise itself within the ongoing stream of history of which it is itself part, its prime concern in studying the records of the past is not simply to reconstruct past events or amass collections of historical facts (though it will do that along the way), but to discover, in the past history of *Dasein*, possibilities of authentic existence which may become *wiederholbar*—literally 'repeatable' or 'retrievable'. By this, he did not mean mere repetition or recovery of the past as such, but a new appropriation and realisation in the present of possibilities opened up by the encounter with the past, possibilities which, realised before, might now be grasped again.

Bultmann by no means took over the whole of Heidegger's philosophy, nor indeed did he grapple with it in such depth as some other theologians, notably the Roman Catholic Karl Rahner, and indeed Barth himself. In the points just outlined, however, he found a formal pattern which he believed could supply the proper framework for understanding and reinterpreting the message of the New Testament. Conversely, he also believed that it is the gospel which enables the transition from inauthentic to authentic existence—a transition which Heidegger's existential analytic could indeed *describe* and *call for*, but not actually *enable*; for it spoke of it 'without power', as Bultmann put it.

What the New Testament mythically describes in terms of bondage to sin, death, the law, the world, the devil, is in fact that fallenness of *Dasein* which is more directly and precisely characterised by Heidegger as the escape into inauthenticity and guilt before the threat of non-being. When the New Testament speaks of redemption from all of these through Jesus Christ, it speaks of the transition from inauthentic to authentic existence. But the heart of its message is that it proclaims that transition as a genuine possibility for us, enabled by the cross. As we face the cross and hear the proclamation of the *kerygma*, we are confronted by God's acceptance of us in our finitude and guilt, and thus set free with the freedom of faith. The Word of the cross is God's Word, conveying to us the challenge and the promise of our own authenticity, calling us to the decision of faith, to our own 'crucifixion with Christ' and victory over 'the world'. Simply as the death of Jesus, the event of the cross is a past event like all others; but in the Easter *kerygma*, it is proclaimed with a universal meaning. Here, what is furnished is not merely information about something which happened once long ago: it bears upon us in the present.

In order for this to be realised, however, the mythical clothing of the message must be replaced by the drawing-out of its existential import. The one thing that must be retained is the fact of the cross itself as that on which the *kerygma* turns. Everything else is but the explication of its significance for faith. Even the resurrection of Jesus is not his 'rising from the grave' in any literal sense, but his continually confronting us in the *kerygma* of the cross: Christ is risen in the message which expresses the faith of the disciples once they perceived the meaning of the cross itself. Therefore, provided the bare fact, the 'that' of the cross is preserved, everything else may and indeed must be reinterpreted existentially, for it is there that its real content lies in the self-understanding of faith. And that self-understanding, that recovery of the possibility of authentic existence, is the bridge which links us today with the early church. It is a proper concern with that that can lead us to approach the New Testament with the right and relevant questions, and find in it what we are most earnestly seeking.

Bultmann's overall position—which is not so much a position as a programme, a method for uncovering and applying what the New Testament has to say—succeeded in a quite remarkable way in combining the diverse contributions of advanced critical New Testament scholarship, of Dialectical Theology, and of his existential hermeneutic, each interlocking and interacting with the others in a powerfully cohesive synthesis. The sharp distinctions between fact and meaning, historical research and faith, stemming in particular from Kähler, were taken up and indeed intensified in the new horizon of Dialectical Theology with its stress on the absolute otherness of God and on faith as encounter with that otherness. But just when it might appear that the New Testament could no longer maintain any enduring significance of its own, the existential and demythologising interpretation restored the *kerygma* to the centre of the picture. It did so by giving the sharp distinctions a further twist, relating them to that between facticity and possibility, and between inauthentic and authentic existence, and linking both sides by the *kerygma* of the cross and its hearing in faith.

Thus the different strands in his thought, though diverse in origin, combine and support each other in a way which makes the whole appear something rather more than the sum of its components. It possesses an extra quality of unified elegance and harmony which adds powerfully to its attractiveness. At the same time, however, the strength and validity of the whole cannot in the end be greater than what the main components can supply. These were much discussed in a debate which ran on well into the 1960s; and although the main focus of theological attention has subsequently moved elsewhere, the questions have by no means been finally disposed of. In the discussion, the main issues had to do with Bultmann's attitude to historical study and the historical Jesus, and with his existentialist reinterpretation. Some of them at least were to be powerfully raised by his own followers.

In 1953 a gathering of former Marburg students heard a paper by Ernst Käsemann on 'The Problem of the Historical Jesus'. He felt that the master's historical scepticism was exaggerated and ultimately damaging; for by concentrating and building everything upon the *kerygma* of the cross, it risked breaking the link, essential to the *kerygma* itself, between 'the preached Christ' and 'the historical Jesus'. He failed to persuade Bultmann, but did provoke within the Bultmann school what has been aptly called 'a new quest of the historical Jesus'—a particularly fine example of which was Günther Bornkamm's *Jesus of Nazareth* (1956; E.T. 1960). The aim of this approach was not to reconstruct an old-style Liberal biography of Jesus, nor was it to 'prove' the validity of faith by historical demonstration. Rather, it was to show that the Easter *kerygma* was not simply the invention of the early Christians, but was rooted in the words and actions of Jesus himself—that even before the crucifixion he had challenged people to respond to him and to his message, and presented that challenge as decisive for their relation to the Father. This looking back *through* (rather than *past*) the Easter message to the historical Jesus linked up with a wider trend in New Testament study, which has in recent decades once more recovered some of its older confidence about the possibility of tracking down reliable evidence in the gospels for what Jesus himself really did and said. Where Bultmann put all the emphasis on the proclamation of the cross, and thus, apart from the fact of the crucifixion itself, on the christology of the early church, the figure of Jesus himself has come back more into the centre of attention.

The new quest can also be seen in the context of a questioning on a wider front of Bultmann's very sharp distinction between history and theology, with its associated disjunctions between *Historie* and *Geschichte*, facts and meanings, and indeed between God and what happens in the world and time. Barth's mature theology represented a concerted effort to hold together *both* the transcendence of God *and* his presence as man in Jesus Christ, and by that means to set history itself in the light of the eternity of God. A different but not unrelated approach was taken by Oscar Cullmann (1902–   ), himself an outstanding New Testament scholar. In his *Christ and Time* (E.T. 1951), he argued that the very kernel of the message of the New Testament is a particular view of history itself, and that it is this that Christian theology must adopt. In it, there is a special, narrow line of 'sacred history' which lies within history in general and is the key to its meaning. The midpoint of that line is Jesus himself, and in his history within history, the sense and purpose of history as a whole is to be looked for.

An important background influence upon approaches such as these has been the impact of the study of the Old Testament, and in particular of those strands in it which describe God as very much bound up with and active within the history of Israel. If these are taken as signposts for theology, it becomes difficult entirely to accept Bultmann's effective scaling-down of God's encounter with us to the single point of the cross and its challenge to the individual in his own self-understanding. A good deal of more recent theology, notably the lines which came to prominence in the 1960s and 1970s, has been concerned to follow up these clues, to paint the divine activity on a broader canvas, and to relate the movement of history itself more closely to it. We shall say more about some of these movements in chapter 7, but this is perhaps the place to mention the most extreme challenge to Bultmann's approach in the work of Wolfhart Pannenberg, born in 1928, and one of the most prominent theologians of the present day.

Pannenberg set out to question not only Bultmann, but the whole disjunction between theology and history running back through Kähler. *Offenbarung als Geschichte*, 'Revelation as

History', which he edited in 1961, put the essence of his thesis in its title. God makes himself known within history; the horizon within which the theologian has to work is that of history itself; and the full meaning of history itself is only opened up when history as a whole is seen in relation to God. So Pannenberg combined, indeed almost fused, history and theology. He laid great weight on 'the unity of universal history', which he maintained to be a necessary 'postulate' for the work of the historian, and argued that ultimately that unity could only be located in a transcendent ground of all history, i.e. in God. He also made much of the idea of 'the end of history', in whose light alone the meaning of history as a whole can be discerned, and saw this end as revealed in the eschatological event of the resurrection of Jesus. Only in the light of this totality and this end could the real movement and goal of history itself be appreciated. Conversely, theology is grounded upon history, and upon historically verifiable events—especially upon the resurrection of Jesus.

Pannenberg thus rejected on the one hand Bultmann's sharp separation between theology and history, and on the other a tendency, which he detected in Barth, Brunner and others, to cut off the special 'history of salvation' from the rest of history as a whole. He then also set out in his *Jesus, God and Man* (1964; E.T. 1968) to move beyond Barth by constructing a 'christology from below'—one which would not argue 'down', as it were, from the *kerygma* or from the Trinity, but rather 'upwards' from the history of Jesus' life, death and resurrection, and in this way arrive at his divinity. At this point, his aims connected up to some extent with those of the new quest, but on a very different theological basis. While the foundations of Pannenberg's approach raise their own questions, particularly concerning the way in which the most far-reaching and all-embracing conclusions tend to be justified on the ground that they are already contained *in nuce* in the presuppositions of the enquiry itself, this questioning of the widely hallowed dogma about the absolute disjunction of faith and historical study certainly demands to be taken seriously.

Equally far-reaching issues have also been raised in connection with Bultmann's Existentialism. One obvious question is whether he did not risk setting the centre of gravity all too firmly in the subjectivity of faith rather than in its object; and on the other hand, whether he was really consistent in holding on as firmly as he did to the 'bare that' of the cross as the irreducible historical datum on which faith depends. Some of his followers have here set out to be more radical than he, and argued that as faith is an event in the present, the idea of God must itself be more radically demythologised and understood essentially as the power and dynamic of the event of faith as it takes place here and now. So Herbert Braun, a leading 'left wing' member of the Bultmann school, could describe God as 'a particular kind of common humanity' in which we are set free for a radically responsible and open kind of life which is 'analogous' to that achieved by Jesus himself. This extreme reduction of theology to anthropology goes very far beyond Bultmann himself; but it has been seen by some critics, as well as by those who subscribe to it, as a consistent following-through of the real drive of his thought, even though he himself drew back from the last step.

There are clear resemblances and connections between this kind of existentialist reductionism and other movements—those of 'religionless Christianity' and 'the death of God'—which we shall briefly encounter later. The weakness which they have in common is not their wish to revise traditional ways of thinking and speaking about God, nor their desire to relate God to the present life of faith, nor even their attempt radically to connect the reality of God with the response of faith to him. It is, rather, their tendency to scale down the whole of theology to that single point, to reduce it to one dimension. A wider trinitarian horizon which made proper room for the presence and action of God as Holy Spirit could include all that they wish to say without risking losing hold of him altogether.

A further, and equally important matter has to do with the question whether, granted that the New Testament needs interpretation and translation for today, the existential analytic of Heidegger can adequately serve as the medium. Does Christian faith really amount to the realisation of our own authenticity in the decision we find ourselves making when confronted by the *kerygma* of the cross? It is by no means evident that the two are really the same, or that Bultmann's exclusive interpretation of 'myth' as an expression of *self*-understanding is enough. There is doubtless truth here, and important truth; but is it the whole truth—or does it need to be grounded and based on something more clearly objective? Can a hermeneutic which moves always within the horizon of human self-understanding do justice to the content of the *kerygma* in which Bultmann does hold that the possibility of authentic existence is opened up? Or does it leave us in the end locked up in ourselves?

Apart from that quite fundamental problem about the viability of a purely existential interpretation of the gospel, a good deal of criticism has also been made of the particular Heideggerian analysis of existence which Bultmann employs. The main reason is a widespread suspicion that there is something more than a little dubious about Heidegger's stress on finitude, fallenness, guilt and death, and his invigorating but rather stark challenge to *Dasein* boldly to embrace its own anxiety and adventure into fresh vistas of authenticity. While Heidegger has offered a profound and perceptive diagnosis of some aspects of human experience, it can be questioned whether he has adequately sketched its deepest and most essential dynamics. Indeed, it can be held that his own thought was too deeply marked by some of the gloomier elements in much traditional Christian thought about man, and that Bultmann's inclination to treat faith very much as an individual matter, having to do with the overcoming of sin and guilt, reflected the same powerful influences.

Dietrich Bonhoeffer, who, as we shall see later, shared Bultmann's concern to reinterpret the gospel for modern man, nevertheless rejected this whole side of Bultmann's programme. He detected in it a debased and demeaning view of human life itself, an emphasis on weakness and vulnerability, which in effect allowed the shadows to dominate the whole picture and so ran directly counter to the message of the New Testament. Bultmann could certainly have answered that that was not his intention, that the centre of gravity must lie in the real possibility of authentic existence rather than in facticity, finitude and fallenness. But just as in his reconstruction, the *kerygma* tends to recede into the distance behind the self-understanding which it is supposed to empower and enable, so too the possibility of authentic existence seems largely parasitic upon the description of inauthenticity. To that extent, Bonhoeffer's charge deserves to be heeded.

Finally, there is the matter of demythologisation itself. Different questions arise here with each of the three main elements in Bultmann's understanding of myth in the New Testament, quite apart from the issue we have already touched upon of

114

whether myth is adequately interpreted as a form of self-understanding. First of all, most New Testament scholars, and indeed most theologians, would recognise some elements in the New Testament as mythical in the sense that they introduce cosmic powers of good and evil, and that the interpretations of Jesus and his meaning may indeed draw on pictures and conceptions of a broadly mythical character. (Whether, on the other hand, there really was a pre-Christian 'Redeemer-myth' of the kind that Bultmann believed, is much more debatable, on purely historical grounds). But many would also hold that what is most significant about these features of the New Testament is the way in which they are used to illuminate the scope and import of Jesus himself, and so re-focused in the proclamation of him. This sets the problem of their translation for today in a subtly different light. What is needed is not only or primarily an adaptation from a 'mythical' to a 'demythologised' view of the world and of Jesus, as if such 'views' were the foci of comparison; it is, rather, the discovery in our world of the bearing upon it of Jesus himself, a discovery which must be as far-reaching as was that of the early church. In a sense, Bultmann's entire project was intended to enable that discovery; but it may well be felt that he too narrowly restricted the field in which it could be pursued. Here, the other two main elements in his account of myth seem to be the prime factors.

These, as we have seen, were, first, his description of the world-view of the New Testament as mythical in the sense of 'pre-scientific'; and, second, his theological concern to avoid a 'mythical' understanding of God's 'presence' and 'action' in the world and history. He did talk, and very powerfully, about God's presence and act in the 'event' of Jesus. But he understood them solely in terms of the eschatological encounter of faith with the Word which, paradoxically, meets us in the historical particularity of the cross. The wedge thus driven between God and the world leads to an almost deistic position, with but one change from the deism of the eighteenth century. Bultmann admitted, indeed insisted upon the reality of God's revelation in the cross of Jesus. But this revelation seems always in his account of the matter to reduce to a kind of shining-through *from beyond* of a God who *remains beyond*. The world of nature and history is taken to constitute a closed system with which God does not interact. There is, however, a tangential contact; for within the world of nature and history there also lies what is qualitatively distinct from that whole *external* realm—the sphere of human existence. *There*, in the inner side of human life, in personal awareness and response, the Word of God in the cross may be heard and answered. Hence everything is concentrated in the existential dimension. This overall conception of God, man and the world supplies the framework of Bultmann's theology; and it was this that he regarded as the only possible modern and scientific understanding of the matter, by contrast with that adumbrated in the New Testament. From this stemmed his sense of the urgent need for radical demythologisation if the gospel of the cross was to be heard. (And it should be underlined that it was 'the Word of the cross' that his whole enterprise was intended to set free to bear with full force upon modern men.)

This overall view, which Bultmann presents with particular sharpness and consistency, is of course very widely shared. But it is by no means the sole possible one, as we shall see in later chapters. One common criticism has been that Bultmann's notion of 'the modern, scientific world-view' was already obsolete by 1941: we shall come back to the topic in our last chapter. Similarly from the side of theology the question must at least be asked whether the presence and action of God can and must always be reinterpreted in terms of revelation, of the Word which challenges us in our existence. Is it adequate or convincing, for instance, to treat the resurrection of Jesus as his 'rising in the *kerygma*' rather than as the basis of the *kerygma* itself? These are far-reaching issues, and it would be wrong to give the impression that any consensus has been reached among theologians on the solutions to them. But once Bultmann's underlying presuppositions are brought into the open, it does become possible to wonder whether they are as solidly established as he believed.

The main effect of Bultmann's work has not been to encourage large numbers of theologians to accept his programme precisely as he outlined it, but rather to stimulate several lines of fresh thinking about the themes he presented. We have already mentioned the 'new quest of the historical Jesus' and the wider debate about the relation between theology and history. To these must be added what became known in the 1960s as 'the new hermeneutic', which set out to develop further Bultmann's concern with interpretation for the present day, and in the process came to see hermeneutics as the essential and primary task of theology itself. On the Continent, the way was led by Gerhard Ebeling (1912–) with his *Theology and Proclamation* (1962; E.T. 1966) and *Introduction to a Theological Theory of Language* (1971; E.T. 1973). Elsewhere, it was chiefly in the United States that the movement grew and was most debated—as, for example, in J. M. Robinson and J. B. Cobb's *The New Hermeneutic* (1964) and C. E. Braaten's *History and Hermeneutics* (1966). Central to this approach is the conviction that the task of critical and demythologising study of the New Testament is *not* to be seen as terminating in *our* deciding what the text is to be allowed to say. Its ultimate aim is to subject ourselves to the message it brings in order to find the new meaning it has for us in our present situation. This makes clear something which Bultmann, too, strongly believed, but which his critics did not always appreciate—that the biblical critic, in the words of Luther, 'does not stand over the Bible and judge it, but below the Bible, and hears and obeys it'. While there is room for questioning how far Bultmann's programme succeeded in doing this, there should be no doubt about his intentions.

The opening up of the discussion on myth, on history, on hermeneutics, is a measure of the impact Bultmann has made. Nonetheless, the main movement of theology in the last twenty years has been in other directions than his. In some quarters, indeed, his work is much too easily dismissed as the last, desperate fling of introspective individualism. This does no kind of justice to his stature and achievement, or to the challenge he posed. The issues he sought to raise are real ones, even if the perspective within which he saw them, and the solution he advanced, themselves require further careful examination.

This is all the more necessary in that a good deal of more recent writing of a shallower kind shows some resemblance to his approach. The language of such writing may not always be that of Existentialism, nor need it necessarily set out deliberately to 'demythologise'. But it is common enough to find books on theology and on Jesus which explain his significance in terms of his 'symbolising for us the meaning of life', which adopt the category of 'myth' (viewed either negatively or positively) as if it comprehensively described the whole character of the New Testament message, or which reduce the 'Christ of faith' to a kind of subjective and shifting 'Christ-image' in the mind of the individual believer or the collective consciousness of the church. To the extent that such approaches sometimes—though not always—go so far as to pay no attention at all to the question of the basis in reality for such a 'mythic' or 'symbolic' christology, they are incomparably less theologically and intellectually rigorous than Bultmann himself was. Beyond that, however, they are exposed to the same critical questions as he by inclining to put the material focus in the same place—in the faith of the individual or of the church rather than in Jesus Christ himself. That is the central problem raised by Bultmann's project; and both those who would wish in some fashion to follow him and those who believe that some other way must be taken need to pay serious attention alike to its strengths and its weaknesses.

6

Some Trends Outside Germany

In the period with which the last two chapters were concerned, from the First World War to around 1960, Barth, Bultmann and the movements springing from Dialectical Theology stand out as dominating the movement of Protestant theology, especially in Germany and Switzerland, but not only there. In these decades there were, however, other major figures in Britain, America and Scandinavia, some with close affinities with their Swiss and German contemporaries, some pursuing rather different approaches. One of the most notable of them, Paul Tillich, was himself German; but it was in the last thirty years of his life, spent in the United States, that he became widely known and gave final form to his ideas. We cannot deal with him or with the others we shall mention here at the same length as Barth and Bultmann; but something must be said to fill out what would otherwise be much too narrow a picture before we go on in the next chapter to look at the new approaches which have attracted most attention in the last two decades.

In the early years of this century, the influence of both Schleiermacher and Liberal Theology was powerful, if diffused, in Britain. There was not a large Ritschlian School as such, but there was a great interest in that approach, reflected, for example, in such books as A. E. Garvie's *The Ritschlian Theology* (1899) and J. K. Mozley's *Ritschlianism* (1909). The general tendency was to adopt Ritschl's approach in modified form, and often to put a

119

stronger emphasis on sin and atonement, on the orthodox understanding of the person of Jesus Christ, and on the distinctive character of the revelation in him—in a word, to combine with Ritschl's emphasis on 'value-judgements' and spiritual and moral values, a theological stance rather more conservative than that of, say, Harnack. Some, notably James Denney (1856–1917) and Peter Taylor Forsyth (1848–1921), made their own transition from a broadly Liberal position to one which anticipated some of the emphases of Dialectical Theology; Forsyth in particular was later described as 'a Barthian before Barth'.

Other British enthusiasts for Ritschl appreciated and welcomed the new approach of Barth and his allies in the 1920s without seeing so great a contrast as its proponents believed there to be between it and that of Liberal Theology. An outstanding example was Edinburgh's Hugh Ross Mackintosh (1870–1936), whose posthumously published *Types of Modern Theology* (1937) is still an admirable introduction to the thought of Schleiermacher, Hegel, Kierkegaard, Ritschl, Troeltsch and the early Barth. This reflects a general tendency in much English-speaking theology to adopt German thought only in a somewhat toned-down form. Opinions differ as to whether this should be ascribed to native Anglo-Saxon sanity, to the cultural gulf between the two spheres, or to something rather less admirable—such as a lack of teutonic toughmindedness. Probably all three factors have been variously at work, and the somewhat complacent habit among some British commentators in particular of pointing to the first alone deserves to be taken with a fair measure of salt.

The inheritance of Schleiermacher was especially explored and cultivated by John Oman (1860–1939). Like almost all of the men just mentioned, Oman was Scottish (on the whole, Scottish and English Free Church theologians have been more powerfully influenced by Continental theology than those in the Church of England), but he spent the greater part of his active life in England, where from 1907 to 1935 he was Professor of Systematic Theology at Westminster College, Cambridge. As early as 1893, he published a translation with critical commentary of Schleiermacher's *Addresses*, and the remainder of his work can be seen as developing from that beginning, an attempt to pursue but also to improve on what Schleiermacher had suggested. In Schleiermacher, Oman detected three main weaknesses: an inadequate conception of religion, a defective treatment of human freedom, and an insufficient appreciation of the causes of disorder in man and the world.

He hammered out his own position in a long series of notable books, among them *The Problem of Faith and Freedom* (1906), *Grace and Personality* (1917) and *The Natural and the Supernatural* (1931). His own classification of religions ranged them according to the fashion in which they conceive of the supernatural and its relation to the natural. They extend from primitive *animism* through *polytheism*, *mysticism* and *legalism* to the highest type, *prophetic monotheism*, whose primary characteristic is that it recognises a transcendent and personal Supernatural whose purposes underly and give meaning to the natural order, and who also relates to us in a personal way.

'Personality' itself was one of Oman's great themes, and it was with its help that he sought to move beyond Schleiermacher. In the idea of personality he combined the 'absolute dependence' which he held to be the hallmark of all genuine religion with the 'absolute independence' which was the equally essential prerequisite of free and responsible moral response and action. God is to be seen on the one hand as 'the environment in which we live and move and have our being', and on the other as standing in a gracious and non-coercive personal relation to us, a relation of which Jesus Christ is 'the one unblurred mirror'. But because man is free, he is free to be bad as well as good, false as well as true, base as well as noble: evil and sin are therefore real because of the reality of personal freedom, and must be taken seriously; but they are overcome in faith, which is a transformation of the person by his relation to God.

In this way, Oman attempted to counter any facile optimism, any too easy belief in progress, and so to advance beyond both Schleiermacher and Liberal Theology. In the main, however, his work was firmly rooted in the same broad line as theirs; and it is scarcely surprising that he had little sympathy for the new thought which began to spread from the Continent towards the end of his life. There is much sensitive discernment in his writing, and his approach still seems to many a preferable alternative to those of a Barth, a Brunner or a Bultmann. In particular, his emphasis on freedom and on personality, and indeed on the religious dimension, has been re-echoed in a good deal of more recent

English theology which has chosen either to ignore or outrigh to reject the Swiss and German influences.

In the Church of England in this same period, a far more extreme form of Liberal Theology (though it owed little enough to Ritschl himself) was being propagated by the Modern Churchman's Union, whose leading light was Hastings Rashdall (1858-1924), author, among other works, of *The Idea of Atonement in Christian Theology* (1919). Here, he reduced the meaning of the atonement won by Jesus to the influence upon us of the inspiring example of his death as a demonstration of divine love—thus conveniently excising the greater part of what the Bible and previous theology had to say on the subject. The aim of the Union, particularly as proclaimed at a famous (or notorious) conference held at Girton College, Cambridge, in 1921, was to rewrite Christian theology on a thoroughly modern and liberal basis. The most significant feature of this movement, historically speaking, was that it reached this height of controversial prominence at the very time when a much profounder type of Liberal Theology was collapsing in its original homeland. It made ripples in its day, but lacked real substance.

The main line of thinking in the Church of England at that time was, however, a very different one, concerned on the whole to engage in a moderate restatement of classical theology along the lines of a 'critical orthodoxy', centred upon the incarnation of God in Jesus Christ, but seeking to reinterpret and reformulate the ways in which the main Christian themes had traditionally been expressed. Important here were two collections of essays, following in the broad tradition of *Lux Mundi*—*Foundations* (1912) and *Essays Catholic and Critical* (1926). (Another collection, *Contentio Veritatis*, published in 1902, was of a more Liberal slant, but did not make the same long-term impression.) Anglican theology has on the whole tended to emphasise the centrality of the incarnation for all Christian theology. It has also been broadly characterised by a concern to hold theology itself in balance, to do justice alike to the authority of the Bible, the witness of Christian tradition down through the centuries, and the claims of critical reason; and in this way to avoid the swing to extremes or to polarisations between revelation and reason, theology and philosophy, traditional belief and the demands of the present.

This has frequently led Anglicans to look more than a little

122

askance at what they saw as the one-sided excesses of Continental theology, and to search for their own kind of synthesis. To this extent, the broad stream of Anglican thinking flows along its own lines, somewhat separate from those of Reformed or Lutheran theology, and cannot be neatly fitted into the pattern of these others. This is on the one hand an undeniable strength: it can and sometimes does supply Anglican theology with a stability which others may well envy. On the other hand, the failure at times to engage in sufficient depth with debates going on elsewhere can lead to a certain insularity, which leaves it ill-prepared to meet radical questions when they are forced upon it from without, or when matters long discussed elsewhere suddenly come to the attention of an Anglican world insufficiently familiar with the background to be able to treat them in the depth they deserve. The Modern Churchman's Union was by no means the last instance of this.

Among the leaders of Anglican thought in the first third of the century, the greatest of all was perhaps William Temple (1881–1944), for the last two years of his life Archbishop of Canterbury. He aimed to reconcile theology and philosophy, revelation and reason, religion and science, in a manner characteristically Anglican, but with marked affinities with the approaches taken by Process Theology and the Jesuit Teilhard de Chardin, both of which we shall mention later. In the background to his thought, which found mature expression in his Gifford Lectures, *Nature, Man and God* (1934), lay a movement in which he himself had taken part away from Hegelian Idealism towards a more 'realist' metaphysics—one which did not dissolve all reality away into the Absolute, impersonal Mind, but which tried to give place to the material world of space and time as existing and knowable in its own right rather than as merely an appearance or a construction of the mind of the knower.

Realist metaphysics as developed by philosophers such as Samuel Alexander (1859–1938), Alfred North Whitehead (1861–1947) and Nikolai Hartmann (1882–1950) was deeply influenced by the rise of modern science, by an awareness of the dynamic process of evolution operating in the universe, and by a sense that there are different levels or strata of being in the natural world, from *matter* through *life* to *mind* and, in the case of at least some of these philosophers, *spirit* and even *God* himself. This offered

123

Temple the framework for a new kind of natural theology which he could connect up with the distinctive and central event and revelation of the incarnation of God in Jesus. He distinguished four levels of reality in the natural order: matter, life, intelligence, and spirit, all coinciding and cohering in man. Further, he maintained that the lower levels derive their meaning and place from the higher: it is man's *spirit* which gives him his distinctive identity, and holds together the material, vital and intelligent levels of his being. Similarly with the universe as a whole: the fact that the process of evolution has led to the emergence of spirit in man points us towards a transcendent Spirit, God himself, who is the supreme unifying and controlling principle of the entire natural universe in its totality. The world as a whole can be seen from this standpoint as *sacramental*, the outward and tangible reflection, form and vehicle of a spiritual reality and purpose.

The final key to this overall vision of the nature of reality is supplied by the Christian revelation, and by the incarnation of God at its centre: this completes and answers to the pointers cast up by Temple's natural theology by binding together the spiritual development within the natural order and God himself. Revelation is thus not reducible to the deliverances of unaided natural reason, but it meets them and may be related to them. Accordingly, Temple regarded 'the Barthian school' as exaggerated in its insistence upon revelation alone, and therefore as erroneous and indeed heretical, though resting upon a valid principle. In this he spoke for a great deal of English-language theology in the last fifty years.

A line lying somewhere between those of a Temple or an Oman and the Dialectical Theology was taken by the brothers John (1886–1960) and Donald (1887–1954) Baillie, who both set off from a broadly Liberal stance, but moved to a more mediating position in which they developed a (distinctly critical) appreciation of Barth and, even more, of Brunner. John held several academic posts in the United States before returning to his native Scotland, where he was Professor of Divinity in Edinburgh from 1934 to 1956. In *The Interpretation of Religion* (1929), he set out to construct a general understanding of religion which would take account of the different religions of mankind—a programme which will by now strike readers as remotely familiar. He defined religion itself as essentially a moral trust in the nature of reality, a trust which rests upon and implies belief in God. The human activity of faith which this involves has throughout history experienced a corresponding divine activity of grace and revelation meeting it. All this then centres in the particular revelation of God in Jesus Christ; but that revelation itself opens up for us the essential texture and sense of human experience and religion as a whole.

Under the impact of Barth and Brunner, he later modified his position slightly. In *Our Knowledge of God* (1939) he put a much stronger emphasis on the otherness and transcendence of God, on the priority of grace and revelation over faith, of God's hold on us over our hold on him. This has led some commentators to describe his later position as a form of 'Neo-orthodoxy'. But the extent of the change should not be exaggerated, for Baillie continued to distance himself very clearly from Barth and Brunner. Alongside the new emphasis, he still wished to preserve a general revelation of God in all religion, and a direct awareness of him in the human heart, even though it might not necessarily be a conscious or reasoned awareness. This immediate awareness he saw as brought out into the open by external mediation—through the world around us, through other people, and most of all through the impact of Jesus himself. The result was what he liked to call a 'mediated immediacy' in our knowledge of God. Overall it is doubtful whether he had really moved very far in point of fundamental method and approach from his more Liberal origins.

Donald Baillie was less widely known than his brother, but was more of a dogmatic theologian. His best book, *God was in Christ* (1948) is rightly regarded for its clarity of thought and style as one of the finest pieces of British theological writing in its day. In it, he criticised the old Liberal attempt to reconstruct the 'historical Jesus' in a fashion which would not and could not make room for his divinity; but he was equally critical of a tendency in Dialectical Theology in all its forms to minimise the importance of the historical issues, and concentrate too easily on a dogmatic theology of Jesus as the Christ. If the incarnation was to be taken seriously, then its historical aspect, the human life and person of Jesus, must be kept in the centre of attention. He worked out his positive account of the meaning of the incarnation by developing the idea of 'paradox', and in particular of 'the paradox of grace'. This points to the fact that in our relation to God, we are aware of our own freedom and of our dependence on divine grace: God makes absolute demands *on us*, yet he also 'gives what he commands', as Augustine had put it. This paradoxical combination of grace and freedom, Baillie took as the key to the dynamics of the incarnation: in Jesus is one who is fully human and lives a fully human life, and yet his whole existence rests solely and completely upon the Father.

He further justified this appeal to the paradoxical by arguing, in terms similar to those of Brunner and the early Barth, that revelation only occurs in a personal encounter—in what is generally now described in the language of the Jewish philosopher Martin Buber as an 'I-Thou' relationship—and that any attempt to represent its meaning in factual, third-person language cannot but distort it and lead to paradoxical modes of speaking. While paradox ought not to be gloried in for its own sake, it could not be avoided in talk about God. So throughout theology, and especially at the very centre where Jesus is spoken of, the two sides must be affirmed and held together.

The approaches of men like Oman, Temple and the Baillies may fairly be taken as representing the trends which shaped theology in Britain up to about the middle of the century, and as illustrating the general difference in climate from the Continent. In some ways that gulf has been partially bridged in more recent years through the impact of Swiss and German influence on British theologians of younger generations. Barth's thought has been followed up by a substantial group, of whom the best-known is T. F. Torrance; we shall come to his special work on theology and science in our last chapter. Bultmann and Heidegger have been important for the work especially of John Macquarrie, whose journey from Scotland and Presbyterianism, via Union Seminary, New York, to Oxford and the Anglo-Catholic wing of the Church of England has made him perhaps the leading Anglican theologian of the present day. On a wider front, we shall see in the next chapter how some of the ideas of Gogarten and Bonhoeffer found an enthusiastic echo in Britain in the 1960s; and more recently still, the work of men such as Moltmann and Pannenberg has been taken up in Britain almost as rapidly as in Germany. But that is only one side of the picture. In other respects the gulf between the German and British worlds of thought seems as great as it was forty years ago, especially in England.

One reason for this is that many of the problems to which

English theologians have given their attention have arisen in connection with developments in British rather than Continental philosophy, so that a broad stream of philosophical theology has developed which has a distinctly Anglo-Saxon character, and which has on the whole tackled quite different questions from those posed by a Barth or a Bultmann, and from a very different starting-point. The traditional topics have been the validity or otherwise of the philosophical arguments for the existence of God; the nature of human freedom and responsibility, and the distinctive character of moral values, and the connection between these and belief in God; and, especially since the Second World War, the analysis of religious concepts and language. The same broad range of issues has also been much to the fore in North American philosophical theology. Among the standard books in this field are John Hick, *Philosophy of Religion* (1963; 2nd edn, 1973), Ninian Smart, *The Philosophy of Religion* (1970) and Richard Swinburne, *The Coherence of Theism* (1977).

The question of the meaning of religious language has come from the 1950s to be particularly important in this whole discussion. In the background lies a rebellion against Idealism at the turn of the century in England, led by Bertrand Russel (1872–1970) and G. E. Moore (1873–1958). Drawing anew on the old British empiricist tradition of John Locke and Hume, they concentrated their philosophical attention on our actual experience of the world about us, disowning the Idealist inclination to treat it as mere 'appearance' which conceals or in some shadowy way reflects pure Mind. As with Hume in the eighteenth century, this approach eventually proved markedly hostile alike to metaphysics and to religion; for it drove in the direction of concluding that any talk about 'God', referring as it does to a reality above and beyond any normal experience, was without any proper basis and uncontrolled by any appropriate criteria. This challenge came into the open with the movement of Logical Positivism, announced by A. J. Ayer's early book, *Language, Truth and Logic* (1936). Ayer advanced the 'verification principle' as the criterion of 'meaningfulness'. According to this principle, a statement has factual meaning if and only if it is possible to specify the actual or possible circumstances which would demonstrate it to be true. Such a statement as 'God loves you,' for instance, or even 'God exists,' cannot be verified in this way: it is not possible to describe a particular set of empirical data which would demonstrate that what they assert is in fact the case. Therefore they are really without any genuine meaning, and only appear to have meaning because they are (misleadingly) cast in the form of factual assertions.

The strict application of the principle of verification relegated a good deal of ordinary language, quite apart from the religious (but including virtually every remotely *interesting* kind of expression), to the realm of meaninglessness, and consequently it was soon abandoned even by its original advocates, at least as an absolute criterion. (One difficulty which was gleefully pointed out by the Cambridge philosopher A. C. Ewing almost as soon as Ayer's book appeared was that the very statement of the principle was itself on its own terms meaningless; for it was presented as a *universal* rule whose truth did not depend on any particular combination of empirical circumstances, and therefore could not be demonstrated.)

Logical Positivism was, however, soon succeeded by the newer and more subtle approach known as Linguistic Analysis. This was inspired above all by the later work of Ludwig Wittgenstein (1889–1951), and by one of his famous *dicta*, 'Don't ask for the *meaning*, ask for the *use*!', as well as another, 'An expression only has meaning within the stream of life.' In this way, Wittgenstein directed attention to the setting and context in which particular 'language-games' were played, and to the diverse aims and purposes which different kinds of language and expression could serve. This general method was developed in a distinctive way by the Oxford philosopher J. L. Austin in lectures which were eventually published under such titles as *How to Do Things with Words* (ed. J. O. Urmson, 1962). Two particularly suggestive applications of this sort of analysis to theology were offered by Frederick Ferré, *Language, Logic and God* (1961) and Donald Evans, *The Logic of Self-Involvement* (1963). The aim here was not to rule out theological statements as meaningless or improper by the application of an arbitrary rule, but to explore the 'logic' by which they worked, and in that fashion to uncover their meaning.

Linguistic Analysis was nevertheless also still concerned to ask what language actually *referred to* as well as how it was used, and in this sense it continued to maintain the challenge presented by Logical Positivism. This became apparent in a collection of papers entitled *New Essays in Philosophical Theology*, edited by Antony

128

Flew and Alasdair MacIntyre in 1955. The force of more than one of the essays was to suggest that statements about God were just as lacking in any factual content as the older Positivism had suggested, and that they therefore could not be taken in any sense literally or as expressing what was claimed to be *true*. The person who sees the world as created by God and the person who does not, on this account, do not actually say anything different from each other *about the world* or their experience of wordly reality as such; the God whom the one introduces and the other does not is not himself an empirical datum about whose presence or absence one can significantly argue. Essentially the same view of the matter was presented in a number of other writings of the period, notably Ronald Hepburn's *Christianity and Paradox* (1958) and Flew's own *God and Philosophy* (1966), and an admirable survey of the issues it raised is to be found in John Macquarrie's *God-Talk* (1967).

The challenge evoked a variety of responses, some more sophisticated than others. One, presented by R. B. Braithwaite, suggested that religious belief is in fact verified by the believer's living commitment to a particular set of moral values, associated with the 'entertaining' of certain 'stories' which need not be taken literally. Another, offered by R. M. Hare, argued that belief involves a 'blik', a way of looking at reality, which cannot be treated as 'true' or 'false' but may yet be both desirable and rationally grounded. More recently, a 'non-cognitive' view of religious language has been vigorously advanced by D. Z. Phillips in *Religion and Understanding* (1967) and *Religion Without Explanation* (1976). Answers of this kind in effect accept the challenge of empiricism as valid; but, not perhaps surprisingly, theologians have tended to feel that they leave altogether too little substantial reality in religious affirmations to be satisfactory. 'I believe in God' may indeed *involve* certain kinds of personal and moral commitment, and a certain way of looking at the world; but that does not mean that it reduces without remainder to them.

A rather different avenue was opened up by Ian Ramsey (1915–72) in *Religious Language* (1957), *Models and Mystery* (1964) and *Christian Discourse* (1965). He found the key to the essential character of religious language in its evocation of 'disclosures' which enable a deeper level of perception, breaking open the enclosedness of our awareness of ourselves, others and the world around us, and setting them in transcendent light. Words and phrases which in the ordinary way refer to the everyday world are 'qualified' in a way which, so to speak, stretches them and makes another dimension transparent through them. (So, for example, the 'model', 'father', is 'qualified' by the adjective 'almighty', and transposed on to another plane of meaning.) In this way, he offered a new slant on the ancient problem of *analogy*, of the way in which this-wordly language can be made the vehicle of beyond-this-wordly sense. And it is most probably via the matter of analogy that the empiricist challenge can best be countered; for this makes it possible to take account of the difference between God and the world of ordinary perception—a difference which the theologian must maintain as much as the empiricist—without falling over into the conclusion that talk about God must therefore be lacking in cognitive content, and justified in a purely non-cognitive way. This cannot of course satisfy the thoroughgoing empiricist who is committed to the proposition that the *only* reality of which we can meaningfully speak is *this* world; but once it has become clear that that is his axiomatic assumption, there is no very obvious reason why the theologian should accept it.

A different style of philosophical theology, with roots in medieval scholastic thought, is to be found in A. M. Farrer (1904–68) and E. L. Mascall (1905–   ). They aimed to defend a more traditional natural theology, maintaining that our finite experience opens out into recognition of the transcendent reality of God. Farrer's *Finite and Infinite* (1943) and *The Glass of Vision* (1948) and Mascall's *He Who Is* (1943), *Existence and Analogy* (1949) and *Words and Images* (1957) combine with this a deep interest in the interplay between theology, perception and imagination—a theme directly related to the issues we have just mentioned, and one whose significance is further underlined by the fact that C. S. Lewis is still apparently the most widely read religious writer in English. We cannot explore it further here, but may mention two recent American studies: Julian Hartt, *Theology and Imagination* (1977) and David Harned, *Images for Self-Recognition* (1977).

In North America at the turn of the century, theology of a broadly Ritschlian type was developed in a distinctive way. W. N. Clarke's widely used *Outline of Christian Theology* (1898) was a classic expression of the Liberal approach. Clarke's younger contemporary H. C. King (1858–1934) took up both Ritschl's theology and Lotze's philosophy of value, gave 'personality' a central place, and interpreted Jesus' divinity in personal and ethical terms rather than in metaphysical, his uniqueness in his perfect moral and spiritual response to the will of the Father, and his power in his evoking in others that love which is the highest motive for noble living. He also laid great weight on the practical outworking of Christian belief; and in general, the ethical stress of Liberal Theology found ready acceptance in an American society and culture marked by a deep and strong practical orientation.

The Ritschlian concern with the kingdom of God also met a warm response among many American theologians, in part at least because the theme of the kingdom had already played a great part in American Christian thought, connecting as it so readily did with the task of building a new nation, and the conscious ambition to construct a new pattern of human community, which bulked so large in the American horizon. There grew up in the United States a movement known as the Social Gospel, whose leading figures included Washington Gladden (1836–1918), Walter Rauschenbusch (1861–1918) and Shailer Mathews (1863–1941).

These men turned their critical gaze upon the social and political situation of their own time in the conviction that the church had a social responsiblity and task to fulfil in the light of the New Testament message of the kingdom. Gladden and Rauschenbusch were Conservative Evangelical rather than Liberal in their theology, whereas Mathews stood much closer to the position of Ritschl. Politically, however, Rauschenbusch was the most radical. (This combination is by no means as unusual as is often supposed: 'conservatism' in theology and politics do not necessarily run together, any more than 'radicalism'.) He pointed searingly to the evils of industrial society, and advocated an alliance between the church and the working classes in a socialist programme which would answer to the original and essential aim of Christianity by transforming human society into the kingdom of God. In previous centuries, he argued, the church had always allowed itself to be diverted from this task; but the time for evasion was now past. In his *A Theology for the Social Gospel* (1917), he insisted that the theme of the kingdom of God must now become the controlling centre of Christian theology, and all else drawn into relation to it. While he himself did not wholly succeed in showing how, theologically, this was actually to be done, his prophetic denunciation of 'the kingdom of evil' paved the way for the more profound analyses offered a few years later by Reinhold Niebuhr.

Matthews' political views were much less revolutionary, but he was more consciously 'modern' in his theology. On the basis of his own understanding of the kingdom as an ideal social order, built around the fatherhood of God and the brotherhood of man, he bent his thought back in *The Growth of the Idea of God* (1931) to reflect critically on our concept of God itself. All our notions of God, he argued, are socially conditioned. This was reflected in the traditional understanding of him as an authoritative sovereign who deals with us as his subjects. Now, however, in our very different form of society and government, that way of picturing him can no longer be accepted. Rather, he must now be conceived of more 'democratically' as the power in the universe who brings personality into being, and to whom we can respond in a personal way. This kind of approach, concerned with the social conditioning of our understanding and with the need today to rethink traditional theological conceptions in that light, was shared by other members of the 'Chicago school' to which Mathews belonged. Something not wholly dissimilar will meet us again in a younger member of it, Charles Hartshorne.

As the century wore on, America experienced its own reaction against Liberal Theology. As in Britain, this can best be illustrated by the work of two brothers, Reinhold (1892–1971) and H. Richard (1894–1962) Niebuhr. As in Britain too, the reaction was a qualified one, which did not always go so far as the Swiss and German theologians. Arguably, however, it went further with the Niebuhrs than with the Baillies. Both the Americans could express their views very sharply indeed about the inadequacies of Liberal Theology—and even more, about the deficiencies of the particular brand of optimistic 'liberal' Christianity which was widespread in American Protestantism, quite apart from any special Ritschlian influence. In his *The Kingdom of God in America* (1937), Richard incisively summed up the grand proclamation at the heart of that brand of Christian faith, 'A God without wrath brought men without sin into a kingdom without judgement through the ministrations of a Christ without a cross' (p. 193). Similarly, in *Faith and History* (1949), Reinhold began by remarking that the perils and perplexities of modern times 'became the more dangerous because the men of this generation had to face the rigours of life in the twentieth century with nothing but the soft illusions of the previous two centuries to cover their spiritual nakedness' (p. 1).

At the same time, however, Reinhold was very sharply critical of Barth, though he felt that he stood fairly close to Brunner. He and Brunner had indeed much in common in their desire to look out—and to look out in lively criticism—on what was going on in the world around them, and to find there a positive base for theological reflection. Barth, by contrast, inclined much more to insist that theology must always begin not from 'the world' but from 'the centre', from God in Christ; and he and Reinhold had a lively confrontation on precisely this issue after the first assembly of the World Council of Churches in 1948. In his opening lecture at the assembly, Barth had criticised the set theme, 'The Disorder of the World and God's Plan of Salvation', saying that it put matters back to front. Reinhold countered this by writing later that Barth's theology was 'in danger of offering a crown without a cross, a triumph without a battle, and a faith which ignores the confusion of human existential life without transforming it'. (Quoted by Heinz Zahrnt, *The Question of God*, E.T. 1969, p. 121. The similarity to Richard's criticism of Liberal Theology is remarkable, and not without its ironic aspect in view of Barth's own attitude to the latter. But it is doubtful if Reinhold really appreciated what Barth was trying to say: certainly Barth felt that the discussion revealed a wide and serious chasm between European and American concerns.) Richard on the other hand stood consciously closer to Barth; but his aim throughout his work was to combine what he had learned from Barth with the insights of Troeltsch.

Both the brothers were thus very much concerned with society, culture and politics, with the interaction between all these and Christian faith and action; and Reinhold regularly insisted that he was not properly speaking a theologian in the strict sense. Both, too, made a great impact beyond the realm of theology, on the study of society and politics. In this way they can be seen as carrying further the concerns of the Social Gospel, but on a more radically critical basis.

Just as Barth's early experience as a pastor in Safenwil had a decisive influence on the shape of his early theology, so too did Reinhold Neibuhr's parish work in Detroit from 1915 to 1928 provide the central challenge to which his later study and writing responded. There he encountered at first hand the nature of industrial society, the character of the machine which rules and can frequently cripple and crush the lives of those who work in it. He moved away from an earlier, rather optimistic view of man and the world to one much more sombre, much more concerned to be realistic in facing evil and destruction and the forces which distort and destroy human dignity and freedom. In the process, he engaged seriously with the Marxist critique of capitalism, and came to accept a good deal of what it suggested to him about the workings of the capitalist system. At the same time, he found the rather deterministic Marxist analysis of man and the movement of history to be ultimately no more satisfactory than that of American liberalism. What he did take from it was the clue to an understanding of the individual and society which came to be central in his work: that a social group is always and inevitably less unselfish than the individuals who make it up. So his first major book was entitled *Moral Man and Immoral Society* (1932)—though he himself later joked that 'Immoral Man and Even More Immoral Society' would have been more accurate.

The main thesis running through his work, which was particularly developed in *The Nature and Destiny of Man* (1941; 1943), was that the Christian understanding of sin was as a matter of demonstrable fact far more realistic, far truer to the realities of human life and experience, than the broadly optimistic humanism which had dominated western society since the Enlightenment and the French Revolution. Following Augustine, he described the essence of sin as pride, pride which engenders a false conviction of self-sufficiency, issuing not only in the particular sinful actions of individual persons, but also in sinful and tyrannous corporate institutions and structures of society. Sin was thus not mere theological theory, but empirical fact; any realistic approach to man and society must reckon with it. He characterised it further by describing it as stemming from the reality of human freedom, and as being *inevitable* (freedom by its very nature can be misused) but not *necessary* (for it comes with the exercise of freedom): thus man remains *responsible* and capable of *guilt*. (Here again, the affinity of Niebuhr to Brunner rather than Barth can be seen—not that Barth denied sin and guilt; but he did not attempt in this way to build upon them.)

In the end, Niebuhr further held, an awareness of sin and responsibility disclose to us the meaning and depth of human existence in a way which cannot be summed up in any set of rational, philosophical, or even theological ideas, or fitted into either a liberal or a Marxist system of thought. It has a dramatic, vital, personal and existential quality which can be better grasped in artistic and poetic terms than by cold and clear-cut explanations; for in those other terms, which are also those which the Bible uses, we find opened up the possibility of self-transcendence through the encounter with the mysterious grace of God, focused in the cross and resurrection of Jesus, and enabling us to live in love reflecting the love and transforming power of God. At the same time, this also involves Christians in a sober appreciation of the wider sinfulness of their society, and in the task of working to transform it too—while always recognising that it is not from ourselves nor from the inevitable movement of history, but from the grace and love of God that salvation is to be looked for.

Reinhold's concern with looking out and bringing the Christian faith to bear upon the whole wider world of society, combined with his suspicion of systems of thought and his preference for dramatic language, to say nothing of his insistence that he was not really a theologian, mark him off quite sharply from most of the other thinkers we have mentioned. His work is nonetheless immensely powerful, penetrating and prophetic. Its main weakness, theologically speaking, is perhaps that he tended too much to take the Christian foundations of his position for granted, and did not sufficiently probe into them to demonstrate their solidity and coherence as the basis for his social and political analyses and criticisms. Nevertheless, he opened up new areas which have become increasingly central in more recent theological work focusing upon the social and political implications and applications of Christian commitment.

Richard was more of a systematic theologian in the ordinary sense, though sharing many of his brother's concerns. His best-known book, *Christ and Culture* (1951), developed and moved on beyond Troeltsch's interest in the sociological study of Christianity by exploring five different ways in which the relation between Jesus Christ and human culture and civilisation had been understood down through the centuries in Christian thought and applied in practice. He observed that, while none of these normally appears in an absolutely pure form, they can be distinguished from each other as marking out the main broad options. At one extreme lies a radical opposition between Christ (and the gospel) and the concerns of the ordinary world ('Christ against culture'); at the other lies an effective identification of the two, in which Christ becomes in effect the symbol of the culture and it is seen as an expression and extension of him ('Christ of culture'). Between these lie three mediating positions which distinguish Christ and what he is about from the aims of the culture, but see different kinds of interaction between the two. These he labelled respectively 'Christ above culture', 'Christ and culture in paradox', and 'Christ the transformer of culture'. Of all these, he felt the last to be the most generally adequate model, the one which does most justice to the realities involved; but he insisted that each of the others too has its strengths as well as its weaknesses, and that the choice between them must depend on the social and cultural context in which the question is being put.

This emphasis on the fact that theology must not only be concerned with culture, but recognise its own entanglement with it, and that it cannot therefore hope to give 'timeless answers', reflects the influence of Troeltsch upon Niebuhr's thought. At the same time, he also attempted to integrate with it Barth's insistence upon the centrality of Jesus Christ and the uniqueness of the revelation of God in him. The whole enquiry in *Christ and Culture* is based on that endeavour; and the same is true of such other books of his as *The Meaning of Revelation* (1941) and *Radical Monotheism and Western Culture* (1961). The broad line of his solution is that it is only in and through our own participation in the 'inner history' of the Christian tradition that the ultimacy of the revelation in Jesus Christ can be recognised or properly spoken of. We cannot take our stand outside that, on the level of a purely 'external history', or seek to establish the uniqueness of Jesus Christ in that way. This therefore leaves open the possibility of other—and valid—forms of revelation in other communities with their own inner history, which we cannot appropriate without abandoning our own. In the eyes of some critics, he thus ends up still balancing unhappily between Barth and Troeltsch; it would perhaps be fairer to say that he discerns a genuine issue and sketches its shape without being able fully to resolve it.

Very different from the Niebuhrs were two others whose work in America was especially influential: Paul Tillich and Charles Hartshorne. They also differed very considerably from each other, but had at least this in common: that both searched for a fresh kind of synthesis between theology and philosophy, and sought to give a positive place to a new kind of natural theology. In this they stood over against the lines stemming from the Dialectical Theology. In other respects, however, the contrasts between them seem greater than the resemblances.

Tillich (1886–1965) was a close contemporary of Barth and Bultmann, and began his career in his native Germany, where in the 1920s he had some contacts with them. Even then, however, his concern to be a 'theologian of culture' set him far apart from the main interests of Dialectical Theology. In 1933 his active involvement in the Religious Socialist movement led to his leaving Germany on the accession of Hitler to power. So, at the age of forty-seven, and with the main lines of his thought already established, he emigrated to the United States, where he became naturalised and spent the last three decades of his life. It was in that period that he came to be widely known, and regarded by many as offering an approach to theology which might improve on those of these others. He did have a certain amount in common with them, and was not unaffected by the revolt against Liberal Theology—of which he too could on occasion be sharply critical. In general, however, his attitude to the nineteenth-century development was much more positive, and his own work stood in greater continuity with it. His special concern was to build bridges between theology and philosophy, religion and culture. He described himself as one who spent his life 'on the boundaries' between such apparently diverse fields with the aim of finding a mediating synthesis between them. In his later years he also became increasingly interested in relating Christianity to other—especially eastern—religions, and searching for the same kind of unifying procedure. He was the author of many books and papers, but the fullest and most detailed presentation of his theological position is to be found in the three volumes of his *Systematic Theology* (1950; 1957; 1963).

Fundamental to Tillich's whole theology is his understanding of God as 'Being-itself'. God is not *a* being but the 'power' and 'ground' of all existence, Being-as-such. Everything and everyone that is, exists by participation in that power, and rests upon, or 'stands-out'—in Latin *ex-sistere*—of it. Thus existence in general and human existence in particular involves a certain kind of separation, of distance from the ground of being. Nevertheless, it is on Being that we all depend, and it is therefore the object of our 'ultimate concern', that which answers to our deepest needs and profoundest questions. It does so, however, not as something purely 'external' to ourselves, as other existing persons and things are 'external' to us, but as the very ground and basis of our existence and theirs, in which the difference and opposition between 'subject' and 'object', 'self' and 'other' is transcended. So Tillich distinguishes three possible states of being: *autonomy, heteronomy* and *theonomy*. Autonomy, self-affirmation and self-assertion, reflects the reality of our distinctness, our personal and individual freedom; but by itself it is ultimately shallow, for it leaves us isolated in ourselves. The antithesis to autonomy is heteronomy, in which we come under the power of other beings or of supra-personal structures and forces. Heteronomy underlines our incompleteness in ourselves, our lack of self-sufficiency; but it substitutes the tyranny of external realities for the authentic ground of our own being. Only in theonomy is that false antithesis between autonomy and heteronomy overcome, and our relation to what is external to ourselves properly grounded.

This identification of falsely polarised alternatives, and the search for a third term in which they can be reconciled in a way which does justice to both, is characteristic of Tillich's whole intellectual approach, and reveals the influence upon him of dialectical philosophy from Schelling (1775–1854) and Hegel onwards. Not the least attractive aspect of his thought to many in Britain and America is the way in which he exploited that (to them) largely unfamiliar philosophical tradition, developing its themes in English terms and categories which opened up a fresh way of seeing and grasping the shape of human experience, and then related that directly to theological questions and to the answers he found in the Christian message. So, for example, he explored the meaning of 'estrangement' or 'alienation' as opened up by art, literature, psychology or sociology, diagnosed it as a fractured relation to Being-itself, and traced the connection between these manifestations and the power of reconciliation and healing which he described as 'the New Being' found in Jesus Christ.

In constructing his system, Tillich used what he called 'the method of correlation' which was intended to bring together 'existential questions' with the answers given in 'revelation'. The analysis with the help of all available philosophical and other tools of the questions which are cast up as the most urgent, pressing and profound issues of human existence, sharpens and deepens them to the point where the answer found in revelation can be heard and appreciated; and in turn, the impact of these answers forces further existential questions. So, for example, awareness of our own finitude, and the existential anxiety which it necessarily involves, constitutes and poses the question to which the answer is found in the identification of God as the ground of all being, including our own. Similarly, an appreciation of the fractured and guilty nature of our existence poses the question to which the 'New Being' is the answer. Thus he replaced a traditional natural theology, independent of revelation, with the forming of the profoundest human questions; and for a 'supranatural theology' of the kind he believed he saw in Barth, he offered instead a theological answering of these questions, which did not simply come 'vertically from above', but met and connected with the questions arising from the human side.

Where, however, are these answers given in revelation to be found? They centre, for Tillich, in the biblical portrayal of Jesus as the Christ. He is presented there as the one who himself is the bearer of the New Being, through whom we too find access to it and the possibility of sharing in it for ourselves. This is not to say that there is no authentic encounter with divine grace, no genuine healing of our brokenness or overcoming of our estrangement, to be found or discerned anywhere else. It is to say that the New Being in Jesus as the Christ is the ultimate criterion of all saving and healing processes. Faith in him is essentially the recognition and reception of the New Being mediated by him and experienced as transforming power; and it is not a matter of historical proof, nor can it be demonstrated by historical study of the facts of his history, his life and death. At this point there emerges a significant ambiguity in Tillich's thought, and one on which many critics have seized. It is essentially the same ambiguity as we have found in some other modern thinkers who have followed this kind of broad approach. Is the affirmation of the New Being in the portrayal of Jesus as the Christ an objective claim *about Jesus himself*, or merely an expression of *the impact he makes upon us*? Where does the centre of gravity lie—in Jesus himself, or in something else which he merely exemplifies or symbolises?

Is Tillich in the end running along the same lines as, say, Biedermann—or even D. F. Strauss? These questions are given a sharper point by two other features of his thought: his concern with 'symbols' and his general conception of 'religion'.

Because God is Being-itself, he can be spoken of only indirectly and symbolically. There is, according to Tillich, only one 'non-symbolic statement' that can be made about God; and that is that he is Being-itself. All other propositions concerning him, because they must be couched in terminology whose primary reference is to existing things or people, can refer to him only in a refracted way. Being-itself cannot be expressed in our words: instead, it must be opened up for our recognition by words and images which direct our attention to the ultimate depths and convey something of its reality to our awareness. It must 'break through' them even as they are used to speak of it. This does not mean that language about God is only metaphorical, let alone purely arbitrary or meaningless. Rather, it is 'symbolic' in a quite specific and technical sense which is essential to Tillich's account of the matter. The prime difference between a 'symbol' and a 'mere metaphor' is that a symbol 'participates in the reality which it signifies'.

Because all existence participates in Being, the things of the world are capable of becoming symbols of the depth of Being-itself. So too, the language which we employ about ourselves, our experience, and the world of people and things about us, can also become symbolic when, beyond its ordinary meaning and reference, it is suffused with a profounder connotation and so discloses and illuminates for us the deeper reality of the ground of being. But the profounder connotation can always and only be conveyed and expressed in this indirect fashion. Thus religious language cannot be taken *literally*, for that is to fasten upon the 'surface meaning' and so to miss its real point. Equally, however—and here Tillich consciously and deliberately distances himself from Bultmann—it cannot be 'demythologised' in the sense of translating the symbols without remainder into some more precise, accurate and literal statements. Instead of demythologisation, Tillich advocates the 'breaking of symbols—that is, the conscious recognition that they *are* symbols, and none the worse for that; that the symbolic way of speaking is unavoidable; but that its symbolic character must be kept in mind, so that the depth rather than the surface meaning is given our attention.

While Tillich presents this position in language which is to some degree his own, it is not in substance original, or even particularly modern. It is in fact a version of one classical view of the nature of religious language which was formulated fifteen hundred years earlier by Augustine. In that view—which involves a certain understanding of the nature of reality as well as of the character of language—this world is seen as a kind of reflection of an eternal realm, of heavenly reality, on which it is grounded and from participation in which it derives its own reality. The visible things of this world can thus be bearers of invisible and heavenly meaning, and so become 'signs' or 'sacraments' of the eternal. This view—whose ultimate inspiration comes from the philosophy of Plato—has worked with immense power in Christian thought in the west. It is however open to many criticisms, both philosophical and theological, of which here we can mention only one which has a particular relevance for Tillich's exploitation of the Platonist Augustinian tradition. It is that in this horizon, there is a strong tendency to treat Jesus himself simply as a symbol, albeit the supreme symbol, of eternity, and of the grounding of all temporal reality upon eternity. The incarnation is interpreted, not as a decisive intersection of eternity and time, of God and the world, not as an altogether distinct and unique event, but as the supreme instance of a more general 'sacramentality' which characterises the nature of the world as a whole. It is not the *actualisation* of the 'New Being' in Jesus that matters, but its *manifestation to us*. And this does seem to be the main drive of Tillich's thought on the matter. The same fundamental questions therefore arise here as were indicated in the case of Bultmann—not whether what they say is not at least partially valid, but whether it drives far enough into the heart of the matter to uncover and bring out the authentic Christian basis of what they desire to affirm.

These suspicions are if anything reinforced by Tillich's handling of religion. He distinguished three key elements in all religion, though not all always present to the same degree in any particular historical form. The first is the experience or discovery of the infinite within the finite. This is the 'sacramental element' which is the basis of all religion. But this element on its own topples over into the idolatrous identification of the infinite with the finite, and leads to the 'demonisation' of religion. It therefore needs to be balanced and complemented by the second element, which

141

stresses the difference between the finite and the infinite and resists idolatry and demonisation. This on its own, however, is equally dangerous; for if unbalanced by the sacramental emphasis, it evacuates religion of any real or ultimate significance and produces the 'secularisation' in which it loses its transcendent reference. (An illustration of how Tillich could apply this dialectic in practice is his comparison between the characteristic attitudes and ethos of Roman Catholicism and Protestantism. On the one hand lies 'catholic substance', the first, sacramental element; on the other, 'protestant principle', the critical rejection of idolatry in the name of the unique holy transcendence of God. The first by itself leads to superstition; the second to secularisation: therefore each needs the other.)

The third essential element he describes as a prophetic concern to attack injustice in the name of the goodness and justice of God—the distinctively ethical component. The three together define the essential nature of pure religion. Tillich also held that this pure essence and balance are never perfectly realised in any actual, concrete historical form of religion. They constitute an ideal form, to which actual versions can only to a greater or lesser degree approximate. At the same time, however, this schematisation makes possible the comparison of particular religions, and the attempt to see ways of drawing them closer together in their shared and complementary concerns.

In offering this analysis, Tillich was following the phenomenological method of study advocated by Edmund Husserl, of which we shall say more in the final chapter. The method has its own usefulness as a means of classifying and comparing religions as well as other forms of expression of the human spirit. One of its weaknesses, however, is that it tends to issue in this kind of rather abstract and theoretical account of 'pure forms', which can often seem rather far removed from any specific and particular instances. (It is not clear, for example, how far comparing and contrasting 'catholic substance' and 'protestant principle' can really take us in grasping the specific Roman Catholic/Protestant points of difference, let alone in reconciling them. The analysis is so theoretical that the impression it gives of a kind of possible complementarity may be almost wholly misleading.)

That is not, however, the only difficulty. In Tillich's account of the character of religion and the key elements which are constitutive of it, the historical rooting of the Christian faith in Jesus seems in danger of being eliminated in the interests of a general and abstract theory which leaves the essential character of religion as fundamentally *un*historical, as floating somewhere in an ideal realm above the real world in which we live, believe, worship, and seek to be faithful; and which secures its attractive openness to other religions as well as Christianity only at the cost of being equally remote from all of them. This account of religion seems in the last analysis to be much less successful than those of Schleiermacher or Ritschl in doing justice to the Christian conviction that Jesus' person and history have a fundamental and essentially central part in the matter. Nor, though this side of Tillich's thought is appreciated and applauded by many who prefer his positive evaluation of 'religion' to the denunciation of it by some of his continental contemporaries, is it clear that he has really succeeded in facing, let alone answering, their critique of religion as idolatry; for in his account, that theme is subsumed, and its sting drawn, within a larger synthesis.

This is not to say or suggest that there are not very many profound, illuminating and challenging things in Tillich's work. The question is rather whether, in the words of one critic, 'the system' is an adequate vehicle for 'the gospel'. This question arises repeatedly. So, for example, his 'method of correlation' as he in fact applies it seems in the end to draw its answers less from any identifiable 'revelation' than from the axioms on which the system itself is built, and above all from the identification of God with 'Being-itself'. There is no doubt about Tillich's intention to offer an account which would do justice to the Christian faith, and in his attempt to do so he opened up wide new horizons for many; but it remains doubtful whether he really established what he set out to do. Nor do questions of this kind arise only from the side of Christian theology. It is the almost inevitable fate of those who seek to work 'on the boundary' to find that they do not satisfy those on *either* side. In spite of the enthusiasm of those who, twenty years ago, were hailing him as *the* relevant and modern theologian, his highly personal work already has a curiously dated quality as the anachronistic survival into the twentieth century of what is really a form of nineteenth-century Idealism.

In particular, Tillich's identification of God with Being-itself has had considerable difficulty in making headway against the criticisms of Anglo-Saxon empirical philosophy. Those in that tradition, whether philosophers or theologians, tend for the most part to be deeply suspicious of the tendency, not only of Tillich but of others too, to speak of 'Being' as if it were something 'substantial', a noun rather than a verb. They argue that this is an elementary confusion, a piece of sleight-of-hand: things and people may be said 'to be', but 'Being' as such cannot be treated as some kind of transcendent entity. This criticism is admittedly sometimes made in a rather patronising fashion in which the way 'Being' is used is somewhat misrepresented. Heidegger once pointed out in answer to it that when he and other Existentialists spoke of 'Being', they were not treating it as an entity, but using it in order to draw attention to the mysterious reality of existence itself, to the wonder of the fact that anything 'is' at all, and urging that that should be recognised as the chief stimulus to philosophical reflection instead of being treated as if it were the most banal fact in the world. In this sense it is perfectly valid and illuminating to say that within and beyond all existing things lies the fascinating wonder of 'Being' as such.

Even if this point is taken, however, as indeed it deserves to be, the simple and absolute equation of *God* with Being-itself still remains more than a little questionable. It is in fact dependent upon further premises—premises which have to do with an understanding of God as the creator and sustainer of all that is—but which it conceals behind its own apparent obviousness, clarity and definiteness. When Tillich insists that God simply *is* Being-itself, the assertion seems something of a short-cut in a dubious direction. It may well be appropriate and helpful to use the language which he also employs, and to apply the metaphors or models of 'ground of being' or 'power of being' to speak of God. Such analogies can indeed be illuminating; and it is, one may suspect, where that has been felt that Tillich's thought has had most appeal. But their underpinning by the ultimate and absolute equation of God with Being is another matter. That equation supplies the very basis of Tillich's system, but here there is certainly room for what he once called, in a notable book of sermons, *The Shaking of the Foundations*.

The thought of Charles Hartshorne (1897–   ) is in many ways quite different from Tillich's. Hartshorne's Process Theology took its orientation from the 'metaphysics of process' of Alfred North

Whitehead (1861–1947). Whitehead had a distinguished career as a mathematician and philosopher in Cambridge and London, where he collaborated with Russell in epoch-making work on the foundations of mathematics. Then in 1924 he crossed the Atlantic to Harvard and embarked on a new course as a metaphysician. His ideas were presented in a series of books, including *Science and the Modern World* (1925), *Religion in the Making* (1926) and *Process and Reality* (1929). His was perhaps the most striking and impressive of several attempts being made around that time to fashion a comprehensive metaphysical system on a basis of 'realism' rather than 'idealism', which would make a place for both 'mind' and 'matter', and trace an organic connection between them. Whitehead himself saw the entire universe as a vast, creative movement, a 'process', involving multifarious levels of inter-related elements which he called 'actual entities'. These ranged from God himself at one end of the scale to the slightest 'puff of existence' at the other. Each of these entities was 'bi-polar', with both a 'physical' and a 'mental' aspect—though only above a certain level did the latter attain the intensification which produced 'consciousness'. The mental aspect at all levels enabled what he called 'prehension', by which the different entities linked up with and related to each other. Through the whole network of prehensions and interactions, the universe was integrated as a dynamic, developing whole, a cosmic symphony.

This had a special bearing on Whitehead's understanding of God. In his 'primordial nature', God was complete and perfect, the source of all else that is; but in his 'consequent nature', he was related to, involved in, and thus also affected by the whole movement of the universe in every part and at every level. He thus participated in all that happened in it, and all that happened made its own impression on him. He could thus be seen as universally sharing in everything, as 'the fellow-sufferer who understands'. In addition, all that happened did not simply pass away and cease to be, like snowflakes upon the water; for it was necessarily retained in the 'memory of God'. Whitehead also believed that the 'religious spirit' was at bottom the recognition of God as the reality 'behind, beyond and within the passing flux of things'. This had been seen by Plato, but realised and demonstrated by Jesus, who in his life and in his death reveals the true nature of God's persuading, non-coercive love. Orthodox Christianity—with which Whitehead believed his own system to be incompatible—had lost sight of this. Nevertheless, the religious spirit was the great hope of the human race, and the religious vision of all-embracing, universally moving and interacting love, and its promise of ultimate triumph, the one element which through history persistently showed an upward trend.

Two sides may thus be distinguished in Whitehead's thought. On the one hand he offered a new metaphysical interpretation of the universe as cosmic process; on the other, a challenge to traditional ideas of a God separated wholly from the world, complete in his own unchanging perfection. This first side could be and was taken up by thinkers such as the English Anglo-catholic Lionel Thornton (1884–1960) in his *The Incarnate Lord* (1928). Here the theme, especially dear to many of the early fathers of the church, of the 'deification' of man in consequence of the incarnation was seen as the climax of the cosmic process; but God himself was not so much drawn *into* the process as seen as its transcendent beginning and goal. There are thus similarities between Thornton and William Temple, whom we mentioned earlier, and also Teilhard de Chardin. These theologians, however, held back from drawing God so completely into the movement of the cosmic process as was done by Whitehead. Hartshorne is less reserved on this point, and the chief characteristic of his Process Theology is the way in which, following Whitehead and developing his thought further, he boldly subjects God himself to the development of the universe as a whole.

Hartshorne's main programme (apart from a great expert interest in ornithology) has been to expound what he calls 'neo-classical theism', a form of philosophically grounded belief in God which nevertheless modifies elements in classical, traditional theism, notably the idea of a static and unchanging perfection in God. In books such as *Beyond Humanism* (1937), *Man's Vision of God* (1941), *The Divine Relativity* (1948) and *A Natural Theology for Our Times* (1967), he takes issue with the way in which the traditional debate between theism and atheism has been conducted. Classical theism has argued for the existence of a supremely perfect Being, one who is in every respect complete, and wholly independent of everything other than himself. Classical atheism has refused to believe in such a Being. But there is a third alternative: that God's being is in some ways absolutely perfect, but in other ways dependent upon a relation to what is other than itself. Following Whitehead's distinction between the 'two poles' of God's being, he argues that God does have an unchanging essence, but that he is also continually developing and completing himself by his own advancing experience of and participation in the universal process and the lives and sufferings of human beings. Because he is in this way implicated in the process, which has at every level its mental or psychical side, an adequate process metaphysics can supply the basis for a proper natural theology which is more tenable than either 'supranaturalism' (classical theism) or an atheistic 'naturalism' which cannot give an adequate account of the natural process itself.

Further, Hartshorne maintains, this kind of understanding of God is far more in harmony with the biblical witness to the God who acts in time and history, and who relates in love to his creatures, than is the notion of a kind of static Absolute. Indeed, even by our ordinary standards of judgement of persons, it is something far higher and better to love and to be affected by those whom one loves, than to be totally untouched by what happens to them. Why then, he asks, should this standard be stood on its head when we come to think about God? Should he not be thought of rather as *eternally* faithful, *always* loving, and *unfailingly* related to his creatures, and in this way as combining an unchanging element (grounded in his 'primordial nature') with his actualisation in relationships, constituting his 'consequent nature'?

This concern to overcome and depart from certain deeply rooted ideas of God's 'perfection' is shared by Process Theology with other movements in recent theological thinking. (Nor, indeed, is this purely a modern phenomenon. One weakness of Hartshorne's work, and of some other Process Theologians, is a tendency to offer a drastically over-simplified account of what 'traditional Christian theism' has amounted to, and thereby to exaggerate the distinctiveness of their own proposals.) It has affinities, for instance, with some of the aims of Barth as these are brilliantly paraphrased by Eberhard Jüngel's *God's Being is in Becoming* (1966; E.T. 1976). Similarly, the concern to move beyond what is felt to be a falsely grounded antithesis between 'theism' and 'atheism' can be found running through the work of other Barthian or post-Barthian theologians, such as Pannenberg and Moltmann. It is in fact fairly easy to show historically

147

that the sort of 'theism' here in view rests upon a conception of God which has less to do with the message of the Bible than with ideas stemming from such ancient Greek philosophers as Xenophanes and Parmenides, ideas which very early fed into Christian theology, and which have remained powerfully at work in it ever since. Deism, for example, represents their logical end-result; and the reaction against deism is certainly justifiable and necessary. Just as in the eighteenth century, that kind of conception of God opens up such a gap between him and the world that it is virtually bound to provoke or itself topple over into atheism in one form or another.

It is not simply in this respect, however, that Process Theology aims to be distinctive, but in its fitting of the *whole* pattern of Christian theology into the framework of the metaphysics of process. It is not merely a matter of seeking to shake up and challenge this or that particular understanding at a particular point—as can equally be done from other theological or philosophical bases—but of presenting *this* conception of reality as *the* true one over against all others, and reinterpreting theology from within it. A good number of thinkers in America, and some also in Britain, have followed Hartshorne's lead and sought in this way to recast the mould of Christian theology, to describe God and his relation to the world in terms of process, and to reinterpret the significance of Jesus in that light as well. This enterprise is not, however, without certain genuine difficulties, both as regards the coherence of process metaphysics itself, and as regards its suitability as a vehicle for the comprehensive re-statement of Christian belief. Without entering into any detailed debate, we may simply mention three of the main issues which have arisen in the discussion.

First of all, one of the essential and laudable aims of process metaphysics is to overcome the one-sidedness of those views of reality which are either crudely materialistic, unable to make any real place for mind, consciousness or spirit, or else dissolve away everything into 'mind' itself. What has concerned even those critics of Process Theology who have to some degree shared that aim has been the question whether either kind of imbalance is really disposed of by positing that every 'actual entity' is 'bi-polar'; and indeed, what it really means to speak in this fashion of, say, subatomic particles. Some have felt that the fabric of process metaphysics is too deeply coloured by *anthropomorphism*: that it does indeed make sense to see human beings in this kind of double light, but not stones, tables and solar systems. Those who take this view may well at the same time appreciate the power of the vision of the 'cosmic process', the sense of dynamic, purposeful relatedness and movement, which is the most exciting feature of process metaphysics; but they are more doubtful about the terms and categories in which that vision is expressed.

The other two issues are more centrally theological, and have to do with the implications of process thinking for the Christian understanding of God and of Jesus. The emphasis which it places upon God's 'consequent nature' produces a God who appears the very obverse of Aristotle's 'Unmoved Mover'—who is indeed, as one critic of the thought of Hartshorne has put it, 'the Moved Unmover'. God becomes the Universal Participant and Experiencer rather than the prime initiator and source of being and action. This certainly does justice to one side of the classical Christian understanding of God; but it is not so apparent that it offers a real basis—apart from simple assertion—for the conviction that the divine purposes will ultimately be fulfilled. Process Theology generally puts some considerable weight on that conviction, grounding it in God's 'primordial nature' interpreted in Hartshorne's fashion as the eternity, stability and universality of God's loving and faithful relatedness. But it is not clear that this conjunction of the two poles is itself coherent or solidly grounded in the general relativity of the metaphysics of process. Certainly this is not only a difficulty for Process Theology: it arises for any theology which affirms *both* the supremacy and distinctness of God himself over everything else *and* his interaction with everything else. But Process Theology has not perhaps come as close to solving it as some of its advocates believe.

The final point is that, at least in some of the forms it has taken, the application of Process Theology to the understanding of Jesus tends to deny his uniqueness in the classical Christian sense. This follows from the fundamental assumptions of process metaphysics, which does see everything in the universe as in one sense unique and individual, but which at the same time puts much more emphasis on the *relations between things*. It cannot easily allow that one particular person or event could be pivotal and determinative for the meaning and direction of the whole: rather, everything is related to everything else, everything and everyone is relative. This seems if anything to underline the doubts of those modern theologians who have questioned whether *any* general 'natural theology' can supply an adequate overall horizon for Christian thinking, and for an understanding of God, man and the world which will have an authentically Christian shape. This is by no means to say that no use can be made in such a Christian understanding of the categories and conceptions of process metaphysics; it is to say that process metaphysics, if it presents itself as *the* universally valid philosophy, cannot expect its claims to be passively accepted by theologians in general.

Lastly, even such a brief and selective survey as this of developments outside Germany in the period of Barth and Bultmann cannot conclude without at least mentioning the resurgence of Lutheran theology in Scandinavia. The names of Gustav Aulén 1879–1977), Anders Nygren (1890–1978), Gustav Wingren (1910–   ) and Regin Prenter (1907–   ) have become very well known, and books such as Aulén's *Christus Victor* (1930; E.T. 1931) and Nygren's *Agape and Eros* (1930; E.T. 1932) more or less standard reading. *Christus Victor* presented with a startlingly fresh vigour what Aulén called the 'classic theory of the atonement'. This saw the life, death and resurrection of Jesus as a victorious conflict with sin, death and the devil, and was sharply contrasted by Aulén with the two conceptions of the matter which had prevailed in much western theology for a thousand years and more—those which saw Jesus either as offering a 'satisfaction' to God, or as simply demonstrating the nature of God's self-giving love. *Christus Victor* found a ready echo in the new climate of fifty years ago, and if Aulén cannot really be classed with the Dialectical Theologians, yet his impact reflects some of the same factors as theirs. While the 'classic theory' there presented is too heavily mythical to be wholly satisfactory, it reflects a line of thought to be found in the New Testament and the early church, and one which certainly cannot be simply left out of consideration in any comprehensive treatment of the matter.

Agape and Eros was a study in what Nygren called 'motif-research', a style of investigation which in some ways resembled the phenomenological method, but which laid greater weight on the differences between particular religions. The aim was to find the essential 'motif' which characterises a particular form of belief:

while religions in general all aim at the union and communion of man with God, they differ in their understanding of the way in which these are achieved. From a comparison of Judaism, Hellenism and Christianity, Nygren distinguished three different motifs: *nomos* ('law'), typical of Judaism; and two different kinds of love, *eros* and *agape*, which characterise Hellenism and Christianity respectively. *Eros* is that kind of love which reaches up to and seeks satisfaction from that which is above and beyond itself. It may be intensely spiritual—the word *eros* as Nygren used it does not necessarily refer to sensual or 'erotic' love—but it is essentially self-seeking, looking to receive from that which is loved and to benefit thereby. *Agape*, by contrast, is that love which gives and does not seek its own, love which a higher may have for a lower, love which is initially and primarily God's own love for that which does not deserve to be loved at all. This is the kind of love of which the New Testament speaks, and which it invites us to receive and to share. Here, according to Nygren, lies the crucial difference between Christianity and all other religions.

This book too made a considerable impact when it appeared, and for similar reasons to *Christus Victor*: here, from yet another angle, was the kind of stress on God's initiative and grace, on the movement 'down' from God to us, which was being so widely rediscovered. While the method of motif-research is not without its weaknesses as a tool for historical and comparative study, Nygren's application of it here did serve to direct attention afresh to what on any reckoning must be seen as an emphasis deeply anchored in the New Testament—and one which Christian theology itself cannot afford to forget for the sake of its own task, even if it need not necessarily follow Nygren in believing that this sense of love is uniquely Christian, or that it in itself is *the* 'motif' of Christianity.

7

Theologies Secular, Radical and Political

In the 1960s theology in the English-speaking world found itself in a new period of excitement and upheaval, of which the most striking symptom was the reception accorded to the little book *Honest to God* (1963) by John Robinson, then bishop of Woolwich. *Honest to God* was not, in itself, a particularly profound (or clear) piece of writing, but it made an enormous impact and served to introduce to a far wider public in and around the churches some of the ideas, questions and answers circulating among theologians. In the discussion which it unleashed the names of men like Bultmann and Tillich became almost household words. The need to 'change our image of God', to engage in bold reconsideration of our most hallowed doctrinal formulations, to reinterpret the gospel and discover 'the meaning of Christ for us today', came to dominate discussion. On every side such mottoes as 'religionless Christianity', 'the secular gospel', and even 'the death of God' were to be heard. These serve conveniently to label three trends which were all much to the fore in the 1960s, though all had roots running much further back, and connecting with the developments outlined in our previous chapters.

The cry for 'religionless Christianity' takes us back first of all to the revolt against Liberal Theology in the 1920s, and in particular to Barth's attack on 'religion' and on the attempt to base theology on something essentially and primordially 'religious' in the human heart. This emphasis of Barth was taken up and carried even further by the man whose name came in the 1960s to be perhaps the best known and most discussed of all modern theologians: Dietrich Bonhoeffer. He believed that even Barth had not gone far enough in eliminating the appeal to the 'religious *a priori'*. At the same time, he did not see the way forward to lie in Bultmann's programme of existentialist demythologisation, for it too rested on 'unreconstructed religious presuppositions', anchored in Bultmann's view of man and his relation to God; it also, in Bonhoeffer's view, eviscerated the New Testament message by its excision of 'the mythic'.

Bonhoeffer was born in 1906, and while still very young came to be known as one of the outstandingly promising theologians of his generation in Germany. In the 1930s he was active in the Confessing Church, which was established in opposition to the Nazis and the German Christians; he also spent some time in both Britain and the United States. Just before the outbreak of the Second World War, he was in America, and under strong pressure from friends there to remain. But he decided that it was his duty to return home—that only if he had borne the heat of the struggle could he hope to share in the rebuilding which he knew would later be necessary. That hope was not to be fulfilled, for during the war he was arrested, and after some years in prison was executed in 1945. Through the 1930s he published a number of books, subsequently translated into English as *Sanctorum Communio* (1963), *Act and Being* (1961), *Creation and Fall* (1959), *The Cost of Discipleship* (1959) and *Life Together* (1954). Mention should also be made of the posthumously published *Ethics* (1955) and the early lectures on *Christology*, reconstructed from student's notes, of which a revised translation was published in 1978. The material which came to be most discussed in the new debate of the 1960s was, however, contained in some of his prison writings, translated in 1953 as *Letters and Papers from Prison* (revised and enlarged edition, 1971).

In *Letters and Papers*, Bonhoeffer repeatedly turns to exploring the question of the bearing of Jesus Christ on life today, of the meaning of faithful Christian life in the modern world. His remarks are often fragmentary, and he himself comments that he cannot entirely see where they will lead or how they should be further worked out. This makes it difficult to construct any clear-cut pattern from them; but if they are taken together with the concerns which can be traced in his earlier work—which does in some places offer valuable clues to his meaning—the key can perhaps best be found in a twofold conviction. On the one hand, Christian faith has an essential 'this-worldly' aspect: it centres on *the man Jesus*, and finds expression in the whole range of our life in the world. Already in his *Christology* this emphasis can be clearly seen: he insists that to call Jesus 'God' is to qualify *the man Jesus* as God, not to superimpose a second 'divine nature' upon him; he works out what he calls the *'pro me'* structure of Jesus' being, his being 'for me'; and he sketches the 'hidden presence' of Jesus in worship and in the life of the Christian community. This underlies the phrase used in *Letters and Papers* to sum up Bonhoeffer's understanding of Jesus: he is 'the man for others', the man whose own identity reaches out to involve us, and to involve us in his quality of radically human life. Similarly, Bonhoeffer's *political* resistance to Hitler was an expression and outworking of *Christian* conviction, rather than the carrying-over of 'religious' concerns to an 'alien' sphere.

On the other hand, supporting and complementing this emphasis, is Bonhoeffer's rejection of what he describes as 'religion', which is essentially a kind of 'other-worldliness' which separates off God from the life of the world, divides the 'sacred' from the 'secular', and thinks in terms of two levels of reality instead of holding all together. His positive aim was to open up what he called 'worldly holiness', his negative to undercut the powerful tendency among Christians to regard 'holiness' as something restricted, mystical and pious rather than practical.

This twofold concern underlies the criticism which Bonhoeffer goes on to make in *Letters and Papers* of the 'religious presupposition'. Religion appeals to 'the God of the gaps', the God who is needed to explain what we cannot explain. So the church, in face of the advances of human knowledge and the increasing control which man has attained over his world, has repeatedly adopted the unedifying strategy of pointing to yet further unexplained fields in order to anchor God there—with the result that it has presented a God increasingly remote and irrelevant. This has also led to the association of Christian faith with those aspects of human life in which men feel most vunerable, most lost and helpless; for it is there that it is easiest to persuade them of the necessity of God. But this too relegates Christianity to the edges of real concern: the gospel, by contrast, must speak to men where they are strong, not only where they are weak. In this way, religion seeks to keep men in a state of 'tutelage', to treat them and persuade them to regard themselves as children rather than adults. But the modern world has 'come of age', and knows it—not in the sense that man today is a better or nobler person than his forefathers, but in the sense that he knows that for good or ill he bears responsibility for what he makes of his life and the life of the world. Religion is thus steadily losing its cultural base. So Bonhoeffer calls in *Letters and Papers* for a 'non-religious' understanding of the Bible, a 'non-religious theology', and challenges Christians to live in the world *esti deus non daretur*, 'as if God himself were not given'.

The appearance of *Letters and Papers* in English made a very considerable impact, though it is a moot point how far Bonhoeffer's own intentions were appreciated by some of those who enthusiastically reiterated the new catchphrases culled from him. He was in fact very far indeed from being 'non-religious' in any ordinary sense of the term, and the last thing he did before his execution was to conduct a service of worship. When he spoke of 'worldly holiness' it was indeed *holiness* that he meant; and in calling for 'religionless Christianity' he did not at all mean a Christianity without prayer, worship and spirituality. Most important of all, the 'God of religion' whom he rejected was the God whom 'religion' conceives in terms of supreme authority, power and control. This God, Bonhoeffer believed, did not exist; but more than that, this was in any case not the 'living God' of the Bible. *That* God is the one who in Jesus allowed himself to be rejected and crucified; and the invitation and call to Christians is to 'share in the sufferings of God in the world'. Life 'without God'—the God of religion—is at the same time life with and before the living God. It is God himself who calls us to live *etsi deus non daretur*; and this God is supremely relevant to life today, a life in which 'only a suffering God can help'. In the words of Luther long before, 'There is no other God for us than the child in the stable, the man on the cross.'

This line of thinking, foreshadowed in Bonhoeffer's earlier writings and opened up slightly more fully in *Letters and Papers*, can fairly be seen as a radicalisation of the christological emphasis of Barth. Rightly or wrongly, however, Bonhoeffer felt that Barth himself had not taken things far enough. In Barth's appeal to

155

revelation, he thought he detected an authoritarianism of a characteristically 'religious' type. But he certainly stood closer to Barth than to Bultmann—or Tillich. Bultmann's philosophy of man seemed to him to be also typically 'religious' in its emphasis on finitude, guilt and death; and, moreover, the way in which Bultmann put the centre of gravity in the 'self-understanding of faith' was very far apart indeed from Bonhoeffer's concern to witness to 'the suffering God'. Similarly, Bonhoeffer was critical of the tendency he saw in Tillich to move away from the radical centrality of Jesus Christ in the direction of a more general 'ultimate concern'. These differences deserve to be underlined, for some popular writing in the 1960s in particular tended to run the three together as if they had the same basic concerns and were offering essentially similar proposals. There are of course similarities and overlaps between them, but there is another side to the picture. In particular, the Barthian note in Bonhoeffer's thought was to be echoed in some of the other movements making the running in that same period.

Bonhoeffer's description of man today as 'come of age' and his concern to move beyond 'religion' lead on naturally to the second leading theme of the new ferment of the 1960s—that of 'secularisation'. The word itself has been used in so many different senses and with so many varying overtones that it is often rather difficult to be sure what a particular writer means by it, let alone how far it really describes what is happening in our contemporary world. Broadly, however, the main use of it in most theological discussion has been to label a turning of attention to the things and affairs of this present world, an awareness of the 'autonomy of the secular realm', and a refusal to subordinate it to 'the sacred'. Thus it serves to characterise the shift which we have previously mentioned taking place in western culture through the recent centuries. One fairly standard theological and ecclesiastical response to that shift has been to condemn it, to diagnose in it the loss of the dimension of spiritual depth which is essential to our humanity, and not uncommonly to denounce the wickedness of the 'worldliness' it reflects. Bonhoeffer was one who sought to set the matter in a different light, and the theologians who made secularisation a central topic in their work had the same aim.

It was Gogarten in Germany in the decades from the 1920s onwards who gave particular attention to the process of secularisation with the aim of developing a positive theological assessment of it. This is especially evident in several books written in the 1950s—*Der Mensch zwischen Gott und Welt,* 'Man between God and World' (1952); *Verhängnis und Hoffnung der Neuzeit. Die Säkularisierung als theologisches Problem,* 'Misfortune and Hope of the modern Age. Secularisation as a theological Problem' (1953); *Was ist Christentum?,* 'What is Christianity?' (1956). In Anglo-Saxon theology, however, it was the work of others, some owing a good deal to him, that brought the question to the forefront of attention. Among the most widely read and debated of these were Paul van Buren, *The Secular Meaning of the Gospel* (1963) and Harvey Cox, *The Secular City* (1965); but a vast stream of other books and articles with the word 'secular' somewhere in their title were published and avidly read in the same period.

In all these, two broad lines of approach can be distinguished. The first, represented by van Buren and others, was primarily concerned to find new ways of expressing Christian belief in 'nonmetaphysical terms'. The modern, secularised world, which no longer had any real sense of the 'transcendent' or 'supernatural' as traditionally conceived, could no longer make sense of talk about 'God' or 'the divinity of Jesus Christ'; and therefore such traditional and hallowed language could no longer serve as a vehicle for the gospel. The 'secular man' could, however, perhaps be caught by the attractiveness of the figure of Jesus himself, and by the kind of living which he represented and inspired. This must therefore offer the avenue of approach, an avenue which might in the end even discover alternative and more viable means of speaking of the reality which had in the past been described in the metaphysical language of classical Christian doctrine. Elements in the thought of Tillich, Bultmann and Bonhoeffer could all be drawn upon to support this analysis of the shift which had taken place in our culture and patterns of thinking, and as suggesting some possible alternative categories; but the established formulations of orthodox belief were generally looked on as at best inadequate and *passé.*

In spite of the excitement which it generated at the time, it has to be said that very little theological work of lasting value seems to have come out of this wing of the movement. Both in its diagnoses and in its positive alternative recommendations it tended to move too much on the surface. In particular, the assumption that the language and expressions which appealed to the 'secular theologian' could really communicate effectively to 'secular man' proved more than a little dubious. It is one thing to offer a new way of thinking which may excite and open fresh horizons for those who are already in some way committed to Christian belief; but quite another to convey the same belief through that way of thinking to those who are quite uncommitted to it, and need to be persuaded that it has any relevance to them at all. In spite of the avowed aim of this approach, its not insignificant successes on the first score were balanced by very little on the second. To this extent, it already has in retrospect a slightly quaint and in-grown flavour, one which smacks less of genuine openness to the real world of men in their 'secularity' and their need than of a private debate among theologians and ecclesiastics.

The second approach to the theme of secularisation was rather different, and considerably deeper in its reflection. It was here, too, that the influence of Gogarten was more powerfully felt. In *The Secular City*, Cox followed up Gogarten's lead, and presented the thesis that what was happening in our modern culture, so far from being alien or opposed to Christian conviction, had deep roots in the Bible itself. The account of the creation in the first chapter of Genesis presents the universe, not as if it were itself 'divine' or ruled by 'magic', but as the handiwork of God. Thus that account 'de-sacralises nature', by contrast with the usual de-scriptions of the beginnings of the universe in other ancient cultures, descriptions which present the cosmos itself as divine, and as inhabited and governed by magical powers and forces. So too, Genesis describes man as created by God to exercise freedom and rule over nature: here already is a witness to that human autonomy which can everywhere be seen at work today. Similarly, the story of the Exodus from Egypt 'desacralises kingship', for it describes the escape of the Israelites from the 'divine Pharaoh', whose defeat and destruction proclaim the true lordship of Yahweh, the God who brought his people out of Egypt. Again, it is in the Old Testament that a sense of history as the field of divine and human action, directed by a purpose and moving on towards a future goal, begins to emerge, by contrast with the idea in most other societies in the ancient world that history is merely an endless, cyclical repetition of the same patterns. The movement of history up to and into modern times witnesses to the same process of 'disenchantment' of nature, society and history: the growth of industrialisation, of urbanised society, of science and technology, are all part of the same overall development.

The significance of this movement is presented by Cox, following Gogarten, as both negative and positive. Negatively, it clears away, by 'desacralisation' and 'disenchantment', the 'false gods' of nature, history and social institutions. Positively, however, this process, with the distance which it opens up between God and the world, and between man and nature, sets man free from entanglement with and enslavement to the inherent divinity of the natural world, and sets him on his feet to live *in* the world *before* God. A central distinction must therefore be made between *secularisation* and *secularism*. Secularism is that form of belief or world-view which rules God out altogether—as, for example, Marxist atheism does. Secularisation on the other hand by no means needs or ought to lead to this result. It offers, rather, that kind of autonomy, of freedom and responsibility, in which the world can be recognised in its own 'secularity', its matter-of-fact 'this-worldliness', as the arena in which man is brought to his own destiny as the one who lives before and answers to the living God. There are therefore clear resemblances between this approach and Bonhoeffer's call to reject 'the God of religion' in the name of 'the suffering God'; and both can be seen to stand in the line opened up by Dialectical Theology. The cry, 'Let God be God!' of the latter is now complemented by its obverse, 'Let the secular world be the secular world!' It is not therefore surprising that critics of this concern with 'the secular', and in particular of its dismissal of 'religion' and 'the sacred', have sometimes seen in it merely the exploitation of the negative influences stemming from the early Barth and his allies.

The same criticism was to be made, even more widely and furiously, of the 'Death of God' movement, represented by William Hamilton and Thomas Altizer in their *Radical Theology and the Death of God* (1966) and Altizer's *The Gospel of Christian Atheism* (1967). Their bold claim was that God had so completely and utterly 'emptied himself' into Jesus that—and here lay the new idea—in the cross God had actually annihilated himself. God really died, really put an end to himself, at that point in history. Henceforth God is dead: there is no God any longer. It has taken the human race some time to catch up on this, but in modern times

159

the cultural experience of the death of God—the loss of any real sense of God, the extinction of the notion of God in human consciousness—has made it both possible and necessary to draw out this most radical implication of the Christian gospel. The message is not, however, simply that God is no more. In some fashion, Jesus remains continually contemporary with us, and we are called to share in his quality of human living, loving the world, embracing even pain and suffering, and so discovering the nature and meaning of his presence today.

In a sense, this is a radically christocentric theology, but its christocentrism is far more exclusive than that of Barth; for it collapses the whole reality of God into the life, and especially into the death, of Jesus. Barth's 'christological concentration', by contrast, opened out into the triune being of God in and through the person of Jesus—a very different method and approach. Nevertheless, it is possible to trace a kind of line running from Barth through Bonhoeffer to Altizer. To this extent, the Death of God theology can be seen as one way of driving extreme christocentrism to its limits, and tends generally to be seen as an object-lesson in the dangers lying along that path. Those, however, who believe that in Altizer they have found a stick with which to belabour Barth, must in all justice ponder the question why Barth's own theology took a quite different road.

To look ahead for a moment, we may notice that a very different kind of 'radical approach' has been attempted in some even more recent writing, especially in England. This aims to hold very firmly on to belief in God—that is, God the Father—but is much more doubtful about the place of Jesus, or about its orthodox expression in the doctrines of the incarnation and the Trinity. The 1977 collection of essays, *The Myth of God Incarnate*, edited by John Hick, is perhaps the best example. Hick's own call, here and in other writings, such as his *God and the Universe of Faiths* (1973), is for a return from a 'christocentric' to a 'theocentric' theology; and the general programme of the contributors to *The Myth of God Incarnate* (though there are very considerable divergences between them) moves in the direction of questioning the uniqueness of Jesus and the 'metaphysical doctrine' of the incarnation. If this project is compared to the Death of God school, it becomes apparent that both are building on certain elements of classical Christian theology, but rejecting others; and the selection in both cases seems more than a little arbitrary. There is, however, a significant contrast between them. The work of the Death of God writers, and especially of Altizer himself, offers some compensation for this arbitrariness by the imaginative power of the vision it presents, by its concern to address the 'cultural experience of the death of God', interpreted with the help of such perceptive (if also disturbing and questionable) thinkers as Nietzsche and Blake, and by its attempt to carry forward, even one-sidedly, impulses which have been both challenging and fruitful in theology in the last sixty years. The contributions to *The Myth of God Incarnate* breathe an altogether blander and more old-fashioned air: their intellectual roots are mostly anchored in the theology of the nineteenth century, and the positive positions advanced offer little that the reader of Schleiermacher or Ritschl will find in any way new.

As the 1960s passed, a striking change came over the theological climate. The slogans most often heard in the last decade have not been those of 'religionless Christianity', let alone of the 'death of God', but rather of 'hope' and 'liberation', associated especially with a loose variety of movements which have come to be generally spoken of as Theology of Liberation or Political Theology. In the eyes of many observers, and especially of its numerous critics, this is simply a natural extension and outgrowth of the earlier Secular Theology; but, while there is some truth in this characterisation, it is at best partial. Secular and Political Theology do have a good deal in common. Both have roots running back to Dialectical Theology, at least in some of their most prominent manifestations. Both have tried to look seriously and openly at the way in which contemporary culture and society are developing, and to reflect theologically upon it. Both have been concerned to uncover afresh the bearing of Christian faith and commitment upon life in the world of today, and are frequently critical of established forms of Christian belief and behaviour. And there are certainly strands in Political Theology which are almost indistinguishable from some of the Secular varieties. Overall, however, Political Theology is different in a series of respects, and these give it a quite distinctive quality. Secular Theology as it grew up to and into the 1960s was very largely a European and American phenomenon, inclined to take the present and projected future development of western industrialised society as the norm for the future of the

161

human race as a whole, and generally confident even to the point of complacency in the correctness of that prognosis. Political Theology in most of its forms sees the world very differently, and tends to be strongly critical both of the present shape of western society and of the role played by the powerful nations of the world in the international arena. It attempts to see the movement of history from the standpoint of the oppressed and exploited whose cry is for justice and freedom, and has developed even more powerfully in some areas of the Third World than in Europe or America.

In this connection, it commonly derives a good deal of its impetus from a Marxist analysis of political and economic forces rather than from the broadly liberal or social-democratic standpoint which is so widely taken for granted in the developed countries of the west. It also fiercely criticises what it sees as the 'liberal' and 'bourgeois' reduction of Christian faith to something private and individual, kept largely in a separate compartment from engagement in the wider life of society; and is in particular strongly opposed to any understanding of theology as mere 'theory', mere 'ideas', ungrounded in specific situations and their demands, and unexpressed in action. Strange, threatening, and incipiently totalitarian as this certainly appears to many Christians, it can nevertheless claim a respectable theological ancestry through the centuries, and indeed right back to the Old Testament prophets, from whose criticism of the religion, politics and society of their own day Political Theology draws much of its inspiration.

The first major impulse to these new movements was the appearance in 1965 of Jürgen Moltmann's *Theology of Hope*. This combined the theological influence of Barth with the thought of the Marxist philosopher Ernst Bloch (1885–1977), particularly as developed in his *Das Prinzip Hoffnung* ('The Principle of Hope'), which was written during the Second World War, and eventually published in Germany in 1959. As a (non-practising) Jew who, like Marx himself, was deeply influenced by the Bible, Bloch used the category of 'hope' to construct a form of atheistic philosophy of man which would preserve what he felt to be the essential truth at the core of the Bible's interpretation of human existence. Man is a being who, by his very nature, is not 'closed' or 'complete'; he does not have an 'essence' which is already 'there' or simply 'given'. Rather, he is open to 'the future' into which he is moving, and in which his identity is yet to be discovered, realised and affirmed. Bloch believed that this openness to the future was the real human meaning of the Bible's speech about a God who is transcendent, who stands over against the present order of things; and that it led on to and involved a demand for a continual readiness on the part of man to criticise and change the present state of things for the better, just as the Old Testament prophets, and Jesus after them, had spoken and acted in opposition to the established institutions and authorities of their own day. Man is not yet himself; he is on the way to what he will become; and this holds both for the individual person and for the wider character of human society as a whole.

In *Theology of Hope* and subsequent books, notably *The Crucified God* (1975) and *The Church in the Power of the Spirit* (1977), Moltmann by no means appropriated Bloch's atheism, though he did accept and assert the validity of atheistic rejection of certain kinds of theism which conceived of God in a deistic or authoritarian fashion. He did, however, adopt the category of hope, and the sense of a movement towards a future that has not yet come, insisting that these supply an essential base for any Christian theology which hopes to be true to the message of the Bible. The eschatology of the New Testament, focused in the resurrection of Jesus, proclaims him as the one in whom the depth of our future, the future which God has for us, is opened up. This is the future to which our own time and history are moving; but, Moltmann argued, Christian theology had almost invariably drawn the teeth of this hope in one of several ways. One had been to relegate Jesus to past history, as if he himself had no future. Another had anchored him safely in a 'timeless eternity' with God, as if he had nothing to do with the onward movement of history. Yet another had diluted and lost the nature of the divine promise in him by interpreting that promise as fulfilled in the establishment of present ecclesiastical or political authorities and institutions, as realised in the church or in what was assumed to be a 'Christian society'.

This development, Moltmann believed, had set in very early in the history of the church, as the original eschatological vision had given way to the establishment and consolidation of the church with its doctrine and ritual. Where, however, other commentators and historians had detected in that same shift, from

163

urgent eschatology to a concern with the continuing life of the church as a 'sacred institution within history', the response to the 'disappointment' which set in as the years passed and Christ did not return, Moltmann reversed the analysis: not 'eschatological disappointment' but a 'pre-empting of eschatology', an illegitimate and presumptuous translation of the eschatological promise, had been responsible. The result could only obscure the real force of the meaning of the cross and resurrection, and obliterate the dimension of real future hope which is central to the gospel and the prime clue to its bearing upon our own present world. As a result, Christian theology itself lost its proper bearing upon mundane reality and its relevance for practice—or, as it is usually called in this connection, 'praxis'. Instead of being a 'critical theory', that is, a way of understanding and interpreting reality which reflects upon and is tested by praxis, it had become a kind of abstract theorising with no practical force. So Moltmann urged that Christian theology itself must once more be seen as a kind of critical theory, enabled by the cross and resurrection of Jesus, which is entered into with a living practical concern and commitment, and which, too, is tested by its fruits.

The concern to engage with Marxist thought, to look for 'orthopraxis' ('right behaviour') rather than simply for 'orthodoxy' ('right belief'), and to open up theological questions from a standpoint of critical and committed social and political engagement, were to become the chief features of the brands of Political Theology which sprang up and flourished from the late 1960s onwards. None of these elements was entirely new, but they were now fused together with a fresh intensity which forged a sense—frequently somewhat exaggerated—of a wholly and uniquely new approach to theology itself. This alternative approach consciously and deliberately distanced itself from what its advocates regularly saw as the irrelevant, unreal, and all-too-dispassionate modes of theological study pursued in the tradition of liberal, academic universities and seminaries in the world of bourgeois capitalism. (This may sound a rather sweeping, not to say arrogant, characterisation; and so perhaps it is; but it is mild compared with some expressions of this sort of attitude that have appeared in the last few years.)

In the background to all this there lies not only the work of thinkers like Moltmann and the German Roman Catholic theologian J. B. Metz (1928–   ), but also a wider Christian–Marxist

164

dialogue which had been pursued in central Europe, in particular, in previous years; the huge explosion of protest, especially among students, which occurred in several western countries in the late 1960s; and, by no means least, the emergence of a new and more assertive self-awareness on the part of nations in the Third World and of ethnic minorities in the west, especially the American Black communities. So recent years have brought on to the stage a variety of movements seeking to approach the Bible and its meaning from the perspective of those who are on the underside of society, and to connect the gospel directly with the call for action for political and social change and with the demand for freedom and justice in the name of the God who puts down the mighty from their seat and exalts the humble, who, in Moltmann's words, 'has a bias in favour of the oppressed and underprivileged'. Insofar as one motto can sum up their central theme, it is that of Gustavo Gutiérrez in his *A Theology of Liberation* (1971; E.T. 1973), 'To place oneself in the perspective of the kingdom means to participate in the struggle for the liberation of those oppressed by others' (p. 203).

The broad spectrum of Political Theology includes several different types and emphases—Black Theology in the United States, as represented by James Cone's *God of the Oppressed* (1975) and *Black Theology and Black Power* (1969); the Feminist Theology of Mary Daly's *Beyond God the Father* (1973); a new political concern among Conservative Evangelicals in recent years; some similar developments among Pentecostalists, described in Walter Hollenweger's *Pentecost between Black and White* (1974); and recent critical reflection upon traditional patterns of Christian mission and education, and upon the role of education itself, as exemplified in Paulo Freire's *Pedadogy of the Oppressed* (E.T. 1972). These are but a small selection from a very wide field. What has made most impact on theology at large, however, is the work of a group of Latin American theologians. Special mention must be made not only of Gutiérrez, from whom we have just quoted, but of Juan Luis Segundo, *A Theology for Artisans of a New Humanity* (5 vols, 1972–4) and *The Liberation of Theology* (1977), and Jose Miguez Bonino, *Revolutionary Theology Comes of Age* (1975). Bonino is something of an exception in the larger group which these men represent, in that he is Protestant rather than Roman Catholic; but while the movement in Latin America is largely Roman Catholic, it has been accorded as much attention, acclaim and criticism from Protestants as Roman Catholics in recent years. Here indeed is one of the points at which Roman Catholic thinking has begun to have a powerful effect in Protestant circles as well.

Among the main contentions of this kind of Theology of Liberation are that the salvation of which the gospel speaks has to do with the overcoming and ending of every kind of crippling distortion of human existence—economic, medical, cultural and political, as well as ethical and spiritual—and that the gospel is therefore inherently and ineradicably political in its scope and implications; that it is impossible for Christians to be neutral or detached in the face of injustice, and that theology must be willing to take sides and engage in conflict with it; that the inequalities inbuilt in, for example, the class system, or the network of relations between rich and poor nations, are in themselves a kind of violence which must be resisted, not simply tolerated in resigned acquiescence; that God is at work in the movement of history to bring about a new future for humanity, and that Christians are challenged to decide whether they will take sides with him in that struggle or not; that the Marxist analysis of the working of economic forces is a valid one, and that to that extent Marxism itself is an authentic challenge to Christians to take the gospel seriously. This by no means implies that Liberation Theology is committed to a kind of Marxist practical atheism. The reverse is generally the case; for their sense of the scale of the task in which they are called to participate generally evokes in its advocates a powerful awareness of the need for worship, for spiritual strength, for the anticipation and celebration of the promise of victory. For the most part, they do not see the world around them as 'godless' or as 'God-forsaken', but as the arena of God's own suffering and struggle. This gives their work a tone rather different from that of at least some of the earlier Secular Theology.

At present, one can only speculate on the likely future development of the Latin American Theology of Liberation. The last ten years have raised a whole series of questions about its approach, and the movement itself has generated a good deal of internal debate, over and above its encounter with criticisms from without. The main issues have to do with the way in which it attempts to hold together theology and politics (in the broadest sense), and

166

with its integration of Christian and Marxist thought in its 'praxis-oriented hermeneutics of liberation'. How far, for example, can the salvation of which the Bible speaks be bound up with what is presented as social, economic or political salvation? Can the use, for instance, of violence be justified in the name of the gospel? Is Liberation Theology in danger of making the same kind of 'translation' of the message of the kingdom as Liberal Theology once did, albeit now in a Marxist rather than 'bourgeois' fashion? Does the 'hermeneutics of praxis', with its concern to read the Bible in the light of the need for present action, really rediscover the authentic message of the Bible itself—or simply look for the reflection of its own face at the bottom of the same well as the quest of the historical Jesus? Does the Marxist interpretation of the movement of history itself represent an 'historicising of eschatology' as illegitimate as that traced by Moltmann in the early church? Here it is of some significance that Moltmann himself has disagreed quite sharply with some of the Latin Americans. Where they have criticised him for failing to draw out the implications of his theology in a Marxist political programme, he has countered by attacking the shallowness of their 'school-book Marxism'. It must also be observed that it is by no means clear that the kind of political approach which arguably makes good sense in Latin America can necessarily be exported to countries like Germany, Britain or the United States: indeed, this is a point which some of the Latin Americans themselves have forcefully made.

While all these questions need to be faced, however, it must be admitted that problems of this kind cannot but arise whenever committed engagement in the affairs of the world is seen as a genuine implication of the gospel. The challenge and the excitement of Liberation Theology flow directly from the seriousness with which it attempts that engagement, and seeks to relate the task of theology itself to it. If it needs to guard more carefully than it has sometimes done against the temptation to transform the gospel into something quite alien, it is by no means alone in that. That challenge is one which Christian theology by its very nature can never escape. Certainly it is *no* escape to assume, as some of the most vociferous critics of Liberation Theology do, that theology has no bearing upon the political realm.

Insofar as there is a single thread linking the main trends we have outlined in this chapter, it is the attempt signalled by

Bonhoeffer to shift the focus of theological attention 'from the world beyond to *this* world'. Clearly, the endeavour is not without its risks, and it has brought its crop of casualties. 'Theology' which finds itself unable to speak of God in the modern world, or reduced to proclaiming his extinction, can scarcely expect to generate enough lasting interest to keep itself in business; and it would appear that that sort of theology has already met its predestined fate. Nor does it seem probable that 'radical theology' of an essentially nineteenth-century stamp will be able to lay any very solid foundations for the future, though it may well flourish happily enough in suitably protected environments. But the endeavour to open up the full bearing of Christian faith upon life in the world of today, resisting its relegation to a narrowly 'religious' sphere, sets an agenda with which future theology will still have to deal. The 'religious captivity of Christianity' to which a Barth, a Bonhoeffer and a Moltmann have so powerfully pointed, and which the main movements sketched here have attempted to counter, is still a most effective instrument for the muffling of the gospel of the Christ who was not crucified on an altar between two candles, but on Golgotha between two thieves.

8

Further Horizons:
Of Ecumenism, Religions and Science

The way in which the movements described in the last chapter have aimed to open up theology to the contemporary world is one indication of a general concern among theologians to avoid any too narrow or restricted understanding of the task of theology itself. We have seen, too, how in various ways theology has been influenced by other disciplines and has attempted to chart its course in relation to them. To conclude what has been a largely chronological account of trends in Protestant theology, this last chapter must now say a little more about three of the frontier areas which are becoming more and more important at present. This will also make it possible to bring together some of the issues which up till now we have only been able to mention incidentally and in passing.

The New Ecumenical Climate

A striking new feature of 'institutional Christianity' in the twentieth century has been the emergence of a whole series of supradenominational bodies which have aimed to encourage dialogue, co-operation and reconciliation between the long divided churches and confessions. A turning-point came with the World Missionary Conference held in Edinburgh in 1910, which inspired a new search for an ecumenical approach to mission throughout the world. The heir of the subsequent series of these conferences, and of others, such as those held by the Faith and Order Movement, was the World Council of Churches, which came into being in 1948. Attempts have also been made, with varying degrees of success, to unite different churches. There has as well been a veritable explosion of ecumenical conversations, in which theologians from a wide range of different traditions have been involved. This has generated fresh thinking, particularly about the theology of the church and about the issues which have for centuries been most divisive—many of them having to do with the place and nature of the church itself, with forms of ministry, with the locus of authority, with patterns of worship. But it has also brought a wider new awareness of the ethos and distinctive theological approaches of the different Christian traditions, and a fresh willingness to attend to what theologians from other confessions have to say. Protestant theology has found itself engaged in a new meeting with Roman Catholic and Eastern Orthodox thought as these other churches have come to play a larger part in the ecumenical movement.

In the latter part of the nineteenth century, the Roman Catholic Church, at least at its official centre, was embarking on a massive programme of retrenchment and consolidation, in which its dominant attitude was on the whole a defensive one—defensive over against the surrounding world, and also over against the developments in Protestant theology. The First Vatican Council, held in 1870, reflected that mood very clearly, especially in its doctrinal definition of the infallibility exercised by the pope when he spoke *ex cathedra* on matters of faith or morals. There were certainly other voices within the Roman Catholic Church itself: Newman in England was one, and another was that of the new 'Tübingen school' of Roman Catholic thinking in Germany, which in its own way sought to reconcile its church's teaching with the fresh impulses in the contemporary world of philosophy and biblical study. But these did not control the stage. When, at the turn of the century, the Modernist movement developed under such spokesmen as Alfred Loisy (1857–1940) and George Tyrrell (1861–1909), it was only to be condemned and suppressed in 1907. The twentieth century, however, brought profound changes, culminating in the Second Vatican Council, held from 1962 to 1965 under the pontificates of John XXIII and Paul VI. While it is still possible to discern, as many Roman Catholics do, an essential

170

continuity between the two Vatican Councils, the observer from without is more struck by the contrasts.

The keynote of the Second Vatican Council can best be summarised as openness: openness to the need for what John XXIII called *aggiornamento*, the adaptation of forms and practices to the needs of new situations; openness to the desirability of setting the relation between pope and bishops, priesthood and laity, on a new footing; openness to Christians in other churches, who were to be seen as 'separated brethren' rather than as 'heretics and schismatics'; openness also to the modern world, and to the adherents of other faiths. The new attitude and spirit ran through many of the major documents approved by the Council, among them the *Dogmatic Constitution on the Church*, the *Decree on Ecumenism*, the *Declaration on Religious Freedom*, the *Declaration on the Relationship of the Church to Non-Christian Religions* and the *Pastoral Constitution on the Church in the Modern World*. This openness was by no means of the kind which dissolves all certainty and conviction into pure relativity: rather it was the kind which a strong and confident Christian commitment enables in facing the realities of the setting in which the church finds itself and with which it is called to deal. With the Council, the Roman Catholic Church began to play its full part in the ecumenical movement. The years since have admittedly been troubled ones for it. It can sometimes seem to be caught between the desire not to change too much and the enthusiasm which wants to change everything at once, and so to lose the kind of balance for which the Council aimed. But these developments have brought a great shift in the pattern of ecumenical relations, one which has profoundly affected both Roman Catholic theology itself and its interaction with the work being done in other traditions.

The way had already been partly prepared for this by some clear shifts in Roman Catholic teaching in the decades before the Council, and in particular by steps taken by Pope Pius XII, who is generally (and not entirely fairly) looked upon simply as a conservative, indeed reactionary figure. Two of his encyclical letters were particularly significant: *Divino Afflante Spiritu* and *Mystici Corporis Christi*, both of 1943. The first of these for the first time gave the highest official blessing of the Roman Catholic Church to the critical study of the Bible with the new tools of scientific literary and historical criticism—tools until then largely forged and applied by Protestant scholars, and regarded with a good deal of suspicion in the Roman Catholic Church since the condemnation of the Modernists. *Divino Afflante Spiritu* followed a new flowering of biblical and historical research among Roman Catholics, and gave it fresh encouragement. As a result, many Roman Catholics are among the leaders in a biblical research in a fashion which contrasts with what obtained in the middle of the nineteenth century.

Mystici Corporis Christi was equally significant, but in a different way. It gave approval to a new trend in Roman Catholic thinking in the previous twenty years or so which aimed to present a different way of understanding the character of the church itself. The conventional Roman Catholic tendency was to think of the church in legal, institutional, hierarchical and authoritarian terms—a tendency which ran back for centuries, but which had hardened in the period after the Reformation, and had fitted particularly well with the outlook and atmosphere of the later nineteenth century, as also with the promulgation of the new and exceedingly comprehensive *Codex Iuris Canonici* ('Code of Canon Law') in 1917. *Mystici Corporis Christi* sought to replace this with a sense of the church as primarily the 'mystical body of Christ', a sense which would place less weight on the external and juridical aspects, and more on worship, on participation in the sacraments, on sharing by the people of Christ in the life of Christ.

This new emphasis had at first been commonly dismissed as rhetorical piety rather than solid, intellectually respectable theology; but it fought its way through successfully, and has come to be one of the characteristic and distinctive features of the Roman Catholic outlook and approach to theological questions in general. Christian theology is seen as resting upon a *mystery*—the mystery of God, the mystery of the incarnation, the mystery of the church, the mystery of the divine purpose in which the whole world is involved and gathered up. 'Mystery' here does not mean simply something dark, obscure, incomprehensible, which cannot be understood at all. Rather, it refers to the infinite, supernatural depth of God, transcendent and inexhaustible, stretching far beyond what we can grasp, and yet opened up in Jesus Christ and touching us in and through the life of the church. This immensely powerful sense of mystery has in modern times been pointed to by many Roman Catholic writers as *the* peculiarly central element in Roman Catholicism, and as supplying an overall horizon within which the risk of trivialising theology by reducing it to mere intellectual enquiry, mere biblical archaeology, mere busy-ness about the manifold concerns of contemporary man, can be avoided. It offers the necessary safeguard by setting these other (and in themselves perfectly valid) interests in a profounder light, one in which 'nature' is preceded, touched and transformed by 'grace', and in which the church itself plays a central role as the medium of the divine disclosure which centres in Jesus Christ.

It is not surprising, against this background, that the main movement among Roman Catholic thinkers in recent generations has been in the direction of an up-dating and re-statement of the theology of the Middle Ages in a form which is nevertheless distinctively modern. 'Neo-Thomism', or, to be more accurate, 'Neo-scholasticism', has been the leading school, represented among philosophers by such as Jacques Maritain (1882–1973), Etienne Gilson (1884–1978) and Frederick Coplestone (1907–   ). In theology it has been carried forward by a considerable number, of whom Karl Rahner (1904–   ) and Bernard Lonergan (1904–   ) have become particularly well known.

Lonergan's system and approach are very much his own; Rahner's owes much to Heidegger. Both, however, have in common what is often called a 'transcendental anthropology'. Human existence, human nature, human experience, are intrinsically connected to and bound up with the reality of God; and through whatever opens up to man the depths of his own being, a doorway is found which leads into experience of God, 'the mystery who surrounds us'. A place is thus made here for a kind of natural theology which bears some resemblance to what can be found in Schleiermacher. But this natural theology does not stand on its own, nor can it be the sole foundation of Christian theology. It must, rather, be met, completed and deepened by the teaching of the church, and by the divine truth on which that teaching rests and which it conveys. The truth is not simply a matter of 'revealed truths', formulated in authoritative statements: it is, rather, the personal reality and truth of God, encountered in Jesus Christ and mediated through the whole life and teaching of the church. Christ and the church are thus seen as the primordial 'sacramental' means of meeting with God. (The charge, still sometimes advanced by Protestant critics, that the Roman Catholic conception of 'faith' reduces simply to intellectual assent to the propositions in which the church has defined what is to be believed, is now well out of date. Theologians such as these have moved far beyond it, and in much the same way as Protestant thinkers such as Barth have departed from the older tendency to identify God's revelation with *the words* of the Bible, and come instead to describe these words as means by which God himself conveys *his Word*. In both traditions, the language of 'personal encounter' has come to displace previous and more literalistic ways of describing the matter.)

Books such as Lonergan's *Insight* and *Method in Theology* (1958 and 1972 respectively), and the numerous volumes of Rahner's *Theological Investigations* (E.T. 1961 onwards) have had an enormous influence in the shaping of recent Roman Catholic thinking, and have been widely studied in other traditions as well. There are two main questions which Protestant theology must put to them in the light both of the classical Roman Catholic/Protestant differences and of the modern debate in Protestant theology itself. The first is whether their integration of transcendental anthropology as a base for theological reflection takes sufficient account of the pitfalls which many Protestant theologians have found to lie along that path, and which the movement we have sketched in our earlier chapters so clearly highlights. One standard Roman Catholic answer to this is that the objection rests upon a typically Protestant viewpoint which tends to oppose God and man, revelation and discovery, divine truth and human meaning; and that this opposition must always issue in most baneful consequences whenever the mediating role of the church is left out of account.

But, while there is most certainly some basis for this counter-charge, it leads on to the second problem. It is very difficult indeed for most Protestants to appropriate, for instance, Rahner's understanding of the role of the church. For he still strongly defends the dogma of infallibility, even to its most recent exercise (in 1950) in the promulgation of the dogma of the bodily assumption of the Virgin Mary. Most other Christians and churches find that this goes much too far; and, while often welcoming the Roman Catholic emphasis on the place of the church as the locus of meeting with God in Christ, would wish to allow for a much greater freedom to criticise what the church may here or there have defined as a matter of faith—and to criticise it in the name of the gospel on which the church itself is founded. The underlying assumption of Neo-scholasticism appears here in its weakest light; for ultimately it cannot allow for any real contradiction between the gospel and the definition of divine truth by the church. The collective subjectivity of the church certainly offers some defence against the excesses of some Protestant individualism; but it too must be open to correction in the light of the object of faith.

The Roman Catholic theologian who in recent years has been most widely read by those in other churches is much more sharply aware of these problems, and has indeed paid rather greater attention to modern Protestant theology than either Rahner or Lonergan. Hans Küng (1928–   ) published his first major book in 1957 under the title *Rechtfertigung* ('Justification'). In it, he tried to bring together the understanding of justification in Barth's theology and the traditional teaching of the Roman Catholic Church. While this undertaking won rather less enthusiastic approval from some other Protestant theologians than it did from Barth himself, it set Küng on a course of ecumenical dialogue which has situated him, frequently precariously, on the very edge of his own church. His *Infallible?* (1970; E.T. 1971), in which he launched a powerful attack on the doctrine of infallibility, provoked a heated debate in Germany and beyond. *Why Priests?* (E.T. 1972), with its criticism of celibacy, had the same effect. His most serious work, however, has been concerned more with positive theological construction, and is best represented by what is still perhaps his finest book, *The Church* (1967). More recently still, his *On Being a Christian* (1974; E.T. 1976) has been widely acclaimed, even more outside the Roman Catholic Church than within it.

Apart from the Latin Americans mentioned in the last chapter, there are many other Roman Catholic theologians whose work is now being read and used in other churches as well. Here it must suffice to name only two others, one from the United States, one from Holland. Avery Dulles (1918–   ), like other Roman Catholic thinkers, is much concerned with the theology of the church, and in particular with the new understanding of the church's nature and calling introduced by the Second Vatican Council. His *Models of the Church* (1974) is an especially illuminating study of the way in which different overall conceptions of the church—as institution, as mystical communion, as sacrament, as herald and as servant—can each offer their own insights, and of how recognition of such diverse but complementary models can enable the mapping of different theological views of the church and also help towards their reconciliation. Like the rather earlier *Household of God* (1953) by the Reformed theologian Lesslie Newbigin, which also distinguished different ways of understanding the church— as sacramental community, as the community gathered round the Word, as the community of the Spirit and showed how these had been emphasised respectively in the Catholic, Protestant and Pentecostal approaches—Dulles' book makes a seminal contribution to new thinking and to the search for better ecumenical understanding.

The same can be said of the work in Holland of Eduard Schillebeeckx (1914–). His *Christ the Sacrament* (1960; E.T. 1963) gives particularly clear expression to the spirit of much modern Roman Catholic thinking, while his more recent *Jesus* (E.T. 1979) shares with Küng's *On Being a Christian* the attempt to work through the complex and technical questions of exegesis and history in order to arrive at a contemporary statement of Christian conviction which will appeal beyond the narrow circles of academic theologians to a wider public. Impulses such as these, issuing from Roman Catholic sources, seem destined to contribute to and enrich the future work of theologians in other churches as well.

There is, however, one observation that may be made with respect to the more 'popular restatements' of Christian belief offered by Küng, Schillebeeckx and some other, less well-known Roman Catholic thinkers—an observation which connects with the criticism made above of Rahner and Lonergan. There is a certain tendency in this genre to slide into positions strikingly similar to those of Liberal Theology, yet modifying them in a characteristically Roman Catholic fashion. So Jesus is quite often presented as if his 'significance', his 'meaning' had its locus in the church's faith in him, as if the dogma of his divinity were an expression of that faith, and as if no further, deeper or more objective grounding of that dogma were either possible or necessary.

In essence, this was the stance adopted by the great Modernist, Loisy, at the turn of the century. In *The Gospel and the Church* (1902; E.T. 1903), Loisy answered Harnack's interpretation of the original message of Jesus and its subsequent 'hellenisation' in christological dogma by reversing the analysis. He agreed with Harnack that Jesus had proclaimed the kingdom of God, and that

176

what had then in fact appeared was the church. But where Harnack wished to return behind the church to what he believed to be the essential message of Jesus himself, Loisy took the contrary road. Christianity has no 'essence': it is continually evolving. Dogma is valid as and insofar as it expresses genuine religious consciousness. To that extent it articulates 'revelation', and it can and should be accepted and affirmed on its merits and in its own right. The danger along this road is that the question of the objective basis and ground of that truth—a question which Harnack at least cannot be accused of ignoring—can all too easily slide under the table as if it were ultimately uninteresting and unimportant. Where that pitfall is not heeded, the result is commonly the presentation of a Jesus whose 'divinity' reduces to his symbolic value as affirmed by the communal Christian awareness down through the ages. Such a presentation—as offered recently, for example, in James Mackey's *Jesus, the Man and the Myth* (1979)—can indeed regard itself as defending orthodox Christian doctrine, and thus as standing over against Liberal Theology; but in substance it appears to be more 'liberal' than 'orthodox'.

This does not, however, represent the main thrust of traditional or of recent Roman Catholic thinking, though it does reflect the fact that in the last two decades the Roman Catholic Church has had to encounter many of the challenges and problems which have emerged more gradually over a far longer period in Protestantism. The central movement in Roman Catholic theology, especially as reflected in the far-reaching liturgical reforms since the early 1960s, has sought rather to uncover and affirm the objective uniquences of Jesus Christ in a way which recalls the theology of Barth rather than of Ritschl (or Bultmann). In the longer term it must be along that line, rather than those of the older Liberal or Modernist approaches, that real *rapprochement* between Roman Catholics and Protestants is sought.

Mention must finally be made of two other Roman Catholics whose thought has a distinctly 'unofficial' character, and whose influence has if anything been greater beyond the confines of their own church than within them. In the early decades of this century, Baron Friedrich von Hügel (1852–1925), a layman who spent most of his life in Britain, was very highly regarded by many Protestants as a Roman Catholic who was ecumenically open to other Christians, who took account of the modern world of science and historical study, but was able at the same time to preserve and convey a profound religious sense of the mystery lying in the depths of human personality, and met and answered by the 'Perfect Reality' of God. He was sympathetic to the cause of the Modernists, but harmonised with their concerns a deep loyalty to his own church, which he believed to be the best historical expression of the religious spirit of mankind. This outlook had a natural appeal to Protestants whose own thought was influenced by Liberal Theology, and highlights again the affinity between it and Modernism.

A bolder and more radical thinker was Pierre Teilhard de Chardin (1881–1955), whose most daring speculative work—e.g. *The Phenomenon of Man* (E.T. 1959)—was only published posthumously. He was a Jesuit priest and a palaeontologist who reached for a synthesis of religion and scientific cosmology which has exercised a vast fascination on many minds, and launched what is virtually a Teilhard cult. His thought has certain affinities with that of Process Theology or of Temple, but it possesses a shape and tone peculiarly its own. Central to it is the idea of evolution: the universe is evolving and unfolding in a fashion which leads through increasing 'complexification' to the emergence of higher and more sophisticated forms of life, culminating in the appearance of spiritual being in man. The entire movement has a destination, which Teilhard calls 'the Omega-point'; and this has already been realised in Jesus Christ. At the Omega-point, mankind will realise its full potential, being drawn towards perfection in an existence of pure, personal love, in which it will be united with the God made known in Jesus. This cosmic vision, suffused with Teilhard's own deep spirituality, his overwhelming sense of the presence of God as the very 'milieu' which encompasses us and of the divine purpose which draws all things upward to itself like a flame, has an enormous attraction and appeal—in spite of a good deal of vagueness at almost every crucial point in the synthesis.

It remains unclear, for example, how the Omega-point and Jesus are really connected; what kind of 'future' existence Teilhard in fact envisages; whether his cosmic evolutionary perspective has any place for failure or sin. But in trying to see Jesus Christ as central to the destiny of the universe as opened up by contemporary science, he has undoubtedly encouraged many people to look afresh at the cosmic horizon which is necessarily involved in the classical Christian understanding of Jesus, but which has all too often disappeared from view. Whatever the defects in his conception, it is a challenge and a stimulus to further reflection, even if the universal scope of Christian faith can (and perhaps also must) be sketched in other ways as well as his.

If recent times have brought an increased familiarity among at least some Protestants with the work of these and other Roman Catholic thinkers, they have also brought a new acquaintance with what, to most western Christians, is something much more strange and exotic: the theology of the Eastern Orthodox Churches, in particular of the Russian, several of whose leading theologians came to settle in the west after the Russian revolution. There is now an Orthodox *diaspora* throughout the western world, and contacts have increased many times over in the last two generations. In addition, the Orthodox Churches now also belong to the World Council of Churches, so that regular communication has been established, not only with the Orthodox in the west, but with their home bases as well.

Eastern theology differs in many respects from that of the west, whether Protestant or Roman Catholic. It draws its inspiration from the Greek fathers of the early church, and from a distinctive eastern tradition which, while it has over the centuries assimilated elements from the (largely separate) development in the west from the fifth century onwards, has fitted them into its own perspective and transposed them into its own key. It is scarcely possible in a few words to sketch that rather different world of thought, but among its most characteristic features may be mentioned a profound sense of the wholeness of things; of the calling of humanity to be 'the priest of the cosmos', in whom nature finds a voice to worship God, and so also to realise its own destiny as God's creation; of the 'divinisation' of human nature through the divine incarnation in Jesus Christ; of the oneness of the church of today with the saints in heaven, powerfully expressed in its iconography, which serves to make visible that invisible but real communion; and, overall, of the transfiguration of the universe by the shining in and through it of the eternal glory of the 'divine energies' of the Trinity. To a striking degree, the life of Orthodoxy is centred in worship, in the great celebrations of the liturgy, and theology itself is seen as an expression of worship rather than as a mere intellectual activity which can, as it were, stand by itself and be pursued simply for its own sake.

It is only fairly recently that some Orthodox theologians have begun to engage seriously in the kind of critical biblical and historical study pioneered in the west in the last two or three centuries; but even in doing so, they have generally been deeply concerned to fit it into a wider coherent theological purpose, and deeply critical of the fragmentation which has so often entered into the theological enterprise in the west. One of the criticisms most commonly voiced by Orthodox thinkers of western theology and the western churches in general is that we in the west tend always to be one-sided, to swing in an unbalanced way from one extreme to another, and so to fall into misconceived polarisations. So, for example, they see Protestant individualism as evoked by a wrong kind of Roman ecclesiastical authoritarianism; an exaggerated stress on pure reason as standing over against an equally exaggerated emphasis on obedient acceptance of authority; a too exclusive focusing on Jesus ('Christomonism') facing a vague relativism which does not well know what special place, if any, he may hold. While these criticisms are no doubt over-simplified, and while, too, Orthodox thought by no means always necessarily offers adequate alternatives, there is certainly enough truth in them for the Orthodox voice to deserve to be heard with respect, even if not uncritically.

A new Orthodox self-awareness, forged in critical reflection upon the movement of theology in the west, began to emerge in Russia last century with theologians such as Alexei Khomiakov (1804–60) and Vladimir Soloviev (1835–1900). Khomiakov's *The Church is One* (E.T. 1948) argued that the church by its nature is a community in which freedom and unity are held together in holiness. To describe this characteristic of the church, he used the untranslatable term *Sobornost* (broadly, 'togetherness', 'community') which has since become a kind of technical term for the organic understanding of the church in Orthodox theology. He contrasted it with the *freedom without unity* and the *unity without freedom* which he discerned in Protestantism and Roman Catholicism respectively. The focus of *Sobornost* was the sacrament of the eucharist: whenever and wherever the eucharist was celebrated, the *whole* church was present in microcosm in the local community. This again he contrasted with the centralism of the Roman Catholic Church and the denominationalism and sectarianism he saw in Protestantism. In a not dissimilar fashion,

Soloviev saw Protestantism as stressing intellectual honesty, Rome as emphasising authority, and Orthodoxy as possessing the spiritual insight which was necessary to hold the other elements together; but he himself towards the end of his life became a Roman Catholic because of his conviction that the whole church is indeed one in east and west.

The next generation produced two provocative and fascinating thinkers, both of whom were for a time Marxist before returning to Orthodox Christianity: Nikolai Berdyaev (1874–1948) and Sergius Bulgakov (1870–1944), who left Russia in the early 1920s and spent most of the rest of their lives in France. Berdyaev was a philosopher rather than a theologian, but he attempted in his philosophy to bring out and emphasise what he believed to be the essential features of the peculiarly Russian Christian outlook—in particular, a desire for freedom, refusing to be subject to external authority, and with it, a feeling of brotherhood and kindliness which he felt was more deeply rooted and more fully realised in Russian than in western Christianity. In his philosophy he drew a sharp distinction between subjectivity and objectivity. In the realm of personality it is subjectivity that matters, not the world of mere objectivity that surrounds us: the fall of man lies in his subordinating himself to the objects around him and so denying and losing his own subjectivity. But what man is called to do is to reverse that process, to transform and redeem the 'objectified order' by integrating it into the purposes of subjectivity. The theological and Christian bearing of this is that, according to Berdyaev, man in his subjectivity is already united with God, and the 'transformation' and 'redemption' of the objectified order is the real point of the eschatological emphasis in the New Testament and in Christian faith.

There are obvious similarities between this and other types of existentialist and personalist philosophy that we have already mentioned, and Berdyaev's work still has many admirers in the west—not least because of a lingering hankering after anarchism in his thought, and also because of the essential continuity he traces between God and ourselves, thus contrasting with the main line of Protestant thought on the matter. But it is debatable whether his frequently convoluted writing is really as profound as has sometimes been believed; and also whether his sharp dichotomy between subjectivity and objectivity is entirely helpful in analysing the real tensions and problems of human life in the world. He was a rhetorical rather than analytical thinker, and his work is best read as offering illuminating hints and suggestions rather than thought-through explanations.

Similar caution is also called for in the case of Bulgakov, whose theories were both condemned by the Moscow patriarch in 1935, and criticised by younger Orthodox theologians as too speculative and as tending towards a kind of pantheistic theosophy. He followed up Khomiakov's conception of *Sobornost*, and used it in a similar way to contrast the Orthodox understanding of the church as a communion united in love with the individualistic and monarchial views expressed in Protestantism and Roman Catholicism respectively. The distinctive element in his own system, however, was that of *Sophia*, of 'wisdom'. This is in a way common to God and man, for man is made in the image of the divine wisdom. This imaging is the basis alike of God's revelation of himself, and of the human reception of that revelation in personal meeting with God. Both the concept of the divine wisdom and that of the image of God were of course long established in theology, and Bulgakov could claim with some justification that he was simply drawing out the teaching of the Greek fathers and the tradition of Orthodoxy. At the same time, however, the *Sophia* took up so much place in his system that it threatened to squeeze out everything else, and to become a sort of diffused, universal communication between God and mankind. It was for this reason that his thought came to be criticised within his own church: in his hands it was and was intended to be Christian, but it could easily take flight and become something quite different without losing its essential characteristics. There is more than a hint of resemblance here to the approach of his friend Berdyaev.

A much more careful and accurate exposition of the Orthodox theological tradition was to be offered by a group of men in the next generation, of whom the most notable were Vladimir Lossky (1903–58) and George Florovsky (1896–1979). Their numerous writings opened up many facets of Orthodox belief, and gave western eyes a new view of its development and crystallisation through the medieval period. Lossky's *The Mystical Theology of the Eastern Church* (1944; E.T. 1957) is one especially fine example. Lossky in particular also had a very sharp and critical eye for what he saw as serious structural weaknesses in the pattern of western theology as it had consolidated through that same period. The key to these he believed to lie in the western doctrine of the *filioque*, which affirms that the Holy Spirit proceeds 'from the Father *and from the Son*'. This, he argued, subordinated the Holy Spirit to Jesus in a fashion which undermined the doctrine of the Trinity, and led western thought to focus simply on 'God' rather than on the Father, Son and Holy Spirit; it effectively downgraded the Holy Spirit to a kind of power given to the church by Jesus, instead of recognising in the Spirit the cosmic and universal transforming and transfiguring presence of God himself; and it led western theology to swing uneasily between an exclusive concentration on Jesus and an obsession with human subjectivity, which became the substitute for the Holy Spirit.

While it is doubtful whether the *filioque* as such can bear all the blame for developments of this kind in the west, and also whether this account of the weaknesses of the western approach is entirely fair to western theology in general, there is certainly some substance in Lossky's critique. Western theology may not accept all of the charges made by the east, but it must at least listen to them and consider what is to be learned from them. Here the work of younger Orthodox theologians, such as Alexander Schmemann (1921–), John Meyendorff (1926–), Nikos Nissiotis (1925–) and John Zizioulas (1931–) may be expected to play a significant role in future years.

Religion and Religions

The encounter between Christianity and other religions in the modern era has stimulated two distinct, though related, lines of study which began to separate out in the nineteenth century. On the one hand there has been a great development of interest in what may be described as 'the scientific study of religion'; on the other, a variety of attempts by Christian theologians to face the question of how 'religion' and 'religions' are to be related to Christian faith. The second of these is of course a specifically Christian enterprise; the first need not be, though Christian thinkers have made major contributions to it. We have already referred here and there to aspects of both lines of enquiry as they arose in connection with particular theologians; but the subject is so important in its own right that some attempt must now be made to draw these scattered threads together.

We saw earlier how in Troeltsch the tension which had been growing between the study of religion as a human phenomenon and the particular concerns of Christian theology finally broke out into the open. Although some theologians—Oman, John Baillie, Tillich among them—continued to follow the older programme with the aim of holding the two together, the general theological trend has inclined to widen the gap. The breach was if anything extended by the rise towards the end of last century of new techniques designed to enable a more accurate and empirically based study of the different elements which could be gathered under the broad rubric of 'religion'. History, anthropology, sociology, psychology could all be drawn upon in an overall perspective which tended to break out of the framework offered by the general definitions of 'religion' used by thinkers like Schleiermacher and Ritschl. In its essence, the new approach which was coming to the fore aimed to be descriptive or, in the term which has since become standard, 'phenomenological'.

The phenomenological method was worked out and given its name by Edmund Husserl (1859–1938). Its aim was to grasp and describe the basic structures of consciousness and experience, which Husserl believed to have a universal character. These are the 'phenomena' which can be, so to speak, distilled out by stripping away all the accidental elements associated with their particular manifestations. This further requires on the part of the phenomenologist what Husserl called *epoche*, a suspension of judgement which is necessary to enable the discernment of the 'pure phenomenon' undistracted by the making of evaluations about any accompanying features. While the whole pattern of Husserl's philosophy is not necessarily taken over by all who seek to adopt a phenomenological approach, this concern to suspend judgement, to describe what is actually there to be found, and to break through to a grasp and recognition of basic forms of experience, is generally characteristic of the method.

A book which Husserl himself regarded as an excellent application of the phenomenological method was *The Idea of the Holy* (1917; E.T. 1923), by Rudolf Otto (1869–1937). Otto had a great admiration for Schleiermacher, who had, in his view, rediscovered religion as a distinct reality in its own right, not reducible to reason or ethics; and his own work moved further along that path. It also had some affinities with that of the English anthropologist Robert Marett (1866–1943), who found in the ideas of *mana* and *tabu*, and the awe, wonder and fear that these evoke, the essential core of the primitive religious consciousness, and the key to the real nature of all religion. Religion, Marett held, was not capable of being analysed simply in terms of intellectual beliefs or of morality, though in its development to higher forms a necessary part was played by a process of intellectual, ethical and spiritual refinement. Its roots, however, lay deeper, and could best be seen in primitive religion.

In Otto's account, the key to the nature of religion is to be found in 'the holy', or, in the term which he used to specify its essential character, 'the numinous'. This refers to the unfathomable and supra-rational nature of God, the *mysterium tremendum et fascinans*, 'the mystery at once terrifying and fascinating'. The sense of the numinous has its own unique quality; it cannot be reduced to something purely rational or merely moral, nor is it simply 'natural' or produced purely from within ourselves. Rather, it is evoked by a genuine recognition of the holy, enabled by what Otto called 'the faculty of divination'. It is at this deepest level of apprehension that the awareness of the numinous arises, and it is then further shaped and qualified in the course of human experience by the addition to it of the rational and moral elements which also form part of our understanding of God. But it, rather than they, is primary: mystery lies deeper than dogmatic theory, and the numinous than any thought.

Some resemblance can be seen between Otto's thought and that of Oman, whose classification of different types of religion we mentioned earlier. Oman himself, however, was somewhat critical of Otto's idea of the numinous, believing that it separated off *feeling* from *valuation*, and stressed *awe* rather than *love* in our relation to God. But while this criticism takes account of the *tremendum* in Otto's description of the numinous, it does less justice to the *fascinans* which is its necessary obverse. It may be too that while both owed a good deal to Schleiermacher, Oman was more inclined than Otto to adopt the Ritschlian emphasis on value-judgements, and with it, a suspicion of a too dark and volcanic notion of God, whether of a mystical or primitive type. However this may be, Otto's work remains an extremely powerful and seminal contribution to the study of 'religious awareness', and makes as strong a case as can well be imagined for regarding religion as qualitatively distinct from the other dimensions of human experience. (It is of course a further and quite distinct question whether or in what way this primordially religious element in man is connected with the God of whom Christian theology speaks.)

The phenomenological approach was further exploited by the Dutch scholar, Gerardus van der Leeuw (1890–1950), particularly in his *Religion in Essence and Manifestation* (E.T. 1938). His reflections on the procedure to be followed in studying religion were especially significant. Religions are not things that can be studied in pure detachment, like objects under a microscope: there must be a sympathetic entering into their meaning in which the student is himself engaged. By the same token, he cannot adopt a purely neutral stance: his own religious beliefs necessarily shape his perception and the comparisons he draws. Van der Leeuw himself believed Christianity to be the fullest form and expression of religion in human history, and his approach was shaped by that conviction. But he believed that it was nonetheless possible and necessary to study the different religions phenomenologically; that in this way the real core of religion itself could be detected, and valid comparisons drawn between its various manifestations. That core lay in the meeting with a strange and wholly other power which breaks into human life; and while the power itself could not be captured by the researcher, the forms which the meeting took could be studied phenomenologically. He distinguished a whole variety of these forms. There is the religion of *remoteness*, where the power encountered is distant, and man seeks to escape further from it: deism is a form of this, and atheism is its extreme limiting instance. The religion of *struggle* envisages a cosmic conflict in which man himself is involved. That of *repose* finds expression in various forms of mysticism. Other types find their focus in *aesthetic form* (Greek religion), in *infinity* (Hinduism), in *nothingness* (Buddhism), in *will and obedience* (Judaism) and in *majesty and humility* (Islam). Finally, Christianity is the religion of *love*, Here, van der Leeuw's classification reminds us of Nygren's *Agape and Eros*, and his work raises similar questions.

Granted that this kind of morphology of religious types can indeed be constructed, the comparisons which it makes possible seem at once too weak and too strong: too strong, in that they are too apparently directed towards the conclusion that Christianity is the highest form of religion; too weak, in that they treat religions as something rather abstract, as 'pure types', in a way which certainly facilitates this arranging of them in a pattern, but does not make wholly clear how they might be connected and related, what place history has to play, nor indeed how far they are really all instances of the same general thing. This difficulty is admittedly inbuilt in the phenomenological approach, concerned as it is with universal structures of pure experience rather than with the concrete particularities of historical development; and it is no doubt unfair to expect the method to deliver more than it is capable of producing. But the serious question cannot be ignored of whether the real distinctiveness of Christianity can be grasped along these lines at all. Does it perhaps lie in another dimension entirely, one which the phenomenological approach systematically excludes? (The same problem, it may be remembered, arose with Tillich's application of the method.)

More recently, the most widely known scholar in this field has been the Rumanian Mircea Eliade (1907–), who in books such as *Cosmos and History* (E.T. 1959) and *Patterns of Comparative Religion* (E.T. 1966) has paid special attention to the role of myths and symbols in various kinds of religion. These express and hold together a unified view of reality, in which the cosmos and man within it are seen as part of an eternally recurring pattern. History does not bring about real change or development, but only the endless repetition of the archetypal symbols, expressed in cult and ritual, by which the present time is related to the original creation, and to the mythical time of the gods and heroes whose original actions are imitated and repeated now. Myths and symbols of this kind gave archaic peoples a sense of security and changelessness, and preserved them from awareness of the burden and responsibility of history. The religion of the Bible, however, broke decisively out of that framework of security by seeing God as acting purposely to bring about historical change, and calling man to live responsively before him. That sense was further sharpened and focused in the New Testament, with its emphasis on the decisive event of Jesus. So the Bible called men out of the paradise of the archetypal myths and challenged them to the creative freedom of faith. This account, very similar to those of some modern theologians we have discussed, makes a sharp distinction between biblical religion, realised in Judaism, Christianity and Islam, and other forms. But the main significance of Eliade's work lies in the way in which he has brought out the functioning of myth and symbol—which he sees as still operative within Christianity, albeit weakened and challenged by the historical orientation of the Bible.

The main line of theological development as we have traced it in the previous chapters has of course been very different from this concern with religion in general, mainly because of the break in a new direction made by Dialectical Theology. That shift has also had its effect on the discussion from the standpoint of Christian theology of its relation with other religions. In the early years of this century, two broad approaches to that question were widely followed. One stressed the complete distinctiveness of Christianity, setting it as 'the true religion' over against all the other 'false religions'. The other was more inclined to see a certain connection, overlap and continuity, and to present the Christian faith as the 'fulfilment' of other religions. This was the approach, for example, of J. N. Farquhar's widely influential *The Crown of Hinduism* (1913), which offered Christianity as the completion and keystone of the real drive of Hindu belief and devotion.

A similar outlook was expressed by the World Missionary Conference in Jerusalem in 1928, when it noted the encroachments of secularisation, and called for the great religions to form a common front for the preservation of spiritual values. Karl Barth was characteristically deeply critical of this appeal, concentrating as it did upon human religion and spirituality rather than upon God's revelation of himself in Jesus Christ. Barth's insistence was not, however, upon the contrast between 'Christianity' and 'other religions', but upon the discontinuity between *all* religion, Christian or other, and revelation, between human 'striving upwards' and God's 'coming down to meet us'. 'Revelation against religion' thus became the new antithesis. And it was in terms owing a good deal to Barth and Brunner that the matter was opened afresh in the preparatory document for the next Missionary Conference, held at Tambaram, Madras, in 1938. This book was *The Christian Message in a Non-Christian World*, and the author was the Dutch missionary theologian Hendrik Kraemer (1890–1968).

Kraemer's aim was not to theorise in a general way about the relation between Christianity and other religions, but to provoke deep reflection on the theological basis for Christian mission. He rejected as inadequate both the 'aggressive approach' which was content simply to reiterate the absolute truth of Christianity, and the 'sympathetic' alternative which presented it as the completion and fulfilment of other religions. He was also sharply critical of the kind of comparative study which isolated particular elements which might appear to be similar in Christianity and other beliefs, and attempted to build upon them; for, he argued, this left out of account the very different overall views of God, man and the world in which these superficially similar features were set, and must therefore build on sand. Instead, he advocated a strategy in four stages: *contact*, *communication*, *controversy* and *conversion*. The first involved acquiring a deep knowledge of the milieu and outlook of those to whom the mission was to be addressed; the second, casting the message in terms comprehensible to them; the third, challenging their beliefs and values, and what Kraemer characterised as the endemic concern with 'self-redemption' in all religion, in the light of Jesus Christ and the Christian understanding of God and man which he termed 'Biblical realism'; the fourth, reintegrating their authentic spiritual and ethical impulses in a fresh and now Christian form. In this way, Kraemer advocated a more dialectical attitude and approach to other religions and to the missionary task than the two previously current.

At Tambaram, however, his theses provoked lively debate and a good deal of conflict, and he was seen by many critics simply as stressing 'discontinuity' between Christianity and other faiths. To some extent, his description of Christianity in terms of 'Biblical realism' could indeed make it appear to be simply an alternative (and, of course, truer) *system of belief*; and that, together with his use of the concept of 'discontinuity', may well have contributed to that impression. Here, Kraemer was in fact less radical than Barth, who was always much clearer that what was at stake was not the comparison of religions or belief-sytems as such, but the contrast between religion and revelation. Most of Kraemer's critics, however, assumed that his views and Barth's were essentially the same. Consequently it is still common to find the two bracketed together as 'theologians of discontinuity'—a description which does less than justice to either, for it ignores both the connections which Kraemer clearly traced between Christian and non-Christian religion, and the fashion in which Barth conceived of the *negation and re-establishing* of human existence in all its dimensions through Jesus Christ.

Among those who disagreed with Kraemer, and aimed to develop an alternative strategy, was the Scottish missionary A. G. Hogg (1875–1954). He drew a double distinction between the *event* and the *content* of revelation, and between the *personal faith* of the individual follower of a religion and *the religion itself as 'a faith'*. Kraemer, he argued, was concentrating so much on the unique *event* of revelation in Jesus Christ that he did not allow for the fact that the *content* of the revelation could and must be formulated in various ways as it was apprehended from different standpoints and circumstances. Again, in distinguishing 'faith' and 'faiths', Hogg recognised in the personal belief of an individual something real and valid which ought not to be lost to sight through an excessive concentration on the macroscopic religious tradition in which he stood, and which supplied the framework of his personal faith. In this way, while himself also asserting the distinctiveness of Christianity, he attempted to work out a more positive approach to the *people* of other faiths, in which what he called 'the challenging relevance' of the message of Christ would become apparent.

From a rather different standpoint, the American philosopher W. E. Hocking (1873–1964) drew attention to the impact of technology on patterns of belief, and argued that all religions, including Christianity, must in the future engage in a process of 'reconception' of their basic premises in dialogue with each other. Out of this, he believed that Christianity could emerge as the universal world religion. These ideas he developed in *Living Religions and a World Faith* (1940) and *The Coming World Civilisation* (1956). In the same period, E. C. Dewick in his *The Christian Attitude to Other Religions* (1953) followed William Temple in arguing that there is a real revelation of 'the larger Christ' in non-Christian religions, and that this revelation is to be seen as completed and fulfilled in the incarnation. Emphases of this kind on the authenticity of the faith and religious experience of adherents of other religions, on the need for dialogue, and on the discovery of Christ already present within them, have been much repeated and developed in more recent work.

Much of the weight of this undertaking has been borne by Christian theologians living in a non-Christian environment, and

190

therefore unavoidably concerned with working out their Christian position in relation to the surrounding culture and traditions. A special and quite outstanding place belongs to a number of Indian thinkers, among them P. Chenchiah (1886–1959), P. D. Devanandan (1901–62), M. M. Thomas (1916–   ) and R. Pannickar (1918–   ), who have aimed to state Christian belief in a form which will integrate into it Hindu spiritual perception, and enable the full participation of Indian Christians in the building of the new India alongside their Hindu fellow-countrymen. For several of them, a leading theme has been that of 'common humanity', the humanity shared by Hindu and Christian, but ultimately founded upon Jesus Christ and disclosed in its full depth and meaning in him. Thus the incarnation on the one hand and common humanity on the other supply a framework within which the search can be made for what Pannikar calls *The Unknown Christ of Hinduism* (1964). Another of their concerns has been to show that the gospel itself need not be cast solely in those forms in which it has been set in western Christianity: a valuable recent exploration of this theme is Robin Boyd's *India and the Latin Captivity of the Church* (1974).

A similar aim informs the work of Japanese Christian teachers such as K. Kitamori (1916–   ), whose 'theology of the pain of God' uses the Japanese idea of *tsurasa*, 'the poignant pain of suffering love', to interpret the cross. Africa, too, has seen considerable theological activity. The distinctive African awareness of reality and its bearing upon Christian thinking, are beautifully drawn out in John Taylor's *The Primal Vision* (1973), while among African theologians a special place belongs to John Mbiti, with his *African Religion and Philosophy* (1970), *Concepts of God in Africa* (1970) and *New Testament Eschatology in an African Background* (1971). Mention must also be made of the meeting with Islam, and especially of the numerous writings of Kenneth Cragg (1913–   ). He has been concerned to enter the Islamic world of thought, to explore its deep sense of surrender to the majesty of God, and has then sought to go on to show that the message of the incarnation and the cross—which to Islam has always seemed the most blasphemous infringement on the majesty and transcendence of God—points to God's own self-surrender as putting our surrender to him on an even profounder and more ultimate basis than Islam conceives of.

In his later work, Kraemer, too, moved in the direction of stressing dialogue and communication rather than controversy and conversion. His books *Religion and the Christian Faith* (1956), *The Communication of the Christian Faith* (1957) and *World Cultures and World Religions: the Coming Dialogue* (1960) reflect this shift; and while he continued to contrast religion and revelation, he tended to emphasise further the positive aspects of other religions and the spiritual awareness they mediated. The pursuit of a critical dialogue was also being advocated by Stephen Neill (1900–) in his *Christian Faith and Other Faiths: the Christian Dialogue with Other Religions* (1961). Around the same time, a distinctively Roman Catholic approach was being worked out by H. R. Schlette (1931–). In his *Towards a Theology of Religions* (1964; E.T. 1966), he followed up a line of thought suggested earlier by Karl Rahner. Rahner had proposed that other faiths stand in the same kind of relation to Christianity as the Old Testament to the New: they could be seen as a 'preparation for the gospel', and their adherents as 'anonymous Christians', that is, as Christians whose commitment to Jesus Christ is only implicit and unconscious, but nevertheless stands in connection with him, and is 'sufficient for salvation'.

The approaches just outlined tended by and large to focus attention on other religions as *religions*, and to concentrate on the religious and spiritual aspects of the lives of their adherents. These were seen as the points of contact and meeting at which dialogue can begin and understanding be fostered. In view of the fact that, contrary to many predictions earlier this century, non-Christian religions in many parts of the world, especially Hinduism and Islam, have experienced a striking renaissance in recent generations, this emphasis certainly cannot be dismissed. But the picture has another side; for that renaissance has itself been accompanied and to some degree provoked by the process of secularisation, fostered by the impact of western technology, the spread of western patterns of industrialisation and community organisation, and the need to build modern nations out of communities whose own traditions and structure reflected a very different type of society. The insistence on 'common humanity' among the Indian theologians mentioned above reflects their sense of this demand. Similarly, we have seen in previous chapters how some recent theology has been concerned to break out of a narrowly 'religious' conception of Christianity itself.

192

These two lines were brought together in what was probably the most hotly debated book on the subject of Christianity and other religions to appear in the last twenty or thirty years: A. van Leeuwen's *Christianity in World History* (1964). Following up the line of Secular Theology, van Leeuwen applied its fundamental theses to the case of non-Christian religions. Their erosion by the process of secularisation, their being eaten away by the 'corrosive acids of modernity', was to be seen as the destruction of 'onto-cratic' patterns of belief and social organisation which paved the way for a more 'theocratic' society. It should therefore be seen as the accompaniment and shadow-side of the gospel itself, as a necessary clearing-away which would set men free to live in the world before God. This thesis was further supported by the observation that it was precisely in the Christian culture of the west that science, technology and secularisation had developed, and that the dynamic thus unleashed must be seen in the light of that culture's Christian foundations. While van Leeuwen's argument generated much debate, it has not been generally accepted among theologians concerned with mission, though many would regard it as containing important, if partial, insights.

A prominent opponent of the secularisation approach has been Ninian Smart (1927–), whose work has taken up the search for a broad and all-embracing understanding of the various religions of mankind under the general rubric of 'a natural theology of reli-gious experience'. In his *The Religious Experience of Mankind* (1969), he traces the rise and development of the main religions, and also of humanism and Marxism as ideological alternatives, and argues that religions must be seen as organic wholes which find expression in several 'dimensions'—ritual, mythological, doctri-nal, ethical, social and experiential. The movement of history has at last brought us to the point where real meeting and dialogue between the major traditions is both possible and necessary: we now live in a single world, and all these streams are beginning to meet in a single history of mankind. Smart does not, however, envisage any simple convergence or accommodation between the different religions; indeed he suspects that an increase in pluralist diversity may well be what awaits us. But he makes a sustained appeal for recognition of the importance of the religious side of human life, and awareness and appreciation of the multifarious variety of its forms. The question which his account raises for

Christian theology is the same one to which we have repeatedly pointed: how far can this broad appreciation of religious diversity be held together with Christian convictions? Smart's approach is at least capable of leading to the kind of relativism which sees Jesus as being central for Christians, Buddha for Buddhists, Muhammed for Islam, and so on.

The issues posed by the gradual drawing-apart of the general study of religion and Christian theology are thus very much still with us; and it may be that in the longer term only some kind of distinction such as is offered by Barth's antithesis between religion and revelation (though not necessarily in those particular terms) can preserve Christian thought from either total relativism or uncontrolled syncretism. Here the more specifically theological approaches of Walter Freytag's *The Gospel and the Religions* (1957) and Lesslie Newbigin's *The Finality of Christ* (1969) point in the needed direction.

A rather different approach to the study of religion has been advocated by Wilfred Cantwell Smith (1916–) in his *The Meaning and End of Religion* (1964). In a style reminiscent of Hogg's distinction between 'faith' and 'faiths', Smith contrasts 'personal faith' with 'cumulative tradition', and gives priority to the former. Personal faith has to do with the individual's own inner awareness of his relation to the divine. It lies deeper than any outward expression, and is not in itself specifically 'Christian' or 'Jewish' or whatever. These labels apply to the developed and developing traditions within which individuals belong, and to the outward, external forms of religious community. The aim of religious dialogue must be to enable the encounter of personal faith with personal faith; and the study of religion must not simply focus on the 'cumulative tradition' as such, for that tradition is itself in a state of continuing development in interaction with the faith of individuals. 'Religions' cannot therefore be treated as fixed, static units, and even the emergence of 'separate religions' in history is itself a secondary and largely accidental matter, so far as the essential core of religion is concerned.

Smith thus offers the framework of an approach which puts the focus squarely on personal faith, and treats religious traditions as dynamic and growing rather than as settled, established and complete. This is not without its own difficulties. Smith's account of 'personal faith' seems rather ill-defined, nor is it clear that one can really treat it as if it were something purely inward and individual rather than specifically Christian, or Jewish, or so on without doing some violence to the understanding of 'faith' itself. But while *caveats* of this sort need to be entered, Smith is surely right to draw attention to the dynamic interaction of individual faith and the wider structures of belief of the religious tradition, and also to underline the fact that religious dialogue does not take place 'between religions' but between persons who believe.

Finally, we have left to the very end an important development whose omission thus far may well appear surprising: the new exchanges between Christians and Jews. We have put it last, not because it is less significant than what has already been mentioned, but because it deserves special emphasis. The roots of Christianity lie in Judaism, though the separation which early entered in between them, and the long and frequently bitter and tragic history of Christian attitudes and behaviour towards Jews, have too often concealed the fact from the eyes of both. Christians have inclined and even today very often still incline simply to dismiss the Jews as the people who rejected Jesus, and so engendered their own rejection by God; and Jews have looked on Christianity as an aberrant and blasphemous deviation from Jewish belief. There have of course been outstanding exceptions to this rule down through the centuries, but they have been relatively few. Even today, meetings between Christians and Jews are burdened by the legacy of that history, by the heritage of Christian anti-semitism and its horrific flowering in Nazi Europe; and also, it must be said, by the critical reactions of many Christians to the modern Zionist movement and to some of its fruits in the present state of Israel. But there has also been positive interaction on a variety of fronts.

The Jewish philosopher Martin Buber (1878–1965) has exercised a wide influence on Christian thought through such books as *I and Thou*, first published in 1923, and *The Eclipse of God* (1953). From the other side, Karl Barth, in many notable passages in the *Church Dogmatics* (e.g. III/3, pp. 210–26) drove home the significance of the Jewish people for the Christian church, insisting that its whole history, so strangely and tragically unique among the nations, is a sign and reflection of the mystery of judgement and of mercy worked out in Jesus Christ the Jew, and therefore a standing witness which Christians dare not ignore or despise. More recently, the efforts of Jewish theologians and philosophers to come to terms with the Nazi holocaust and its meaning for their faith in the God of Israel have connected with attempts of Christians to face the same questions, and 'theology after Auschwitz' has become a common theme in Jewish–Christian meeting. Again, in the field of biblical study Christian scholars have come increasingly to recognise that there is a distinctively Jewish approach to the Old Testament which demands respect, and have moved away from the negative stereotypes of much earlier Christian interpretation of Jewish faith and practice in the time of Jesus. Conversely, there has been a fresh attention to the New Testament and to the figure of Jesus himself on the part of Jewish biblical scholarship, well represented by Geza Vermes, *Jesus the Jew* (1973).

Admittedly wide tracts of Jewish and Christian thinking remain utterly unaffected by all of this: contemporary Judaism is in its own way as diverse and as open to anti-religious secularism as western Christianity. But seeds have been and are being sown which should yet bear fruit in the future; and, we may add, Christian theology which fails to take the Jews seriously risks cutting itself off from its own vital roots. The question here is not merely that of co-existence in an increasingly pluralistic world: it has to do with the identity and calling of the church itself, grafted as it is 'on the stock of Israel'.

Theology and Science

The choice of this final topic in our survey may well seem a surprising one. Many people today see theology and science as so utterly different, not to say diametrically opposed to each other, as to be capable at best of some uneasy co-existence in which the concerns and boundaries of each are sharply marked off and distinguished. Among theologians many would hold that the main impact of the sciences has been to restrict the area of theological concern, and that only by a clear demarcation of that area can theology and religion preserve any space for themselves in a world increasingly dominated by science and technology. This essentially defensive strategy is commonly expressed in the appeal to such rules-of-thumb as, 'Science deals with facts, religion with meaning,' or 'Science investigates the world of things, theology the realm of persons in relation to God.' Of those theologians to whom we have given most attention, Rudolf Bultmann most clearly illustrates

196

that outlook; but he was by no means alone. Karl Barth too, for instance, was anxious to draw a sharp line between the theological understanding of the world in the light of Jesus Christ and its investigation by the enquiries of the natural scientist.

Yet others whom we have mentioned—Temple, Teilhard de Chardin, the Process theologians—had a different view, and have tried to combine, and in some cases even to fuse together, a theological and a scientific view of the world. The aim on the one side has been to maintain the distinctiveness and integrity of theology, on the other to ensure that theology does not cut itself off from what is on any reckoning an enormously important dimension of our modern understanding of reality and of truth. Between the extremes into which either can fall lies a field in which positive interaction between theological and scientific understanding is clearly desirable, and in which recent years have seen significant initiatives. The world of thought of the natural sciences has come to be seen by at least some theologians as opening up new frontiers for theology itself.

These frontiers are of course of no interest to those who see such an absolute dichotomy between science and theology as to render them incapable of any kind of dialogue. But there are good theological reasons not to rest content with such a view, however it may appeal to some theologians—to say nothing of those scientists whose attitude to theology is wholly negative, or who preserve their own religious sense only by shutting off their science and their religion in separate compartments. If Christian faith is, in the words of the Nicene Creed, in 'God the Father Almighty, Maker of heaven and earth, and of all things visible and invisible,' and in Jesus Christ as 'God of God, Light of Light ... through whom all things were made,' the exploration of 'all things' is clearly within rather than without the overall horizon of theological interest. Nor can the impact of science and technology on the shape of modern life be treated as if it were without theological significance—at any rate, not without a disastrous narrowing of theological vision. Nor, finally, if truth and reality are ultimately coherent—as both theology and science generally presuppose, whether consciously or unconsciously—is it apparent that *absolute* disjunctions can be set up between 'things' and 'persons', 'facts' and 'meanings', 'physical' or 'material' and 'personal' or 'spiritual' in the way that a radical separation between theology and science seems to imply. These contrasts must rather be seen as representing genuine but relative differentiations within a larger and more complex unity. From this standpoint, the question is not whether theology and science could possibly have anything to say to each other, but rather, why it has been so widely assumed that they have not.

The main reason is perhaps to be found in the way in which the development of the natural sciences up to the nineteenth century fostered widespread conceptions of science itself in which it was seen as at best neutral, at worst actively hostile to religion and theology, and the modern scientific world-view as incompatible with the Christian, or at least as demanding radical revision of the latter. While the story of the rise of science and its interpretations is immensely complex, the general development in mind here can be briefly illustrated by reference to three major stages, which also fit into the wider cultural and intellectual movements sketched in our opening chapters.

First, the great surge forward in physics in the seventeenth and early eighteenth centuries was assisted and characterised by an understanding of the natural world as 'mechanical', as functioning in a regular and patterned way, and by the excitement generated by the discovery of the 'natural laws' governing its operations. This outlook reached its height in the work of Isaac Newton and in his sytem of physics, in which the entire physical world was seen as composed of material objects moving according to the 'laws of motion' within the framework of absolute (and theoretically infinite) space and time. Newton himself believed that these 'laws' had been imposed by God, and that in tracing them he was thinking God's thoughts after him; but their grasp and articulation appeared such an immensely impressive attainment of the human mind, and the 'laws' themselves so evidently and inherently rational, as to support the increasing inclination of the rationalism of the day to relegate God to the edge of concern as a marginal and eventually redundant hypothesis. The result was to forge a view of science as an autonomous enterprise, based on the twin pillars of the objective discernibility of the 'speculative principles' by which the universe was ruled and the capacity of the human mind to explore and discover them. It also encouraged a sense, still powerful today—and still commonly expressed in histories of science—that the rise of science was chiefly due to the liberation of the human mind from the fetters of religious doctrines and assumptions. To put it crudely, 'Science uncovers the truth about things, but it could only begin to do so when it broke out of its religious cocoon.' So God—and theology—were in effect driven out of the 'natural order', and 'universal laws' took their place.

Second, came the great shattering of the confidence of rationalism, and with it, the new sense of historical development which we earlier noticed in connection with Hume, Kant and other figures in the latter part of the eighteenth century. One of their consequences was the rise of the school of thought known as Positivism, initiated by the French philosopher of science Auguste Comte (1797–1857). Positivism rejected any idea that science can 'break through' to a grasp of hidden realities or universal, rational truths about the governance of the natural order. Instead, it held that all that science really knows and can really deal with are the phenomena of our own experience, the measurable and quantifiable data resulting from scientific experiment. Everything else—all 'theories', 'hypotheses' or 'principles'—is simply the construction of the scentific mind, but does not in fact tell us 'how things really are'. So Comte developed his own view of 'three stages' in the development of individuals and of cultures as a whole. In the first, 'religious' or 'fetishist' stage, events are explained by reference to supernatural powers; in the second, which is 'metaphysical', these powers are reinterpreted as speculative 'essences' or 'forces' of a more abstract kind; in the 'positive' this supernatural and metaphysical scaffolding is finally found to be unnecessary, and explanations of this kind give way to the simple recognition and description of the pattern of events.

A similar form of Positivism was later held by the influential German scientist and philosopher Ernst Mach (1838–1916). He insisted, like Comte, that science cannot tell us *why* things happen, but only describe *how* the events we experience are regularly connected; and he vigorously attacked the 'animistic' idea of 'causes' or 'forces' operating in the world, seeking to substitute for them the calm discernment of logical and abstract patterns of interdependence which would leave no place for any sense of the 'wonderful' or 'marvellous'—a sense which seemed to him 'religious' and 'fetishist', and the very antithesis of a properly scientific attitude. Reality, he held, begins, ends and is entirely contained in 'sensations': 'persons' and 'things' alike are not objectifiable entities, but collections of experiences, or constructs out of experiences. The 'inner' and 'outer' world are thus one and the same: there can be no dichotomy between them because there is no 'real' objective world apart from our 'sensations'. Mach, consistently perhaps with this general stance, came to subscribe to a Buddhist form of religious philosophy; and this helps to underline the fact that Positivism of this kind, while certainly undercutting the confidence of Enlightment science in its grasp of objective truth, was in no way inclined to restore the God of Christian faith to the centre, or even the edge of the stage. Rather, the conviction of the objective reality and rationality of the world beyond ourselves had gone the way of the belief in God as its guarantor from which it had grown and which it had then displaced. That indeed was the essential meaning of Comte's 'three stages'.

A third development of far-reaching import was the shift in perspective enabled by the appearance in 1859 of *The Origin of Species* by Charles Darwin (1809–82). His theory of 'natural selection' for the first time offered a coherent and credible key to the idea of evolution—an idea which was already widely current in a variety of forms, but which up till then lacked the scientific basis supplied by Darwin. The impact of his work was immense, not only upon science as such, but upon the whole climate of the modern world. Unfortunately, accounts of the matter—especially where the topic of 'science and religion' is under discussion—tend to focus upon its less-significant features, such as the 'shock' to religious sensibility of the idea that man was descended from the ape, or that the process of creation had not been completed in six days, as Genesis recorded. In spite of the attacks launched upon Darwin in his own day—notably by the ill-advised Bishop Wilberforce, who denounced Darwin's ideas as incompatible with the teaching of the Bible—and in spite too of those in Christian circles who still have the same attitude, theologians in general had relatively little difficulty in coming to terms with his work. The way had already been at least partly prepared by the advances in geology and palaeontology, which had demonstrated the immense age of the world and shown the need either to reinterpret or wholly to depart from the six-day chronology of Genesis; and the idea of evolution readily lent itself to assimilation to the notion of onward and upward progress, culminating in man—an idea equally popular in theological and humanist thought in modern times. The really significant issues lay on another level altogether; and they were as challenging to the established science of the day as to religion and theology. Indeed, much of the strongest resistance to Darwin came from scientists rather than from theologians, and on grounds which had to do with their scientific conception of reality rather than with their religion or their reading of the Bible.

The heart of the matter lay in the way in which Darwin's theory combined the elements of *law* and of *accident* or of *randomness*. All living organisms were seen as growing and developing in a fashion which involved the spontaneous appearance of new characteristics capable of being transmitted to their descendants; those characteristics which had a positive value in assisting their survival were thus retained and spread through the hereditary group, so changing its character, and leading eventually to the emergence of quite new and distinct species. There was thus a 'law' at work here, the 'law of natural selection'; but its functioning involved a spontaneous and unpredictable capacity for change in the structure of living forms. Species as such was not 'simply given', nor was it unalterable: the story of living creatures, from the humblest cell to the most complex animals, was one of continual change and transformation, of the appearance of new types and of the obsolescence of those which could no longer hold their place in the struggle for survival. Chance and change thus had to be seen as central elements in the whole business, and as determining the very shape and nature of living beings themselves.

Darwinian biology therefore opened up a perspective very different from that of earlier science, and especially of physics as developed by Newton and his successors. They thought chiefly in terms of unchanging natural laws which governed the behaviour of essentially unalterable basic materials in the form of atoms. But physics too was in the end to experience its own kind of Darwinian revolution, above all through the work of Max Planck (1858–1947), the founder of quantum theory and of those who developed and extended it in various ways—notably Albert Einstein (1879–1955), Niels Bohr (1885–1962) and Werner Heisenberg (1901–76). While there were very deep differences between Einstein and the others, and while, too, their work has bequeathed many as yet unsolved problems, it has driven physics to operate with a view of reality very different indeed from the classical Newtonian type.

Newton's understanding of space and time, his laws of motion and the Euclidean geometry upon which his work was based, are now seen as holding good only under certain conditions and within definitely limited parameters; they do not apply either to the macroscopic structure of the universe as a whole or to the realm of subatomic particles. Einstein's theories of relativity present space and time as a 'continuum' which interacts with and is distorted by its contents—contents which may be thought of both as 'energy' and as 'matter'—so that 'space tells matter how to move, matter tells space how to bend'; the one constant absolute around which everything turns is the velocity of light; and the rate of passage of time is itself a function of velocity, which in turn determines mass. At the subatomic level, quantum theory describes the building-blocks of which atoms are composed not only as 'material corpuscles' but also as 'waves of energy', as 'processes' with their own—frequently infinitesimally brief and fleeting—history. The 'models' of wave and of particle are both valid, and both are needed to grasp their behaviour (Bohr's principle of complementarity). Further, their activity appears to be in part random, and to be describable and predictable only in terms of statistical probabilities rather than of absolutely determined causal necessity. In addition, account has to be taken of the fact that the 'interference' of the observer or experimenter imposes its own limits on his observations, and makes it impossible to establish precisely *both* the position *and* the velocity of a particle at any moment (Heisenberg's principle of indeterminacy): this too restricts the scope and reliability of the predictions he can make and test by subsequent observation, and introduces an unavoidable factor of uncertainty into his calculations. (Einstein, it should be said, was never willing to accept this emphasis upon randomness in the later development of quantum physics. He insisted, 'God does not play dice,' and, 'God is mysterious, but he is not malicious.' His own attempt to evolve a 'unified field theory' which would overcome these deficiencies (as he saw them) was, however, unsuccessful—though it may be that such a theory will eventually be found.)

One far-reaching set of conclusions which some scientists and others have felt compelled to draw from all this may be summed up as follows. Chance and randomness are inbuilt factors in the very structure of the physical universe; science itself has driven us to see this, and in the process has revealed the inevitable limitations imposed upon its own attempts to understand and explain reality; scientific theories are simply constructs of the human mind in its attempt to impose intelligibility and order upon the chaos of experience, and cast only a fitful and ambiguous light upon the true nature of things; and man himself is the product of an unthinkably lengthy series of accidental occurrences, and is therefore a stranger in a cosmos which is ultimately without sense or meaning. It is of course possible to subscribe to one or more of these propositions while rejecting others; but taken together, they express what is currently a common attitude, well illustrated by Jacques Monod's *Chance and Necessity* (E.T. 1972). Where this view of the matter is accepted as 'the truly scientific one', it is not surprising if theologians in retreat from the abyss of meaninglessness opening up before their feet have been tempted either to abandon the doctrine of creation as no longer tenable or to reinterpret it in a fashion which will preserve it from any direct connection with the conclusions of science— and to take the path to one or another of the cities of refuge labelled 'inwardness', 'personal and spiritual values', 'human existence', 'religion' or even 'revelation'. In this way, the erosion of the sense of God as Creator, and of the natural world as his creation, which can be traced in the development of modern science, has found its mirror-image in a good deal of theology as well; and on the basis of this shared conviction (or lack of it) theology and science have been driven apart, settled in hermetically sealed compartments.

This sharp disjunction has been further reinforced in many quarters by a kind of composite picture of science itself in which its most characteristic features are seen as being utterly different from those of religious and theological study. In its most extreme versions, this picture depicts the scientist himself as a kind of cold, calculating manipulator, interested only in torturing and exploiting nature in order to control it, and concerned with 'bare facts' and their organisation and classification. While there are no doubt scientists who fit that description, it can only be regarded as a ludicrous caricature of the species as a whole—but it is deeply anchored in the collective mind of our culture, and has certainly affected the attitude of some theologians, who react with horror to the idea that theology and science might be in any way related. But even where the picture is not drawn in this exaggerated form, the principles and procedures of science can appear so alien to those of theology as to open a vast divide between the two. Science aims by carefully controlled experiments to discern patterns in the behaviour of things, and by a cautious process of interpretation, generalisation and testing in fresh experiments seeks to build up an ever more extended and comprehensive network of hypotheses and theories which are in principle open to public verification or falsification through the further work of the scientific community. On the face of it, there appears little resemblance between this and the enterprise of theology as traditionally conducted; for it clearly does not apply the same kind of experimental method as the natural sciences, nor does it develop and test hypotheses and theories in the same fashion, while the 'authorities' to which it appeals seem to restrict its freedom and openness in a style radically different from what is taken for granted in scientific work.

This whole view of the matter, though widespread, is however by no means the only possible one, nor is the essentially defensive rearguard action the only tactic open to theology in the light of the rise of science; for modern scientific thought offers many points of potentially fruitful connection with theological interest. It is admitted somewhat dangerous to generalise about 'the modern scientific outlook', for closer inspection soon discloses a good variety of competing views among scientists and philosophers of science themselves. Further, the fact that certain scientific ideas may be linked up with theology should not be taken as offering a scientific 'validation' of theology, much less as binding theology to a particular scientific viewpoint, which itself may well be a passing one. It is nevertheless quite possible to identify suggestive analogies and convergences which open up the possibility of a constructive meeting between the scientist and the theologian. This has been done from both sides and along a variety of lines in recent decades. While there has been a good deal of meeting and mixing between these lines, it may be helpful to distinguish them in a rough way. The following classification is by no means exhaustive, but helps to indicate the shape of the field.

1. As has already been mentioned, Process philosophy has from its beginnings in the work of Whitehead been very much influenced by the vision of reality opened up by modern physics. It has been applied especially to the re-thinking of the doctrines of creation and providence, and of God's relation to the natural

world. Among many others, special mention may be made of L. C. Birch, *Nature and God*, and J. B. Cobb, *A Christian Natural Theology* (both 1965). Some use of Process thought is also made by I. G. Barbour, *Issues in Science and Religion* (1966). (A selection of papers illustrating a variety of approaches to the whole area is given in Barbour (ed.), *Science and Religion. New Perspectives on the Dialogue*, 1968.) More recent studies taking the same general direction include some of the papers published in two collections edited by E. H. Cousins—*Process Theology: Basic Writings* (1971); and *Hope and the Future of Man* (1973); also W. N. Pittenger, *Process Thought and the Christian Faith* (1968). On the whole, however, Process theologians seem more inclined to focus on relating theological doctrines to Process thought than on probing further into the more recent movement of natural science itself.

2. While many eminent scientists are atheist or agnostic many others have found in their scientific work support for their religious convictions, have argued powerfully that theology and natural science can not only co-exist, but interact creatively, and have traced parallels and resemblances between them. A full list of writings in this vein would cover many pages, but by way of illustration we may refer to C. A. Coulson's *Christianity in an Age of Science* (1953) and his *Science and Christian Belief* (1955); to A. R. Peacocke, *Science and the Christian Experiment* (1971); and to H. K. Schilling, *The New Consciousness in Science and Religion* (1973). The reader who comes to books such as these with the conception of the nature of science which we outlined above will be astonished to see how very different is their perspective on the matter. They present science itself as an enterprise combining controlled, factual observation with creative imaginative theorising; as opening up the mysterious complexities of the universe in a way which both evokes immense humility and a sense of the strange affinity between the enquiring human mind and the world out of which it has evolved; and as itself resting upon convictions of the intelligibility of the structure of that world which are ultimately unprovable, but which reflect an attitude analogous to religious faith. Similar emphases are to be found in the work of the scientist and philosopher Michael Polanyi (1891–76), whose many writings—among them *Science, Faith and Society* (1946), *Personal Knowledge. Towards a Post-Critical Philosophy* (1958) and *The*

205

Tacit Dimension (1967)—have become increasingly influential in some theological circles in recent years.

3. Historians of science were for a long time inclined to explain the rise of science from the sixteenth and seventeenth centuries onwards as resulting from the recovery of the mathematical and scientific heritage of ancient Greece alongside a general emancipation from the domination of the intellectual world by theology. This view has increasingly been challenged in the last fifty years. In his *Science and the Modern World* (1927) Whitehead pointed to the importance of the religious and theological context in which science became possible, and R. G. Collingwood advanced the argument further in his *Idea of Nature* (1945) by maintaining that the distinctively Christian belief in an omnipotent, transcendent Creator was a necessary prerequisite for the attitude to the natural world which made science possible. This line of historical study has been further followed up in closer detail by others, such as R. Hooykas, *Religion and the Rise of Modern Science* (1972); S. Jaki, *Science and Creation. From Eternal Cycles to an Oscillating Universe* (1974) and *The Origin of Science and the Science of its Origin* (1978), as well as in his Edinburgh Gifford Lectures of 1975 and 1976, *The Road of Science and the Ways of God*; and E. M. Klaaren, *Religious Origins of Modern Science* (1977). Jaki, in particular, powerfully advocates the view that natural science not only emerged from a Christian theological matrix, but by its achievements as a self-sustaining enterprise witnesses to the validity of the convictions of the reality of the Creator and the intelligibility of his creation which it first inherited from Christian faith. So he sees science and Christian theology as mutually supportive for the present and the future as well as for the period in which science first took wings.

4. Finally we come to the work of theologians rather than Process philosophers, natural scientists, philosophers or historians of science (though there have been theologians who have combined one or more of these other trades with their theology). Here again, a variety of approaches has been taken, reflecting the diversity of modern theology itself. A full survey would have to include, for instance, the stream of literature influenced by Teilhard de Chardin; the work of many Roman Catholics who believe they can find

in a repristinated metaphysics the bridge between theology and science; the flourishing in England in the first half of the century—or, to be more precise, in the second quarter—of the kind of scientifically based natural theology represented by Temple, or by C. E. Raven's *Natural Religion and Christian Theology* (1953); and the very considerable writing on the whole subject which appeared even earlier—a good impression of the state of play fifty years ago can be got from J. Needham (ed.), *Science, Religion and Reality*, published in 1925. More central to our story than all of these, however, and of greater contemporary significance, are the endeavours of a relatively small number of theologians in the last thirty years to engage in depth with the phenomenon of science in a way which would cast fresh light on theology itself. This is not merely a matter of looking for elements in the discoveries or theories of science which can be harmonised with theological convictions, nor of making piecemeal adjustments of the theological map in the light of scientific correction or criticism. It involves, rather, a much more probing search into the nature, aims and presuppositions of the scientific quest and its implications for our conception of reality, truth, knowledge and the place of man in the universe, and at the same time and as part of the same enquiry an equally profound examination of the same issues as they arise in theology.

This kind of approach, though anticipated to some degree by thinkers like Temple, took a fresh turning and opened up a new horizon with two books by Karl Heim, both translated into English in 1953: *Christian Faith and Natural Science* and *The Transformation of the Scientific World View*. Heim's writing combined a personalist, 'I-Thou' philosophy of human existence, inspired chiefly by Buber and stressing the absolute distinction between the personal 'self' and the 'objectified order' investigated by science, with what at first sight might seem something utterly alien to and quite incompatible with it—close attention to the current development of scientific thought, especially of quantum physics as expounded by Heisenberg and by C. F. von Weizsäcker in his *The World View of Physics* (E.T. 1952).

In that development Heim traced the collapse of three 'absolutes' in which the science of a former age had axiomatically believed—the 'absolute object', 'absolute time and absolute space' and 'absolute determination in natural events'. The consequence of this was that the enquiring, experimenting, theorising *subject* must be seen as intrinsically necessary to the development of scientific understanding. It was not the task of science, as had been assumed in the era of Newton and Laplace, simply to discern a purely 'objective' structure, a mere 'given' in the pattern of things; nor was it reduced, as some post-Kantians and positivists had later concluded, to imposing artificial constructs hatched in the mind of the scientists upon an inherently unordered nature. Rather, scientific knowledge was the product of an interaction, with both an objective and a subjective component, and issued in genuine understanding, even though that understanding might frequently find expression, not in any kind of 'picture' that could be visualised or imagined, but rather in more abstract, mathematical terms. In this way, the bridge between subject and object could be and had been found; the ideal of pure objectivity had been shown to be a mirage; and so science itself had come up against the limits necessarily imposed on any purely objective approach to its material. Thus science itself disclosed the need for 'objective space' to be supplemented by the radically different 'space' of personal being.

Opening out further from there, Heim sought to sketch the further, transcendent 'space' of the God who is omnipresent and all-encompassing. Within this horizon, Heim also took issue with the old, rationalist definition of 'miracle' as 'suspension of natural law', 'interference by the supernatural with the natural process'. What characterises a miracle, he insisted, both in biblical and in modern times, is the use of natural causes to serve the beneficent divine will, usually associated with the direction of human willing in faith and prayer to the same purpose. While events in the past are 'signed, sealed and delivered', and thus give us the impression that history is ruled by unalterable fate, the future (as we know from our own experience as active agents) is more open than that, and can be altered and affected by human decision. In a similar but more comprehensive way, God is at work in all that happens, and 'miracle' thus by no means to be ruled out on 'scientific' grounds.

Heim's approach was in many ways a highly individual one, and not without debatable aspects. His use of the concept of 'space' has seemed to some critics singularly inappropriate in connection with the realm of *personal* being, while the epistemological conclusions which he drew from the work of Heisenberg are by no means universally accepted. (It is still a highly contentious question whether the 'revolution in physics' amounts to a philosophical revolution as well. Many do believe that it does, but the point is one on which there is no universal agreement among scientists or philosophers even today.) But Heim was far from alone in holding that the new scientific outlook opened up fresh vistas for theology, and allowed it more room to move than the commonly aggressive mechanistic determinism associated with earlier physics. The same issues have been tackled since in a number of ways and from several different theological viewpoints—e.g. W. A. Whitehouse, *Christian Faith and the Scientific Attitude* (1952); E. L. Mascall, *Christian Theology and Natural Science* (1956); and, more recently, W. Pannenberg, *Theology and the Philosophy of Science* (E.T. 1976), and L. Gilkey, *Religion and the Scientific Future* (1970).

The theologian who has given the most sustained attention to this whole subject over many years is, however, T. F. Torrance (1913–), whose characteristic interests and emphases are well reflected in the titles of some of his recent books—*Theology in Reconstruction* (1965), *Space, Time and Incarnation* (1969), *Theological Science* (1969), *God and Rationality* (1971) and *Theology in Reconciliation* (1975). Among his leading themes are that theological study is itself a rational discipline which can properly be called 'scientific'; that it has profound affinities with other sciences as well as differing distinctively from them; that natural science sprang from and can and should still interact constructively with Christian theology; and that the particular development of contemporary science both reinforces the Christian understanding of God, the world and man, and also offers fresh light upon the nature and proper procedures of theology itself.

In particular, he forcefully maintains that if theologians paid heed to the way in which science operates, and to the nature of scientific knowledge, they would find that some of the most intractable problems in theological debate are generated by ways of thinking and posing questions which science has shown to be inadequate, and from which theology too must depart. His chief target here is what he calls 'the damaging dualism' which drives such a sharp wedge between the self and the world, subject and object, fact and meaning, reality and interpretation, that it posits an unbridgeable gulf, despairs of finding any objective truth, and so falls back into pure subjectivism. Not altogether surprisingly, Bultmann is seen by him as the prime (but by no means the only) example, of this tendency. Torrance's main aim is not, however, simply to criticise what he believes to be inadequate theological method, but through that criticism to open up a creative and dynamic understanding of the nature of theology as an exploration of the divine intelligibility opened up to human minds through God's giving himself to be known by us in Jesus Christ.

Torrance's writing covers so many scientific and theological questions that the brief comments which are possible here cannot touch on more than one or two aspects. But the points just outlined can be partially illustrated by summarising one of his main lines of thought concerning scientific method and scientific understanding. First of all, he traces in the development of recent science a new appreciation of the role of the human subject in all knowing. Knowledge is not and cannot be 'purely objective'; it arises rather in the 'cognitive relation' between subject and object. This destroys the 'objectivism' of classical physics, and the model of purely detached 'knowing' with which it worked. It does not, however, issue in what might at first sight appear to be the natural alternative—pure subjectivism, in which 'knowledge' evaporates away into the 'constructs' of the subjective mind. Rather, it opens the way to a profounder notion of 'objectivity', in which our concepts and systems are seen as necessarily subjective, but at the same time as 'tools' which serve to disclose to us the rationality of the structure of the world, and enable us to enter into it, while recognising that that rationality infinitely transcends our grasp. It is 'apprehended' rather than 'comprehended', but in this apprehension, it is genuinely encountered.

The idea that we can 'picture' reality simply as it is gives way to the enterprise of fashioning 'open concepts' and patterns of understanding—most commonly of a mathematical sort—which lead our minds on beyond themselves to the reality which they enable us to explore. Through further experiment and theorizing the enquiry is extended and deepened, and more and more complex structures of rationality uncovered. In all this, creative imagination and speculation play a necessary part; but they are not uncontrolled or free-floating, but subject to critical testing of the validity of the interpretations they offer of the 'clues' by which we seek to decipher as yet hidden meanings. Scientific study is thus 'bound' to its object: it is, in the technical sense of the word, 'dogmatic' rather than purely inventive.

What it opens up is a mysterious and awe-evoking affinity between the human intelligence and the objective intelligibility of the natural world—an affinity which not only makes science possible at all, but justifies us in seeing the scientific enterprise as itself part of the 'expanding universe', the giving of new expression in a fresh way to the hidden rationality of things. In this respect, science can be seen as performing a role which Christian thought has traditionally ascribed to man—that of being 'the priest of the universe' in whom dumb nature finds a voice to worship the Creator by expressing the wonder of his creation. So far from being a stranger and an accident in a cosmos without sense or meaning, man is 'at home' in the universe, and has a central role to play in it—a theme which, Torrance points out, some modern cosmologists have also emphasised. (One line of thought opened up by the 'Big Bang' theory of the origin of the universe is that only a universe which exploded into existence at a particular speed, and which attained the immense size which astronomy reveals to us, could have generated the possibility of the emergence of life and consciousness in our world. The vastness of the cosmos, on this view, does not render man insignificant, but quite the reverse.)

This concern to set science itself in a theological light is one of the chief characteristics of Torrance's work. Another is his insistence that, at bottom, theology follows the same basic way of knowing as does science: it too is a human enterprise, concerned to bring to expression the rationale of God in his relation to the world and to ourselves. It differs from other sciences in that its object is different, and therefore its method must also be that appropriate to its object. But it is not for that reason 'unscientific', any more than chemistry can be called 'unscientific' because it applies different techniques of investigation from those in use in other branches of science. The broad canons of rationality do not dictate the specific methods and techniques which are necessary in any particular field, nor can these be dictated from any other field, or predicted in advance. They must be discovered and developed in the course of the enquiry itself. Torrance powerfully argues that Christian theology as it has developed through the centuries is in many ways similar to any of the natural sciences, and in particular that it has its own logic, its own structures of understanding, its own reference to reality, and that the great dogmas function in a fashion similar to scientific discoveries by grasping and focusing for us the central truth and reality of God himself in his own being revealed in his dealings with us, and by directing our minds to Jesus Christ as the centre in whom God and man, Creator and creature, are bound together.

Yet a third feature of Torrance's thought, flowing directly from his sense of the centrality of the incarnation as well as from his parallels between the work of the theologian and the scientist, is his aim to bring theology and science together in an integrated vision of reality. In what is perhaps the clearest and most succinct summary of his recent thinking, the address which he gave on receiving the Templeton Prize for Progress in Religion in 1978, he referred to 'a number of changes which are proving to be highly significant in overcoming the split between the natural and the human sciences and between both and theological sciences'. These were changes occurring in science itself, forced upon it by its own development and apprehension of reality, and he selected four in particular as especially significant.

First was the move away from a purely 'abstractive' conception of science which 'tended to tear the surface pattern of things away from its objective ground' towards one which 'is concerned to understand the surface patterns of things in the light of the natural coherences in which they are actually embedded, and therefore operates with the indissoluble unity of form and being, or of theoretical and empirical elements in human knowledge'. Second was the contemporary displacement of the 'analytical methods and their disintegrating effects' by a more 'unitary approach' which 'operates with an integration of form', and in which 'atomistic thinking is replaced by relational thinking'. Third, recent work applying the laws of thermodynamics to 'open or non-equilibrium systems'—to which in their classical formulation these laws did not apply—had opened a new avenue to the comprehension of 'the so-called random elements in nature'. This implied 'that the old way of thinking in terms of the couplets chance and necessity, uncertainty and determinism must now be replaced by a new way of thinking in terms of spontaneity and open-structured order'— which could be directly connected with the theological 'understanding of the spontaneity and freedom of the created universe as grounded in the unlimited spontaneity and freedom of God the

212

Creator'. Finally, 'Science has been moving away from a flat understanding of nature to one that is characterised by a hierarchy of levels or dimensions' which 'cannot be flattened downward by being reduced to connections all on the same level'. Consequently, 'the new science gives ample room for the human sciences and the sciences of the spirit, and all sciences concerned with living connections, within the framework of an open-structured, dynamic universe in which the human person is not suffocated but can breathe freely transcendent air, and yet be profoundly concerned with scientific understanding of the whole complex of connections that make up our universe'. So he ended his address with these words,

> It is more and more clear to me that, under the providence of God, owing to these changes in the very foundations of knowledge in which natural and theological science alike have been sharing, the damaging cultural splits between the sciences and the humanities and between both and theology are in process of being overcome, the destructive and divisive forces too long rampant in world-wide human life and thought are being undermined, and that a massive new synthesis will emerge in which man, humbled and awed by the mysterious intelligibility of the universe which reaches far beyond his powers, will learn to fulfil his destined role as the servant of divine love and the priest of creation.

Only time will tell whether or to what extent Torrance's vision can be realised. To some it may appear utopian to hope for such a grand synthesis of science and theology, however, desirable it may be in principle. Others may feel that he lays too much weight on the one hand on 'pure science' and on the other on the intellectual aspects of theology, and that this brings its own dangers of a kind of abstraction combined with an excessive stress on *understanding*. They would perhaps sympathise with some very sharp words spoken by Jürgen Moltmann at a conference on Hope and the Future of Man held in New York in 1971—though Moltmann's target there was not Torrance, but papers written from a Process and a Teilhardian standpoint,

> Our attention has been called to the religion of the human 'self' in the world process, that is, concretely and critically we presumably spoke of the white self, the capitalist self, of the American and European in the process of *his* world. Next we'll probably go on to *extrapolate his* future and speak of science and scientific knowledge to which religion must adjust in order to satisfy scientific reason. Liberal theologians of the white bourgeoisie have always talked that way. They overlooked that

their concrete starting-point was involved in institutional oppression of their neighbours. They spared no effort in making theology scientific and their dialogue with other sciences equally scientific, while overlooking the social and political context of science and of their own theologies.

I am not so much interested in Whitehead in regard to his process-thought and his 'becoming God' with a primordial and consequent nature, though I like his phrase about God as 'the great companion—the fellow-sufferer who understands'. My co-suffering reason would wish to know what is going on in his divinity in relationship to those abandoned, starved, bereft of their own name and their honor, and what practical consequences follow for the philosopher and theologian. Electromagnetic fields do not interest me relative to a *religious Weltanschauung* congenial to my scientific reason, but relative to the electrification of the shacks of sharecroppers in North Carolina and the slums of Nairobi ... Of course we say $2 \times 2 = 4$. But for some two days of work times two days of work easily equals eighty dollars; for others it equals only eight dollars. Practically $2 \times 2 = 4$ is something different in East Harlem than in Wall Street, and in Botswana something different than in Tübingen (E. H. Cousins (ed.), *Hope and the Future of Man*, 1972, pp. 56, 58–9).

Powerful and eloquent though Moltmann's words are, however, and undeniable as is the validity of his practical concern, they veer perilously close to a form of obscurantism of which Moltmann himself would be the last to approve. His own real attitude to the matter as sketched in the last chapter of his *Hope and Planning* (E.T. 1971), 'Theology in the World of Modern Science', includes a much more positive appreciation of the role of the sciences, though not indeed engaging with them in such depth as Torrance. Here surely theology must avoid the false dilemma of an artificial either/or. It has to do with understanding as well as with practical action, with the epistemological and cosmological implications of the advance of science as well as with its technological fruits and their use or abuse. The field which Torrance has sought to explore is one which theology today can ignore only at its peril, and it is a striking testimony to the vitality and vigour of theology in the last third of our century that it has brought forth pioneers of this stature.

Select Bibliography

A selection of the major writings mentioned, with some further suggestions for reading in the different areas.

GENERAL

Cragg, Gerald R. *The Church and the Age of Reason, 1648-1789.* Harmondsworth: Penguin Books, 1960; revised, 1970 (Pelican History of the Church, Vol. 4); Grand Rapids: Wm. B. Eerdmans Publishing Co., 1964.

Cunliffe-Jones, Hubert. *Christian Theology Since 1600.* London: Gerald Duckworth & Co., 1970.

Mackintosh, Hugh R. *Types of Modern Theology: Schleiermacher to Barth.* London: James Nisbet & Co., 1937; New York: Charles Scribner's Sons, 1937.

Macquarrie, John. *Twentieth-Century Religious Thought: The Frontiers of Philosophy and Theology, 1900–1970.* London: SCM Press, 1971.

Nicholls, William. *Systematic and Philosophical Theology.* Harmondsworth: Penguin Books, 1971 (Pelican Guide to Modern Theology, Vol. 3); Baltimore: Penguin Books, 1969.

Vidler, Alexander R. *The Church in an Age of Revolution, 1789 to the Present Day.* Harmondsworth: Penguin Books, 1961; revised, 1971 (Pelican History of the Church, Vol. 5); Grand Rapids: Wm. B. Eerdmans Publishing Co., 1962.

Zahrnt, Heinz. *The Question of God: Protestant Theology in the 20th Century.* London: William Collins Sons & Co., 1969; New York: Harcourt, Brace and World, 1969.

CHAPTER 2

Barth, Karl. *Protestant Theology in the Nineteenth Century.* London: SCM Press, 1972; Philadelphia: Judson Press, 1973.

Welch, Claude. *Protestant Thought in the Nineteenth Century,* Vol. 1: 1799–1870. Yale University Press, 1972.

Niebuhr, Richard R. *Schleiermacher on Christ and Religion.* London: SCM Press, 1965; New York: Charles Scribner's Sons, 1964.

Reardon, Bernard M. G. *Liberal Protestantism.* London: Adam and Charles Black, 1968; Stanford: Stanford University Press, 1968.

Richmond, James. *Ritschl: A Reappraisal.* London: William Collins Sons & Co., 1978; Cleveland: William Collins + World Publishing Co., 1978.

Ritschl, Albrecht. *The Christian Doctrine of Justification and Reconciliation,* Vol. 3. Edinburgh: T. & T. Clark, 1900; Clifton, N.J.: New Jersey Reference Book Publishers, 1966.

Schleiermacher, Friedrich D. E. *The Christian Faith.* Edinburgh: T. & T. Clark, 1928; Philadelphia: Fortress Press, 1976.

————. *On Religion: Speeches to Its Cultured Despisers.* Harper & Brothers, 1958.

Diem, Hermann. *Kierkegaard's Dialectic of Existence.* Edinburgh: Oliver & Boyd, 1959.

Feuerbach, Ludwig. *The Essence of Christianity.* Harper & Brothers, 1957.

Harris, Horton. *David Friedrich Strauss and His Theology.* Cambridge University Press, 1973.

Kierkegaard, Søren. *Philosophical Fragments.* Princeton University Press, 1962.

Clayton, John P. (ed.). *Ernst Troeltsch and the Future of Theology.* Cambridge University Press, 1976.

Kähler, Martin. *The So-called Historical Jesus and the Historic, Biblical Christ.* Fortress Press, 1964.

Plantinga, Theodore. *Historical Understanding in the Thought of Wilhelm Dilthey.* Toronto: University of Toronto Press, 1980.

Schweitzer, Albert. *The Quest of the Historical Jesus: A Critical Study of Its Progress from Reimarus to Wrede.* London: Adam & Charles Black, 1910; New York: Macmillan Co., 1968.

Troeltsch, Ernst. *The Absoluteness of Christianity.* London: SCM Press, 1972; Richmond: John Knox Press, 1971.

CHAPTER 4

Barth, Karl. *Church Dogmatics,* Vols. I/1 to IV/4 (Fragment). Edinburgh, 1936–1969; revised translation of Vol. I/1, Edinburgh: T. & T. Clark, 1975.

————. *The Epistle to the Romans.* London: Oxford University Press, 1933.

————. *Evangelical Theology*. London: George Weidenfeld & Nicolson, 1963; New York: Holt, Rinehart & Winston, 1963.

Brunner, Emil. *Revelation and Reason*. London: SCM Press, 1947; Philadelphia: Westminster Press, 1946.

————. *Truth as Encounter*, 2d ed. London: SCM Press, 1964; Philadelphia: Westminster Press, 1964.

Brunner, Emil, and Barth, Karl. *Natural Theology*. London: Geoffrey Bles, 1946.

Busch, Eberhard. *Karl Barth*. London: SCM Press, 1976; Fortress Press, 1976.

Smart, James D. *The Divided Mind of Modern Theology: Karl Barth and Rudolf Bultmann, 1908–1933*. Westminster Press, 1967.

Sykes, S. (ed.). *Karl Barth: Studies of His Theological Methods*. Oxford, 1980.

Torrance, Thomas F. *Karl Barth: An Introduction to His Early Theology, 1910–1931*. London: SCM Press, 1962.

CHAPTER 5

Bartsch, Hans-Werner (ed.). *Kerygma and Myth,* Vols. 1 and 2 combined. London: S.P.C.K., 1972; New York: Harper & Row, Harper Torchbook, n.d.

Braaten, Carl E. *New Directions in Theology Today, Vol. II: History and Hermeneutics*. Westminster Press, 1966.

Bultmann, Rudolf. *Faith and Understanding* (E.T. of Vol. I of the 4-volume collection of essays *Glauben und Verstehen*, 1933–1965). London: SCM Press, 1969; New York: Harper & Row, 1969.

————. *Jesus and the Word*. London: S. J. R. Saunders & Co., 1960; Charles Scribner's Sons, 1960.

Cullmann, Oscar. *Christ and Time: The Primitive Christian Conception of Time and History*. London: SCM Press, 1951; rev. ed., 1962; Philadelphia: Westminster Press, 1950; rev. ed., 1964.

Galloway, Allan D. *Wolfhart Pannenberg*. London: George Allen & Unwin, 1973.

Heidegger, Martin. *Being and Time*. London: SCM Press, 1962; New York: Harper & Row, 1962.

McArthur, Harvey K. (ed.). *In Search of the Historical Jesus*. Charles Scribner's Sons, 1969.

Macquarrie, John. *An Existentialist Theology: A Comparison of Heidegger and Bultmann*. London: SCM Press, 1958.

Ogden, Schubert M. *Christ Without Myth: A Study in the Theology of Rudolf Bultmann*. Harper & Row, 1961.

Pannenberg, Wolfhart. *Jesus — God and Man*. Westminster Press, 1968.

CHAPTER 6

Baillie, Donald M. *God Was in Christ*. London: Faber & Faber, 1948; New York: Charles Scribner's Sons, 1948.

Baillie, John. *Our Knowledge of God*. London: Oxford University Press, 1939; New York: Charles Scribner's Sons, 1939, 1959.

Macquarrie, John. *God-Talk: An Examination of the Language and Logic of Theology*. London: SCM Press, 1967; New York: Harper & Row, 1967.

Oman, John W. *Grace and Personality*. Cambridge, 1917. 2nd ed.: London: William Collins Sons & Co., 1960; New York: Association Press, 1961.

Ramsey, Arthur M. *From Gore to Temple*. London: S. J. R. Saunders & Co., 1960; New York: Charles Scribner's Sons, 1960.

Swinburne, Richard. *The Coherence of Theism*. Oxford: Clarendon Press, 1977.

Temple, William. *Nature, Man and God*. London: Macmillan Co., 1934.

Niebuhr, H. Richard. *Christ and Culture*. Harper & Brothers, 1951.

Niebuhr, Reinhold. *The Nature and Destiny of Man*. 2 vols. London: James Nisbet & Co., 1941, 1943; New York: Charles Scribner's Sons, 1941, 1943.

Thomas, John H. *Paul Tillich: An Appraisal*. London: SCM Press, 1963; Philadelphia: Westminster Press, 1963.

Tillich, Paul. *Systematic Theology*. 3 vols. University of Chicago Press, 1951, 1957, 1963.

Cousins, Ewert H. (ed.) *Process Theology: Basic Writings*. Paulist/Newman Press, 1971.

Hartshorne, Charles. *The Divine Relativity*. Yale University Press, 1948.

Whitehead, Alfred North. *Process and Reality: An Essay in Cosmology*. London, 1929; New York: Macmillan Co., 1929.

Aulén, Gustav. *Christus Victor: An Historical Study of the Three Main Types of the Idea of the Atonement*. London: S.P.C.K., 1931; New York: Macmillan Co., 1951.

Nygren, Anders. *Agape and Eros: A Study of the Christian Idea of Love*. London: S.P.C.K., 1932; Philadelphia: Westminster Press, 1953.

CHAPTER 7

Altizer, Thomas J. J. *The Gospel of Christian Atheism*. London: William Collins Sons & Co., 1967; Philadelphia: Westminster Press, 1966.

Bethge, Eberhard. *Dietrich Bonhoeffer*. London: William Collins Sons & Co., 1970; New York: Harper & Row, 1970.

Bonhoeffer, Dietrich. *Lectures on Christology*. Rev. trans. London: William Collins Sons & Co., 1978.

———. *Letters and Papers from Prison*. Rev. and enlarged ed. London: SCM Press, 1971; New York: Macmillan Publishing Co., 1972.

Cox, Harvey. *The Secular City*. London: SCM Press, 1965; New York: Macmillan Co., 1965.

Gutiérrez, Gustavo. *A Theology of Liberation*. London: SCM Press, 1973; Maryknoll, N.Y.: Orbis Books, 1973.

Kee, Alistair (ed.). *A Reader in Political Theology*. London: SCM Press, 1974; Philadelphia: Westminster Press, 1975.

———. *The Scope of Political Theology*. London: SCM Press, 1978.

Moltmann, Jürgen. *The Crucified God: The Cross of Christ as the Foundation and Criticism of Christian Theology*. London: SCM Press, 1974; New York: Harper & Row, 1974.

Robinson, John A. T. *Honest to God*. London: SCM Press, 1963; Philadelphia: Westminster Press, 1963.

van Buren, Paul. *The Secular Meaning of the Gospel*. London: SCM Press, 1963; New York: Macmillan Co., 1963.

CHAPTER 8

Flannery, Austin (ed.). *Vatican Council II: The Conciliar and Post-Conciliar Documents*. Dublin: Dominican Publications, 1975; Collegeville, Minn.: Liturgical Press, 1975.

Goodall, Norman. *The Ecumenical Movement*. London: Oxford University Press, 1961.

Küng, Hans. *On Being a Christian*. London: William Collins Sons & Co., 1976; New York: Doubleday & Co., 1976.

Lossky, Vladimir. *The Mystical Theology of the Eastern Church*. London: James Clarke & Co., 1957.

Rahner, Karl. *Foundations of Christian Faith: An Introduction to the Idea of Christianity*. London: Darton, Longman & Todd, 1978; New York: Seabury Press, 1978.

Teilhard de Chardin, Pierre. *The Phenomenon of Man*. London: William Collins Sons & Co., 1959; New York: Harper & Brothers, 1959.

Ware, Timothy. *The Orthodox Church*. Harmondsworth: Penguin Books, 1963; Baltimore: Penguin Books, 1963.

Fleischner, Eva (ed.). *Auschwitz: Beginning of a New Era? Reflections on the Holocaust*. KTAV Publishing House, 1977.

Hallencreutz, Carl F. *New Approaches to Men of Other Faiths*. Geneva: World Council of Churches, 1970.

Kraemer, Hendrik. *The Christian Message in a Non-Christian World*. London: Edinburgh House Press, 1938; New York: Harper & Brothers, 1938.

Otto, Rudolf. *The Idea of the Holy*. Oxford, 1923.

Smart, Ninian. *The Religious Experience of Mankind*. Charles Scribner's Sons, 1969.

Smith, Wilfred Cantwell. *The Meaning and End of Religion: A New Approach to the Religious Traditions of Mankind*. Macmillan Co. 1964.

Barbour, Ian G. (ed.). *Science and Religion: New Perspectives on the Dialogue*. London: SCM Press, 1968; New York: Harper & Row, 1968.

Heim, Karl. *The Transformation of the Scientific World View*. London: SCM Press, 1953; New York: Harper & Brothers, 1953.

Hooykaas, Reijer. *Religion and the Rise of Modern Science*. Edinburgh: Scottish Academic Press, 1972; Grand Rapids: Wm. B. Eerdmans Publishing Co., 1972.

Jaki, Stanley L. *The Road of Science and the Ways to God*. Edinburgh: Scottish Academic Press, 1977; Chicago: University of Chicago Press, 1978.

Peacocke, Arthur R. *Science and the Christian Experiment*. London: Oxford University Press, 1971; New York: Oxford University Press, 1971.

Torrance, Thomas F. *Space, Time and Incarnation*. London: Oxford University Press, 1969; Grand Rapids: Wm. B. Eerdmans Publishing Co., 1976.

—————. *Theological Science*. London: Oxford University Press, 1969.

Index of Subjects

Absolute Dependence, 25–32
Absolute Mind, 39–40, 44, 123
Agape, 150–1
Aggiornamento, 171
Alienation, 45–6, 138
Analogia entis, 77, 87
Analogia fidei, 87
Analogy, 56, 59, 129–30, 144
Anglicanism, 3, 97, 122–4, 126
Anglo-catholicism, 63, 65, 146
Angst, 47
Anonymous Christians, 192
Anthropology, 11, 44, 46, 79, 84, 105, 113, 173–4 (Transcendental), 184
Anxiety, 107–8
Apocalyptic, 53–4
Assumption of the Virgin Mary, 174
Atheism, 43–6, 146–8, 159–63, 166, 186
Atonement, 62–4, 120, 122, 150
Attributes of God, 65, 93
Authentic Existence, 107–10, 113–14
Autonomy, 138, 158

Barmen Declaration, 86
Begriff, 39–40
Being, 106, 137–44
— New Being, 138–9, 141
Bible, Authority of, 2–8, 11, 18, 20, 27, 57, 61, 64–6, 122
Biblical Criticism, 5–6, 42–5, 51–4, 57, 61, 64–6, 68, 99–118, 171–2, 180, 196
Biblical Realism, 188–90
Biblical Theology, 102
Black Theology, 165
Buddhism, 194, 200

Calvinism, 62, 66, 80, 88–9, 92
Categorical Imperative, 18

Cause and Effect, 13–6, 199–200, 207–9
Christendom, 1–3, 50–1, 70, 75–6
Christocentrism, 62, 64, 66, 88–95, 155–6, 160, 212
Christomonism, 180
Church, 27–8, 35, 50, 54, 58, 64, 67, 82–3, 85–6, 100–1, 131, 150, 154, 163–4, 167, 170, 172–7, 179–81, 183, 196
Coincidentia Oppositorum, 39
Complementarity, 202
Conservative Evangelicalism, 22, 131, 165
Correlation Method, 138–9, 143
Cosmological Proof, 14
Covenant, 88–9, 91
Creator, Creation, 5, 27, 40, 85–9, 91–2, 179, 187, 200–1, 203–4, 206, 211–13
Creeds, 8, 20, 67, 197
Cross, 54, 62, 77–8, 93–4, 108–11, 113, 115–16, 132–3, 135, 155–6, 168, 191
Culture and Theology, 135–7, 158–61

Dasein, 106–8, 114
Death of God, 113, 152, 159–61, 168
Deism, 7–8, 115–16, 148, 163, 186
Demonisation, 141–2
Demythologisation, 97, 99–118, 140, 153
Design Argument, 13–16
Dialectic, 38–40, 43, 48, 67, 78, 138, 142
Dialectical Theology, 78–81, 83–4, 103, 109, 119–20, 124–5, 137, 150, 159, 188
Dogma, 20, 26–8, 30–1, 36–8, 40–2, 44, 51–2, 59, 63, 81–3, 97–8, 125, 152, 157, 176–7, 212

Randomness, 8, 201–3, 212–13
Rationalism, 4–12, 15, 18–19, 44, 50, 61, 198–9
Rationality of the External World, 200, 203, 205–7, 210–13
Rationality of Faith, 84, 210–13
Realism, 123–4, 145
Reason, 4, 6, 10–18, 20, 31, 38–40, 56, 88, 122–4, 180 (see also Enlightenment)
Reconception, 190
Reconciliation, 34–5, 62, 64, 67, 89, 94
Redaction Criticism, 101
Redeemer myth, 103–4, 115
Redemption, 29–31, 35, 57, 69, 89, 103, 108–9, 181, 189
Reformation, Reformers, 2, 6, 34, 79, 87–9
Relativity Theories, 202
Religion, 3–4, 8–11, 23–38, 44–6, 57–60, 68, 71–2, 76–9, 121–5, 127–30, 137, 141–3, 145–6, 150–1, 183–96
— Religionless Christianity, 96, 113, 152–6, 161, 168
— Religious Language, 27–8, 33, 35, 37, 127–30, 140–1
Renaissance, 2
Resurrection, 54, 76, 87, 93, 109, 112, 135, 150, 164
Revelation, 8, 10, 13, 20, 29, 31, 33–4, 37, 56, 74, 79, 81–8, 96–7, 103, 111–12, 115–16, 120, 122–6, 136, 138–9, 143, 156, 173–4, 177, 182, 188–90, 192, 194
Revival, Revivalism, 11, 67
Roman Catholic Church, 1, 33, 67, 142, 165–6, 170–9
Romanticism, 12, 26, 32, 38–9, 84

Sacrament, Sacramental, 67, 124, 141–2, 172–3, 175–6, 180
Salvation, 135, 166, 167, 192
Science, 2–8, 12, 15, 22, 41, 58, 66, 70–1, 97, 104, 116, 123–4, 126, 177–9, 193, 196–214

Secularisation, 70, 142, 188, 192–3
— Secularism, 159, 196
— Secular Theology, 97, 152, 154, 156–9, 161–2, 166, 193
Self-understanding, 84, 104–5, 109, 111, 113–14, 156
Sin, 30, 37, 44, 47–8, 50, 62, 64, 69, 87–9, 93–4, 114, 120–1, 132, 134–5, 150, 178
Sobornost, 180–2
Social Contract, 9
Social Gospel, 131–3
Socialism, 64, 75, 131–2, 137
Son of Man, 54
Sophia, 182,
Sorge, 106
Source Criticism, 100–1
Space, 17, 91–2, 198, 202, 207–9
Subject and Object, 16–17, 25, 28, 40, 55, 77, 106–8, 113–14, 138, 175, 181–2, 207–11
Subjectivism, 90, 210
Subjectivity, 31, 47, 112–13, 175, 181–3
Symbol, Symbolic, 117–18, 140–1, 177, 187–8

Tabu, 185
Theonomy, 138
Time, 17, 91–2, 106–7, 198, 202, 207–8 (see also Eternity and Time)
Tractarians, 63
Trinity, 8, 28, 40, 82–3, 91–3, 97, 112–13, 160, 179, 183
Tsurasa, 191
Tübingen Schools, 42–3, 170

Ultimate Concern, 138, 156
Unitarianism, 8, 37, 160–1

Values, Ethical and Spiritual, 11, 37, 49, 69, 131, 188
— Value-judgements, 35, 37, 120, 185
Vatican Councils, 170–1

Index of Names

Abraham, 48, 50
Adam, 89
Alexander, S., 123
Altizer, T., 159–61
Anselm, 84
Aquinas, 13
Aristotle, 149
Augustine, 104–5, 126, 134, 141
Aulén, G., 150–1
Austin, J. L., 128
Ayer, A. J., 127–8

Baillie, D. M., 24, 124–6, 132
Baillie, J., 124–5, 132, 184
Barbour, I. G., 205
Barth, K., 66, 73, 74–98, 100, 108, 111, 112, 119–21, 124–6, 127, 133–4, 136–7, 147, 150, 152–3, 155–6, 160, 168, 174–5, 177, 188–90, 194–5, 197
Bartsch, H.–W., 99
Bauer, B., 45
Baur, F. C., 23, 42–3, 52, 67
Berdyaev, N., 105, 181–2
Biedermann, A. E., 23, 41–2, 43, 140
Birch, L. C., 205
Blake, W., 47, 161
Bloch, E., 162–3
Blumhardt, J. C., 76
Bohr, N., 201–2
Bonhoeffer, D., 96, 114, 126, 152–6, 157, 159, 160, 168
Bonino, J. M., 165–6
Bornkamm, G., 110
Bousset, W., 57
Boyd, R., 191
Braaten, C., 117
Bradley, F. H., 41
Braithwaite, R. B., 129
Braun, H., 113
Brunner, E., 75, 78, 80–1, 84–91, 95, 112, 121, 124–6, 133–4, 188

Buber, M., 105, 126, 195, 207
Buddha, 194
Bulgakov, S., 181–2
Bultmann, R., 42, 57, 73, 75, 78, 80–1, 84, 90, 99–118, 119, 121, 126–7, 137, 140–1, 150, 152–3, 156–7, 177, 196–7, 210
van Buren, P., 157–8
Busch, E., 91
Bushnell, H., 62–3
Butler, J., 8

Caird, E., 41
Calvin, 6, 87–8
Campbell, J. McL., 62–3, 64, 89
Chenchiah, P., 191
Clarke, W. N., 130
Cobb, J. B., 117, 205
Coleridge, S. T., 61–2, 63
Collingwood, R. G., 206
Collins, A., 8
Comte, A., 199–200
Cone, J., 165
Constantine, 70
Copernicus, 5, 16
Coplestone, F., 173
Coulson, C. A., 205
Cousins, E. H., 205, 214
Cox, H., 157–9
Cragg, K., 191
Cullmann, O., 111

Daly, M., 165
Darwin, C., 200–1
Denney, J., 120
Descartes, R., 11, 13
Devanandan, P. D., 191
Dewick, E. C., 190
Dibelius, M., 100
Dilthey, W., 57–8
Dodwell, H., 8
Dostoievsky, F., 47, 75, 105
Dulles, A., 175–6
Durkheim, E., 45